What Went Wrong, Gordon Brown?

Colin Hughes is an associate editor of the *Guardian*. Having started his career as a journalist at the *Sheffield Star* in 1979, he worked at the Press Association and the *Times* before joining the *Independent* in 1986 as a political correspondent. He went on to become policy editor, education editor, and US correspondent, and spent his final six years there as managing editor of the *Independent* and *Independent on Sunday* and deputy editor of the *Independent*. He joined the *Guardian* in 1998. He is a governor of Middlesex University and author of *Labour Rebuilt: the New Model Party*.

What Went Wrong, Gordon Brown?

EDITED BY COLIN HUGHES

Additional editing and research by Amelia Hodsdon

guardianbooks

Published by Guardian Books 2010

2 4 6 8 10 9 7 5 3 1

First published in Great Britain in 2010 by
Guardian Books
Kings Place, 90 York Way
London N1 9GU

www.guardianbooks.co.uk

A CIP catalogue record for this book
is available from the British Library

ISBN 978-0-85265-219-0

Designed by Two Associates
Typeset by seagulls.net

Printed and bound in Great Britain by
CPI Bookmarque Ltd, Croydon, Surrey

Contents

Introduction

COLIN HUGHES

In 1998, a year after 'New' Labour swept to power in that over-whelming 179-majority election victory, the *Guardian* suggested I write an extended profile of Gordon Brown for its Saturday *Review*. The occasion was the first party conference afer a full session of Labour in government. Why Gordon? Well, though he had failed to win the leadership of the party after John Smith's death, Brown clearly remained the fulcrum figure for the party, and therefore the government.

However, few knew very much about him – his character, personality, history. Though he'd been politically prominent for a decade and a half, his naturally reserved character, and his tendency to keep counsel only with an intensely loyal and private personal cadre, meant that the wider world knew little of Gordon the man. The idea was to write a piece that revealed more of Brown's humanity, and how that married with his self-evidently huge political brain.

The piece that finally appeared began like this:

Walk out on the street this morning and ask the first 10 people you meet what they most want to know about the chancellor of the exchequer. You can bet your life it won't be what he's been up to at Ecofin this morning, or what he's going to tell the party conference on Monday, or what message he's taking to the World Bank meeting in Ottawa on Tuesday. No, the first nine will probably ask: 'When will the wedding be?', and the tenth: 'Is he still mad at Blair about the leadership?'

As it happens, the answers are: 'Probably next year, but he and his fiancee, Sarah Macaulay, are not telling' and: 'No, in a way he never was'. But the galling thing for Gordon Brown is that what people want to know about him is all personal, and personal things are what he hates to talk about. Politics, yes, till the mountains fall into the sea. But not personal.

It's not because he's evasive by nature. Brown is as capable of deviously ferocious political street-fighting as the next cabinet member, but he is also, in front of a camera or a tape-recorder, one of the straightest politicians around, courteous and unassuming to a fault. It's just that he finds any personal inquiry excruciating. Try and imagine him doing that gushy number Tony Blair did on the Des O'Connor show earlier this year. It doesn't bear thinking about.

Talking to Brown about his upbringing, football, his career, a bit more football, the Third Way, more football, he is warm, modest, friendly. He tells funny stories about Scottish soccer disasters and laughs at them, enjoying himself. But as soon as the Sarah Macaulay question is asked he slides back into his seat, still smiling, not looking away, but visibly curling. All his body language says: 'Oh God, do we really have to do this?' So you ask anyway: 'How's it going with Sarah?'

'Well,' he says.

Long pause.

'It's going well.'

Stones sweat more comfortably.

There's an interruption (a call from John Monks [the general secretary of the TUC]) and the relief is palpable. He bounces off into the adjacent private office to take it. Chance for a walk round the chancellor's elongated office admiring the Sutherlands he's dug out of the government vaults, along with a lovely Pissarro, some other impressionists: good stuff, and different. Mostly chosen by Sue Nye, his close personal assistant. Gordon returns, plonks back in his chair. Smiles.

'Where were we?' 'Sarah.' 'Oh yes.'

Another silence. 'Well?' he says. 'Well, when are you going to get married?' 'Oh, I don't think the Guardian *is the appropriate place to discuss these things, do you?' Big nervous smile. Hands fold in lap. Emphatically end of subject.*

On the Saturday morning that the article appeared, I travelled to the Labour party conference by train. Walking through the carriage, packed to the aisles with journalists and politicos, I noticed Sarah Macaulay sitting alongside Sue Nye apparently reading a copy of the *Daily Telegraph* together. Being slightly acquainted with them both, I stopped, and they rather guiltily scrambled the newspaper closed. Both were suppressing titters, as if they'd been caught in some back-of-the-class naughtiness. I raised my eyebrows, and asked what was amusing them so much in the Saturday Torygraph? They looked at each other, and then at me, and then sheepishly re-opened the paper. Inside the *Telegraph* was the *Guardian Review*, open at that Brown profile. And they were laughing at the passage you've just read. 'What's so funny?' I asked. 'Funny?' Sarah replied, 'It's hilarious – it's just not fair to ask Gordon a question like that!'

I recall this moment often when people ask, 'So what's Gordon really like?' It's a question that has fascinated, bemused, and occasionally infuriated everyone interested in politics for more than a decade. Who's the real Gordon? The one who chews his own jaw while wrestling with economic abstractions? The charming, kind and actually rather gentle man you encounter privately, the loving husband and father? The brutal boss and scheming fixer? The strategic super-brain, or the petty infighter? The planner of grand schemes and great change, or the endlessly prevaricating, indecisive, fiddling tactician?

The purpose of this book is to reread Brown's premiership as both a story, and a rolling commentary – not to retail every incident and event in that period, but to see how the *Guardian*'s and *Observer*'s writers wrestled with interpreting and understanding the central conundrum of Gordon's time in No 10: how did a man who started with such goodwill see it slip so easily from his grasp?

This book does not present my view, nor that of my co-editor. In fact, even though most of those who write in its pages naturally view Gordon from a left-of-centre stance, they also differ profoundly in their views of him, and their explanations of both his successes, and his failures. But for what it's worth, having watched Gordon Brown over 25 years, both closely and from afar, as a political correspondent, newspaper editor, commentator, and latterly as a newspaper manager, I continue to find him, and his political trajectory, a curious enigma.

A final anecdote. Shortly before that 1997 election I dined with Peter Mandelson. Mandelson: the man who adored Brown prior to Blair securing the leadership; who fought Brown during the Blair years; and who returned to try to rescue Brown's premiership as it floundered. At that dinner, I asked Mandelson how good a government he thought they'd be. He said: if you looked back in history, what determined a powerful government, and distinguished it from a shallow one, was whether or not the government contained enough of what he called 'big cats'. If a government contained only two or three, it would be unconvincing; if the cabinet held four, five, six big jungle beasts, it would succeed. Didn't matter that they would contend with each other – that, he thought, was natural in politics. What mattered was that they were big politicians. And he added: in Gordon Brown, we have one of the biggest politicians of our era.

I agreed with Peter then, and I agree with him now. Gordon Brown has been, and is, one of the biggest political animals or our era. As a chancellor, his growl continually echoed through the Westminster undergrowth. Understanding why he has seemed unable to carry that personal and political strength into the wholly different role of prime minister will continue to baffle many of us for years to come.

CHAPTER ONE

'I WILL TRY MY UTMOST'

Exactly one year before Gordon Brown took over the premiership, Jonathan Freedland followed the 'prime minister designate' on a visit to Northern Ireland, taking the opportunity to speculate on how the newly anointed leader would change the political temper. It's a good place to start – not only because any of Freedland's speculation was well-informed by years of watching Gordon at close proximity, but also because his article soberly summarises what most reasonably sympathetic political observers felt at the time. Gordon will be different, he'll have his own style, he'll do something radical, he'll still be New Labour ...

So from the word go there was the knowledge that Brown needed to carve out a new and distinctive position, make some bold, defining moves to separate himself from the evanescent Blair aura. But how hard is that to do, when you have been a politician (and in this case, consistently the same politician) all your long adult life? In truth, Gordon could only go on being Gordon – as he demonstrated instantly when he made his last major speech on the eve of his long-awaited accession.

No one yet felt euphorically optimistic, and certainly nothing akin to the thrill of New Labour's 1997 arrival in power; but, nestled inside the inevitable scepticism, there was a sense of at least the chance of a new dawn. Few, however, expected the first months to be quite so emphatically positive as they turned out. Perhaps through relief at Tony Blair's exit, maybe in part because voters were as yet unconvinced that David Cameron carried substance, Brown received a warm support from an electorate that evidently hoped that he could refresh what had become a stale political atmosphere.

21 JUNE 2006

What Gordon Brown is planning for his first 100 days in No 10

JONATHAN FREEDLAND

The Ulster press corps were frustrated. Denied a chance to interview the chancellor of the exchequer, they could only photograph or film him as he opened Belfast's new science park, shook hands with a fresh batch of police recruits or paid a visit to army HQ. 'It's like a bloody royal visit,' fumed one television reporter.

And so, in a way, it was. Lots of chitchat – 'And where do you come from?' – and plenty of rictus smiles for the cameras as Gordon Brown took his ongoing UK tour to Northern Ireland on Monday. All that was missing were the flag-waving children and a few bouquets.

Officially it was simply a visit by a government minister. Several of those who met Brown tried to play along with that fiction, framing their remarks in terms of costs and budgets. But they all knew what it was really about: they were there, Northern Ireland's chief constable as much as the leaders of the main political parties, to meet the next prime minister.

Such a dynamic is entirely new in British politics. The US might have its three-month transitions between presidents, but Britain has had no equivalent. Until now. For Brown has emerged as that most novel entity: a prime minister designate.

Following him for the day gave a glimpse of how he will be seen. How a Prime Minister Brown, no longer chained either to the dispatch box on budget day or the inner corridors of the Treasury, might look. And we should brace ourselves: it will be very different.

He has little of the slickness that marks out his presumed predecessor, Tony Blair, and imminent rival, David Cameron. When he spoke at the science park he made no spontaneous reference to his hosts or warm-up joke – as Blair and Cameron do everywhere and always – but went straight into his prepared text. He told one gag, but it fell flat. When he unveiled a plaque he stood in the wrong place as he pulled back the curtain, ruining the shot for television. Blair wears TV makeup for public appearances, to give him colour. Brown was pale, his jacket rumpled, and he had a visible shaving cut on his left cheek.

None of this seems to bother the chancellor unduly. He does not share the pessimism of the Brownite MP Michael Wills, who made what the camp insist was an unauthorised prediction at the weekend that Labour will be out of office for 15 years. Brown believes the doomsayers are underestimating the British public; that, in the end, voters will react to substance, not style, deciding what's best for themselves and the country, not which candidate is more likable. People liked Jim Callaghan in 1979 and actively disliked Margaret Thatcher – but they voted for her because they thought she was right.

Brown will have another advantage too: a stint in power before taking on Cameron, a chance to remake the political weather. The chancellor is a keen student of US politics, where the notion of the magical 100 days was born. So what will he do in his first 100 days in power?

His opening move will, of course, be the appointment of a team. Watch for promotions for those who aim for quiet competence rather than headline-grabbing prominence: the top rank of the Brown administration will be more Alistair Darling than John Reid. Aware that the public has lost confidence in Labour's basic ability to manage things properly, Brown will favour ministers who keep out of the papers and get on with running departments well, restoring essential confidence. He will also seize on new blood, to signal that this is a new government. Stand by for promotions for the Miliband brothers, his confidante Ed Balls and the rising stars James Purnell and Andy Burnham.

It's a fair bet that he will make at least one radical move very early. The precedent here is the independence of the Bank of England, granted by the new chancellor 24 hours after the 1997 election. That was planned for years in advance, but still had the power of surprise; Brown clearly wants to repeat the trick if he moves next door. What does he have in mind? No one will let on.

It's a racing certainty, too, that Brown will move fast to secure both his flanks, left and right. To reassure the *Sun* and others bent on casting him as Red Gordon, the new PM is bound to announce some unambiguously New Labour initiative. So far this government has privatised anything not bolted down: my hunch is that Prime Minister Brown will get out his spanner, unbolt the rest and sell much of it off. The bosses of Channel 4, for example, should prepare for the worst.

Brown will not abandon the *Guardian*-reading tribe; he's always had more respect for that part of the core Labour vote than the current incumbent. They can look forward to House of Lords reform that will make it 'fully accountable' while still respecting the supremacy of the Commons. Translation: a fully elected Lords, its role explicitly confined to that of a revising chamber.

There will also be more constitutional change, again modelled on Bank of England independence. Brown will transfer the power to make war from the executive to parliament, and shed Downing Street's patronage over honours and the appointment of bishops. In 1997 he denied himself the right to set interest rates; now he wants to tie his hands once more, again to boost public trust. It's not impossible that he'll propose all this be set down in a new, written constitution.

Sometimes there will be simultaneous straddling of left and right. I expect a Brown government to crack down just as hard on terror suspects, perhaps extending again the period of detention without charge from the current 28 days, but sweetening the pill with safeguards that civil liberties campaigners would struggle to reject: regular judicial oversight, a formal report-back to parliament to check on potential police abuses. On antisocial behaviour there could be a similar blend, with no rowing back from Blair's Asbo agenda, but a new emphasis on helping delinquent kids as much as on punishing them. It could be night football games or pirate-style radio stations – schemes that give disadvantaged teenagers something to do. Or, to revive a slogan coined by Brown: tough on crime, tough on the causes of crime.

Perhaps the trickiest question the coming man will face is the one that destroyed trust in the incumbent: Iraq. The most straightforward option would be to ape the Italian prime minister, Romano Prodi: declare the war a 'grave mistake' and announce imminent troop withdrawals. But that option is not open to Brown. He voted for the Iraq war and did not resign over it: he cannot possibly claim now to be against it. Yet he has to do something to win back those whose faith in Labour was broken by the invasion. The likely solution is some kind of admission that terrible mistakes were made in the conduct of the war and afterwards, and a strong signal that nothing like it will ever happen again.

Will it work? Gordon Brown does not look like a man preparing for failure. He may not have the glad-handing skills of a PR professional, but as a big-picture strategist he has few rivals. So long as he gets to ask the question – Who best prepares Britain to face the threat and opportunity of globalisation? – he's sure voters will see him as the answer. He believes his moment is finally coming, and he is nothing if not prepared.

25 JUNE 2007

Brown handover: We must have a soul, new leader tells party

TANIA BRANIGAN

Gordon Brown's speech yesterday was 13 years in the making, but harked back more than 50, to his boyhood. Around the nuggets of policy came personal reflections on his upbringing, beliefs and values – on the 'soul' that should be at the heart of his party.

In one of his stronger speeches to Labour, he attempted to resolve the paradox that faces him: to build on the government's successes, while offering a new start that can tempt both the party's base and the swing voters flirting with the Conservatives. Like Tony Blair before him, he suggested that only by changing can Labour remain true to its values.

As he attempted to reach out to sections of the party and of the electorate that remain suspicious, his essential message was one of humility. His remarks on service and the 'awesome responsibility' of leadership were not just an attempt to tackle Tory charges of arrogance, or doubts about his unopposed ascendance, but an echo of his two predecessors, John Smith and Blair.

'I grew up in Kirkcaldy, the community I represent in parliament ... I went to my local school and was one of the people in my class to get to university. When at 16 I suffered an injury and lost the sight in one eye, I was fortunate to have the NHS, which saved the sight in my other. It is for me a matter of fundamental principle that the best education and health care I received should be there ... for all families in all parts of Britain.

'All I believe and all I try to do comes from the values I grew up with: duty, honesty, hard work, family and respect for others. I am a conviction politician ... My conviction is that everyone deserves a fair chance in life ... that when the strong help the weak it makes us all stronger. Call it the driving power of social conscience, call it the better angels of our nature, call it our moral sense, call it a belief in civic duty. I joined this party as a teenager because I believed in these values. They guide my work, they are my moral compass. This is who I am.

'And because these are the values of our party, too, the party I lead must have more than a set of policies – we must have a soul.'

Brown stressed that he wished to continue the New Labour project, in an implicit rebuke to those who want to steer the party back to its 'old Labour' roots. 'It is in this spirit of advancing economic progress and social justice that I wish to serve ... Successful progress depends not on quick fixes or taking the easy option – that is not the New Labour way – but on having the strength to take the long-term course and see it through.

'If people think we will achieve our goals in future by retreating to the failed approaches of the past, then they have not learned the lesson I have learned from the last 10 years.'

25 JUNE 2007

All change,
but all rather familiar

SIMON HOGGART

Gordon Brown yesterday told us he wants change. He wants us to meet the challenge of change. He will heed the call to change, and will face the challenge of change everywhere. He is champing at the bit, cheerleading for change, facing the changing challenges yet realising you cannot chop and change these challenges.

In other words, he is going to be Blair Mark II, following another man who was obsessed with change. At times, if you closed your eyes and ignored the accent, it could have been Blair, right down to the verb-free sentences.

Even his opening line: 'It is with humility and pride ... ' was straight out of an old Blair speech, one of those fake oxymorons, like: 'it is with modesty and vanity', the besetting sins of most politicians. The weird pledges: 'democracy strengthened by citizens' juries'. What are they when they're at home?

Even the odd clunky phrases: 'call it "the better angels of our nature",' could have been the master, returning after being gone for approximately two minutes. Or given the past week, could it be that Gordon wants to get Gabriel in his cabinet? And the religious overtones: 'We must have more than a set of policies – we must have a soul', whatever that might mean in a political party. On Iraq he (and his new deputy) have contrived a magnificently evasive formula, also worthy of the swami Blair: 'We will learn the lessons that need to be learned, and at all times be unyielding in our support for our dedicated armed services ... ' Sounds terrific, but tells you nothing. Another New Labour triumph!

Actually the whole conference was a classic New Labour event familiar from the last 10 years: the magenta and lime-green lighting. The thunderous, ear-splitting, eye-watering, brain hemisphere-cleaving rock music. The videos in which happy smiling people of all ages, sexes and races, praise New Labour achievements, their words echoed by the cheering in the hall. More verbless non-promises, such as 'towards full unemployment'. They cheered that wildly too. This was Glastonbury without the mud, a North Korean rally without the missiles.

John Prescott and his wife arrived to more massive huzzahs. They loved him, especially because the press didn't. Prezza looked close to tears. The six deputy leadership candidates marched in, as if manacled together by invisible chains.

A young apparatchik, who looked as if he was in nappies when Blair became leader, told us that under Blair the British people always came first. Yeah, we thought, first right after millionaire businessmen and George Bush. Hundreds of meetings of thousands of people had already met to endorse Gordon as leader. It had been a 'stunning logistical operation'. What, an election with one candidate?

We had the results of the deputy campaign, percentage point by point, a total of 80 statistics over all the rounds, 277 different digits. Everyone loved that. Next Harriet Harman, winner by less than 1 per cent, rose to speak – or perhaps lecture – and you could almost hear them thinking to themselves: 'My goodness, we have to listen to this for the next 10 years?'

Then Blair introduced his successor with lavish, slathering praise. So it was necessarily a very short speech, ending: 'He will give his best, and his best is as good as it gets!'

Another video, with Gordon touring schools, travelling by tube and bus (how long will that last?) dropping in on seemingly startled strangers, like characters in a staged reality TV show.

And after the speech (received happily but without that extra edge of demented delight) Brown told us: 'I am ready to serve' – perhaps an echo of John Smith's last words, 'a chance to serve, that is all we ask'. Finally, joined by his wife, Sarah, he plunged into the crowd, smiling, slapping backs and shaking hands with his imaginary friends – many of them Labour MPs.

27 JUNE 2007

Blair exits British politics as new era begins with a Tory defection

PATRICK WINTOUR

A new political order in Britain will take shape this afternoon when Tony Blair flies to his Sedgefield constituency to resign from parliament with immediate effect, and Gordon Brown enters No 10 to prepare a shakeup of government that will see at least six ministers quit the cabinet.

Brown's allies said the new ministerial line-up would be deliberately inclusive, and not settle scores with Blair's supporters.

Blair had planned to keep the decision to quit as an MP secret until after his 318th and final prime minister's questions at noon today. But news leaked that his local party was being called to an extraordinary meeting to be addressed tonight by Blair.

One of his closest friends said: 'Tony is already psychologically out the door of No 10, and on to new challenges.' He 'had no desire to hang around Westminster for two years waiting for votes aged 54', the friend added. He will spend the next four days in Chequers before moving to his London home, north of Hyde Park.

Brown will go to see the Queen at 1.30pm today to be asked to form a government, still buoyed by his engineering of the defection to Labour of the pro-European Tory MP Quentin Davies.

The timing of the announcement yesterday and the criticism of David Cameron in Davies's resignation letter secured maximum impact for Labour on the eve of Brown's move into No 10.

The satisfaction in the Brown camp was all the more intense after the failed attempt to reach out to a group of Liberal

Democrats, including Lord Ashdown, and bring them into his government.

28 JUNE 2007

The accession: Hewitt leads exit of women from Brown cabinet

WILL WOODWARD

Patricia Hewitt resigned from the government last night after six years in cabinet and a tumultuous two years as health secretary. She thanked Gordon Brown for an offer to stay in a top post, although she had been certain to be moved from health.

The leader of the Lords, Lady Amos, the first black female cabinet minister, also left the government, nominated by Brown for the new post of EU representative to the African Union.

The resignations mean that, along with that previously announced of the social exclusion minister Hilary Armstrong, Brown is losing at least three experienced women from the cabinet; Margaret Beckett's position in the cabinet is also in doubt.

Brown was quick to establish control at No 10 yesterday. His first formal act as prime minister was to revoke the order in council allowing special advisers to instruct civil servants. The prime minister's spokesman, Michael Ellam, said it cleared the way for Brown to formally appoint his team. It also re-established Whitehall formality eroded over 10 years. Tony Blair's 1997 order enabled two political appointees, Jonathan Powell, chief of staff, and Alastair Campbell, press spokesman, to give orders to officials; one went in 2003, the other left yesterday.

29 June 2007

Brown's cabinet: Shrewd, inclusive and unthreatening

MICHAEL WHITE

Unless one of his new ministers is caught robbing a petrol station overnight, Gordon Brown's run of good luck and judgment still holds. The new cabinet won fair-minded plaudits yesterday as being shrewd and inclusive.

The contrast with the reshuffle shambles that marked the Blair years is tempting. But the new prime minister is a strategist rather than tactician. Almost uniquely he has had months to pick his team, not a weekend scramble under the lash of events. That will come later.

Even so, things can go wrong on the day, as they routinely do in a house sale chain. Nominees can change their minds or sulk. Prime Minister Brown – the title stills jars on the news bulletins – has picked competent managers from the restricted parliamentary talent pool, though few of the colourful characters of yesteryear. On Radio 4, Alistair Darling boldly made the case for dull as this season's colour, though he can surely afford more jokes now. He may need them as the economic weather darkens.

Brown has also refrained from putting all known Blairites up against a wall. As the Latin American general said 'treason is a matter of dates' and last autumn's young 'Blairites for Brown' – notably James Purnell (culture) and 'Handy Andy' Burnham (Treasury No 2) have prospered. Both are a mere 37 and clever, but are not any kind of threat. To the extent that Brown's well-constructed cabinet contains threats at all they have been gently parked. John Hutton, who was capable of standing up to the Treasury on pensions policy, has been given the rebranded and reduced Department of Trade and Industry, a hard task.

As for the current heir apparent, always a dangerous title, David Miliband gets the Foreign Office plum and the grandest office in Whitehall. Bags of opportunity to broaden his range there, but also lots of travel, lots of time away from the domestic agenda where Brown will concentrate his efforts as Tony Blair fatally did not.

To underline his own authority, Brown has nevertheless given Douglas Alexander international development with an enhanced brief on trade. It includes the world trade talks, where he will mark the Blairite Brussels exile Peter Mandelson.

The appointment of Mark Malloch Brown, ex-UN apparatchik, to the Lords, so far the sole imaginative appointment from outside the Westminster tent, may help persuade a suspicious Brown that diplomacy sometimes matters more than even his beloved economics.

Brown's overriding interests – Britain's deficient skills base and poverty, both home and abroad – are evident in the restructuring of Whitehall departments. There may be more to come. Today the cabinet meets for a rare Friday session to discuss constitutional reform, perhaps a convention on the Scottish model.

All the same, some sensitivities and quirks remain to be teased out. New Labour's 'Scottish raj', which so inflamed the Tory press, is reduced to four, including the top two spots, Brown and Darling, who along with Jack Straw are the sole survivors of the 1997 cabinet. Margaret Beckett, first a minister in 1976, is finally out. But Jacqui Smith, a popular colleague, becomes the first female home secretary in a job that has been divided and diminished.

Five women against eight last week are buttressed by three female attendees, including the steely QC, Lady Scotland, who inherits Lord Goldsmith's file of horrors. Harriet Harman, very much a love-her-or-loathe-her politician, will be leader of the Commons after all. Some MPs fear that will strain her diplomatic skills.

In a distinctly family cabinet, the Brothers Miliband plus the Cooper-Ballses, there is only one peer, Lady Ashton, surely a record, and one 60-plus (Straw) against five under 40. As unpaid Northern Ireland secretary, Shaun Woodward may be the first supermarket-sponsored cabinet member (his wife is a Sainsbury heir).

Apart from Des Browne, left at defence, it is all change and yet the Brown cabinet will feel familiar until new personalities have had time to grow. It remains New Labour elitist, only one non-graduate, Postman Johnson (health). Thirteen of the 22 went to Oxbridge, most of the rest to ancient Scottish universities.

How it works out, time will tell. But one Labour MP felt moved to tell Brown recently that he has a big advantage over Tony Blair: 'You won't have Gordon Brown to deal with.' The MP is not waiting by his phone for a job.

30 JUNE 2007

Brown effect propels Labour to election-winning lead

JULIAN GLOVER AND PATRICK WINTOUR

Gordon Brown's first three days in office have produced a surge in Labour support, putting the new prime minister in an election-winning position, according to a *Guardian*/ICM poll published today.

The poll, the first since Brown became prime minister on Wednesday, shows Labour soaring seven points to 39 per cent, a clear four-point lead over the Conservatives and its first lead in an ICM poll since March 2006.

The result is Labour's best performance in an ICM poll since David Cameron became Tory leader in 2005. If repeated at a general election it would see Labour increase its majority at Westminster.

After a difficult month, Cameron will be relieved to see the Conservatives rise to 35 per cent, up one on last month.

The main losers are the Liberal Democrats, whose support has shifted to Labour. The party is on 18 per cent, down three on last month. The rating suggests the Lib-Dems have been trading too heavily on Labour's unpopularity, especially over Iraq. It also suggests that the orderly transition betweeen Tony Blair and the new prime minister has gone down well.

The Conservatives had been bracing themselves for a Brown bounce, and privately believe the new prime minister is going to dominate the agenda for at least a fortnight. Cameron's staff were relieved the Tory vote remained solid, but will be worried that leads on a raft of policy issues, including health, have dissipated. The Tories are holding back their policy review reports for some weeks and Cameron will soon reshuffle his shadow cabinet.

1 JULY 2007

Will Gordon Brown really change the face of British politics?

NICHOLAS WATT, THE *OBSERVER*

As an early riser who likes to flick on his radio every morning on the dot of 5.30am for BBC Radio 5 Live's *Wake Up to Money*, Gordon

Brown is bright-eyed when the rest of the nation is asleep or mumbling obscenities at their alarm clocks. Early on Friday morning, however, Britain's new leader experienced his first prime ministerial wave of irritation in his Downing Street flat.

Brown was 'annoyed' and 'surprised' that no official had woken him to pass on the news that Britain had faced one of its most serious terrorist threats since the bombings of July 2005. Unlike the new home secretary, Jacqui Smith, who was woken with the news that a massive car bomb had been found in central London, Brown was left in bed by his officials.

As a meticulous political strategist, who spent months planning his first week in office down to the minutest detail, Brown knew he needed to be briefed immediately on any crisis to ensure he avoided slipping up on what even his admirers admit could be his weak spot as prime minister.

'Events, dear boy, events': the famous warning by Harold Macmillan of the greatest challenge facing a statesman has haunted the Brown camp. They know only too well that the new prime minister must show the sureness of touch displayed by Tony Blair in response to the unexpected.

With the sound of police sirens echoing round his No 10 flat as central London faced shutdown on Friday morning, Brown agreed a plan with Smith to demonstrate he could master the unforeseen. Within hours he had interrupted a trip to a pre-school centre in Islington to warn that Britain faced a 'serious and continuous security threat'. A few hours later, once he had returned to Downing Street, a cabinet meeting to discuss constitutional reforms was extended to an hour and 45 minutes to allow Smith to brief ministers after she had chaired a meeting of the government's Cobra emergency response committee.

The attempted bombing was the only item that did not appear on the new Downing Street 'grid' for Brown's first 72 hours in office, which went, as even his opponents were having to admit, remarkably smoothly. In a feat rarely achieved by Blair, Brown carried out a gaffe-free cabinet reshuffle on his first full day in office. This marked the new prime minister out from his predecessor in another key respect. Blairites, who struggled to prosper under their patron, were catapulted into key jobs at all levels.

The appointments were meant to provide a dramatic illustration of Brown's key theme of the week, which he outlined as he assumed the reins of power on Wednesday: that he would head a government of change. 'I have heard the need for change,' Brown said in remarks which cut two ways.

Brown hopes this week will show a change from the Blair era as he beefs up the role of the cabinet and parliament. But there will also be change in his own habits as he goes out of his way to show that the days of acting as a factional leader are over.

Brown will be hoping that the initial 'bounce' in Labour's fortunes – two opinion polls gave him a clear lead yesterday – will develop into a sustained lead that will undermine both the Tories and the Liberal Democrats.

On a crisp and sunny evening last week, the House of Commons terrace was packed as members of the Labour tribe gathered on the eve of the most momentous day in the party's history since Tony Blair swept into power a decade ago. As the wine flowed at one of London's most exclusive venues, with its views across the Thames, normally earnest members of the Fabian Society broke into fits of laughter as their august chair took to the stage.

'What is the difference between Gordon Brown and Stalin?' the prime minister's closest ally, Ed Balls, asked the gathering as he recalled a question he was asked by David Dimbleby shortly after the former cabinet secretary Lord Turnbull had accused Brown of 'Stalinist ruthlessness'. 'I thought for a moment that I should say one is a ruthless and determined dictator who brooks no opposition, and the other was the leader of the Soviet Union,' a beaming Balls said to widespread laughter. He paused before adding: 'Then I thought, maybe not.'

The joke by Balls on Tuesday night, which would have been unthinkable just a few days before, showed how the atmosphere had been transformed as the Blair era finally drew to a close. The seven-week Brown coronation had passed off better than his team could have hoped as the dour chancellor finally opened up at Labour hustings and at book festivals to show a more natural side, even if he still lacks the ease of the former MP for Sedgefield.

With just 24 hours until he achieved his lifetime's ambition on Wednesday, Brown drove home the political advantage by master-minding the defection of the former Tory shadow cabinet member Quentin Davies. Labour glossed over the record of the pinstriped former merchant banker – he turned up in full morning suit from Royal Ascot to vote in favour of the imposition of VAT on domes-tic fuel bills in the early 90s – to hail his arrival on the Labour benches as a sign of Brown's wide appeal.

While Davies decided not to rub shoulders with the casually dressed Fabians, his name rang round the Commons terrace as Balls whetted the appetite of the faithful by saying that other Tories were thinking of following Davies's example. Buoyed by the defection, Balls spoke in remarkably candid terms of how Britain's 'political lens' had until now focused on divisions between Blair and Brown, to the detriment of Labour. Labour's success in achieving a 'stable and orderly transition' meant that the lens would, for the first time in years, focus on divisions between Brown and Cameron, a prospect he relished after the Tory divide on grammar schools.

The public declaration of confidence by one of the most senior figures in the new order set the scene for the emotional scenes in the Commons the following day when Blair took his bow at his last prime minister's questions.

'That is that. The end,' a nervous Blair said as he left the Commons for the last time as an MP after 24 years, to an unprecedented cross-party standing ovation watched by his family, including seven-year-old Leo, seated in the gallery above. With Blair gone, attention turned rapidly to his successor. What kind of leader would he really be?

Tapping the microphone in the manner of a nervous compere, Brown had none of the elan of Blair as he prepared to address the nation in Downing Street for the first time as prime minister at 2.52pm last Wednesday. Fresh from his 50-minute audience with the Queen, who had just asked him to become the eleventh prime minister of her reign, Brown walked slowly up to the entrance of No 10 in a deliberate attempt to demonstrate his key theme of change.

No hand-picked crowds waving union flags lined the street. Only the media were on hand to hear Brown's brief statement, which was shorn of the grand rhetoric of Blair's first appearance before ecstatic crowds on 2 May 1997. Flanked by his wife, Sarah, Brown spoke of how his schooling in Kirkcaldy, Fife, had inspired him. 'On this day I remember words that have stayed with me since my childhood and which matter a great deal to me today: my school motto, "I will try my utmost". This is my promise to all of the people of Britain,' he said. 'And now let the work of change begin.'

With that, the Browns turned and walked into Downing Street, where the new prime minister deliberately chose once again to break with the past. No cabinet ministers were appointed on his first day as his team put into action the main item of Day One on the Brown grid: let the nation digest the arrival of the new prime minister in Downing Street. 'You cannot underestimate the simple political fact that changing prime minister is a major event in itself, and people should be given a chance to appreciate that,' one aide said.

The steady approach meant that Brown was able to put the finishing touches to his reshuffle in a calm manner inside No 10. Within an hour of his arrival his trusted Treasury gatekeeper, Sue Nye, who is now head of government relations in No 10, had a full cabinet list that did not change. 'This is unprecedented,' the cabinet secretary, Sir Gus O'Donnell, said of the reshuffle, which contrasted with Blair's notoriously chaotic upheavals.

Journalists at Sky News and BBC News 24, who had hoped – as was traditional – to film happy ministers and dejected ex-ministers walking the length of Downing Street the next morning, were disappointed when the reshuffle took place out of reach of their cameras. The sight of armour-plated cars in the courtyard outside the Speaker's House within the precincts of the Palace of Westminster showed that the prime minister had decided to conduct his first, and most delicate public task, in peace.

The reshuffle, which was generally regarded as one of the most polished in the modern political era, was the culmination of months of thinking. This focused both on people, and on how departments should be reorganised.

Once the names had been made public in the early afternoon of Thursday, the new ministers began arriving in Downing Street – mostly ark-like, two by two – for their first cabinet meeting. Jowell arrived with Purnell. Miliband was with Smith. Cabinet lasted 40 minutes, and a further 105 minutes when it met again on Friday in a meeting where every minister made a contribution to a discussion on constitutional reform. 'The young members of the cabinet will not realise that this is not how it was,' Straw told colleagues. Brown, it appeared, wanted to show a new discursive side.

Heath Robinson, the cartoonist who famously drew convoluted contraptions for achieving the most mundane of tasks, would have been proud of the sight that greeted visitors to the Downing Street office once occupied by Ruth Turner, the No 10 official at the centre of the cash-for-honours investigation, on Friday afternoon. A pair of whiteboards propped up against the backs of armchairs were at the centre of a military-style operation that was conducted with what one aide described as a 'nicely amateurish' feel. The boards allowed Brown, in his shirt sleeves, O'Donnell, Nye, Hoon and other officials to take an overview of the fiendishly complex task of conducting the reshuffle for government members outside the cabinet.

The boards were decorated with 23 magnetic white cards representing each department – plus whips' offices – that needed to be filled with 96 names. Once a post was agreed the minister's name would be placed on the magnetic card with a tick.

Fuelled by bacon sandwiches, Brown stood in front of the boards as he worked out which minister to place where. The process took hours, and was completed only late on Friday evening, partly because of the attempted bombing, and also because Brown insisted on calling every minister who was appointed, every minister who was sacked and every MP who had expected to get a job.

To complicate matters, he telephoned cabinet ministers to check they were happy with the appointments in their departments. 'Gordon made between 110 and 120 telephone calls on Friday afternoon,' one aide said.

One minister was impressed. 'I was called by the No 10 switch, which put me through to Gus for a few seconds, immediately followed by Sue and then Gordon for about 20 seconds. It was very friendly and very professional. I remember once being kept waiting on the line for seven minutes for Tony Blair.'

A series of outsiders who were appointed to government, in a move by Brown to shed his image as a tribal politician, received treatment normally afforded to cabinet ministers. Sir Mark Malloch Brown, the former UN official who becomes a foreign office minister, Sir Digby Jones, the former CBI director general who becomes a trade minister, Admiral Sir Alan West, the former head of the Royal Navy who becomes security minister, and Professor Sir Ara Darzi, the pioneering surgeon who becomes a health minister, were also seen personally by Brown, who had wooed them all. 'Brown was completely hands-on – this was not done through intermediaries,' a friend of Malloch Brown said. 'They really got to know each other at the G8 summit in Gleneagles two years ago.'

Peter Hennessy, the Attlee professor of contemporary British history at Queen Mary college, University of London, said Britain had seen nothing on this scale since the cross-party war cabinet in 1940. 'This looks like the greatest import of experts of a non-political background since World War Two, which was a vacuum cleaner for people who knew about things rather than believed things.'

Brown hopes his gesture towards outsiders will convince voters that he is not a partisan politician and that he is genuinely interested in changing the way government does its business – a point he will reinforce tomorrow when he talks of cross-party co-operation in reforming Britain's constitution. If Brown achieves his key objective – to distinguish his government from Blair's without vacating the centre ground occupied by New Labour for more than a decade – he may well outfox the Tories and pave the way for an early election.

Brown will be up, as ever, in the early hours of this morning. As his two young sons noisily wake up the rest of the household, Brown will slip out of his bedroom and into his study where he will sit down at his computer to prepare for his first encounter as prime minister with Andrew Marr on the BBC1 Sunday AM programme.

'So far so good,' one departing cabinet minister said of Brown's debut. 'Let's just see what happens when the going gets tough.'

1 July 2007

The new prime minister is master of his universe

ANDREW RAWNSLEY, THE *OBSERVER*

Enthroned in the prime minister's seat at the cabinet table for the first time, Gordon Brown cracked a faintly menacing joke to his colleagues. 'It's very interesting to look across at the chancellor and to think I'm no longer the man who says, "No".' With a glance at Alistair Darling, he added: 'I'm looking forward to my first battles with him.' How they all laughed, carefully.

Lurking just beneath the surface of that remark was a very serious question: who precisely will dare to do battle with the new prime minister? For the moment at least, Gordon Brown is lord of all he surveys.

True, there are enormous challenges ahead of him if this long-awaited premiership is not to turn into a relatively short one. True, as I suggested to you last week, he will be surprised and defined by events beyond his control. He's had early warning of that with the car bomb plot to wreak carnage in the West End of London. True also, he did not look like the master of the universe when he arrived at the address that he has yearned for all those years.

When he spoke to the country as prime minister for the first time, he looked becomingly hesitant, attractively clumsy. He was unsure where to stand for the cameras and then tapped at the microphone, apparently unconfident that anyone would have bothered to switch on the sound system for the nation's new leader. After 10 years of watching Tony Blair, this was like time-warping back several decades, an effect heightened by the new prime minister's invocation of his school motto to summarise himself. Does anyone still say 'try my utmost'? Well, Gordon Brown does.

He begins his time at No 10 in an exceptionally powerful position. The Labour party has cheered up, not least because a 'Brown bounce' has put them ahead in a few opinion polls. It is possible for Labour MPs to start believing that they might win the next election. It is now Conservatives who are misted in fear about their prospects. David Cameron is telling friends that he will stick to his centrist strategy. 'We mustn't lose our nerve,' the Tory leader has told allies, which demonstrates his fear that his party will succumb to panic. Things are not going according to the script that the Conservatives wrote for themselves as Brown proves to be a lot more imaginative and supple than either his opponents or quite a few in his party had expected.

Follow the money. Business leaders don't like to be seen anywhere near a loser. So it helps Brown to look like a winner when he successfully recruits the bosses of BP, Marks & Spencer, Tesco, HSBC and Vodafone to one of his new advisory panels.

Most of the media have decided to give him a honeymoon. The new PM may lack the presentational skills of his predecessor, but he was once a journalist himself and he understands what animates them. The media hunger for novelty and he has dished up plenty for headline writers to feed on. In Jacqui Smith, there is the first female home secretary. In David Miliband, there is the youngest foreign secretary in 30 years. In David and his younger brother, Ed, the first siblings to sit in the cabinet for more than 50 years. In Patricia Scotland, the first female attorney general. In Shaun Woodward, the first Labour cabinet minister to have a butler. In Quentin Davies, the defector from the Tories, the first Labour MP to be called Quentin.

The other way in which Gordon Brown has gone about surprising people is by confounding expectations of what he would be like as prime minister. As his appointments were announced, I could hear the great calculating machine that is the Brown brain as it worked down the list of everything negative that anyone has ever said about him.

You thought he was a man who can't bear criticism and nurtures his grudges like other people do their geraniums? He gives a cabinet job to John Hutton, who was of the opinion that Gordon Brown would make 'a fucking awful prime minister'. You reckoned he was a sectarian tribalist? Into his Big Kilt he has beckoned non-Labour figures such as Digby Jones, late of the CBI, and Alan West, formerly head of the Royal Navy, and Shirley Williams, darling of the liberal classes. You thought he preferred slavish loyalty in a colleague over talent? He has given big promotions to promising proteges of the departing prime minister while letting down some of his best friends.

His most difficult meeting was with Margaret Beckett, an old ally who declared her support for him long before most of her colleagues. That did not save her from having to spend more time with her caravan. The able Blairites James Purnell and Andy Burnham have seats at the top table. So has Brown's closest ally, Ed Balls, who has a portfolio packed with the new prime minister's domestic priorities. But Yvette Cooper, who might reasonably have expected to join her husband as a full member of the cabinet, only gets visiting rights for the moment. Nick Brown is so close to the new prime minister that they share the same surname. He is resurrected, but only as deputy chief whip. Ten years ago, he was chief whip. He may feel that is poor reward for all those years of loyal service, but it demonstrates that Gordon Brown can be ruthless with old friends as well as generous to old foes.

He told his new ministers that he wants the cabinet to be the forum for decision-making that it has not been during the Blair years. As a token of that, he held two cabinet meetings in his first two days as prime minister and the second of them lasted for two hours. In future and in contrast to the previous regime, so he told them, policy will be made in cabinet, Whitehall and parliament, rather than by advisers and in the media. It suits Gordon Brown to increase the status of the cabinet because he will be so powerful within it. Apart from him, only two other people – Jack Straw and Alistair Darling – have sat at the top table continuously since 1997. Neither the new chancellor nor the justice secretary has a power base independent of Brown. There is no deputy prime minister. There is no heir-apparent. The bookies might have made David Miliband the favourite, but he is too smart to waste time trying to rival the prime minister.

This puts Gordon Brown in a peculiarly dominating position. John Major was never a commanding figure, even after he'd won the Tories an election they had all expected to lose. His majority was ever-shrinking and his authority was shot to pieces as his party went to war with itself and its leader. Margaret Thatcher was regarded as a domineering prime minister. A Spitting Image sketch had a waiter asking her what she wanted for dinner. 'Steak,' replied the Great She Elephant. 'And what about the vegetables?' Withering the cabinet, she delivered the punchline: 'They'll have the same.'

Though that was the popular perception of her relationship with her cabinet, Thatcher was always surrounded by other big personalities such as Michael Heseltine, Norman Tebbit, Nigel Lawson, Geoffrey Howe and Ken Clarke. She did not always get her own way. It was her cabinet that gave her the bullet.

Blair was depicted as a presidential figure, but he would privately excuse his inability to do things on the opposition of the 'Big Beasts'. Brown will not have to deal with a John Reid, a David Blunkett, a John Prescott or a Charles Clarke. Most of all, he will not have to contend with a Gordon Brown, an alternative prime minister running a rival government from the Treasury. Every big beast starts life as a small beast. Some of the younger cabinet members will grow in reputation to become substantial figures in their own right. For the moment, though, there is no one Gordon Brown needs to be scared of in the way that he breathed down the neck of Tony Blair.

I want to be a fly on the wall on the first occasion when Alistair Darling – or any of the rest of them – does try to say no to Gordon Brown.

2 JULY 2007

Fast, agile, ruthless: Brown's start is a Tory nightmare

JACKIE ASHLEY

Gordon Brown's opponents have long claimed that as soon as he is hit by 'events', he will be left floundering. As a long-term strategist, Brown has had little practice at reacting quickly. Well, the terrorist attempts in London and Glasgow gave him an instant test. With his beefed-up security team, now including a retired admiral and the former head of the Met police, Brown easily passed – no amateur dramatics, no histrionics, nothing silly. He may be a days-old prime minister, but he didn't sound like one. With his sober assessment of the danger and warnings of the inconvenience we will have to face, he made it clear that knee-jerk responses to atrocities will be a thing of the past.

That's about as much as the current terrorist crises tell us about the new government. The really interesting signs have so far come from behind the scenes, and in particular the way the first two cabinet meetings have played out. Those attending who had experience of the Blair cabinet style are still recovering from the shock.

In the Blair years, what happened was that everyone would trip in, listen to the report on forthcoming business, and then sit back while a pre-selected minister explained his or her latest moves on health, or transport, or what have you. There would then be a round of congratulatory harrumphing and everyone would trip out again. At Friday's cabinet meeting, by contrast, there was already a real debate. Jack Straw brought his plans for constitutional reform to the table. Two ministers, who had chatted before the meeting, were dubious about parts of this and, after checking with Brown, raised their concerns. A vigorous debate followed, with everyone contributing. Straw argued back, accepted some points, repelled others, and went off to modify his plans.

There were no tantrums, no leaking and, it seems, no hard feelings. But despite the fact that the plans are scheduled for announcement today (the terrorist incidents may cause delay), they are being refined because of a collective discussion. You may think this boring, humble common sense. The truth is that, after the past decade, it's a small earthquake.

Other early signs suggest the same seriousness about running things better. As leader of the Commons, Harriet Harman wants to brief MPs about the government's business rather than the lobby journalists. Brown was punctilious in his BBC interview yesterday not to give details of the constitutional changes ahead, because he wants parliament to find out first. Jacqui Smith has been put in at the Home Office precisely because she has a more consensual approach to dealing with problems than her tub-thumping, aggressive predecessor, John Reid.

It may be bad news for journalists and broadcasters looking for a scoop or a fight, but it's good news for parliament and politics. And though all these good intentions may fray and decay as the pressure builds up on the new lot, so far Brown and his team are delivering what they promised.

This may simply be high-minded piety, but it is also ruthless, bruising party politics. Not only did Brown insist that all the former Tory advisers, Liberal Democrats and others invited into his big croft must take the Labour whip, his plans for destabilising the other parties are moving ahead. The offers to Paddy Ashdown and Shirley Williams, and the roles for Julia Neuberger and Anthony Lester, may not have been the final deadly daggers in Menzies Campbell's back (there were too many worried Lib Dems already), but it looks as if a plot to oust him is gathering force. If it produces a new leader, such as Nick Clegg, who will give the Conservatives a tougher time in their marginals, Brown will be delighted.

The Tories themselves are reeling. Yes, they may well get their balance back, and David Cameron is tougher than he looks. But there are several reasons to suggest Labour's poll bounce may be more than a blip. First, Brown's determination to rebuild trust and restore faith in the Commons robs the Tories of one of their easiest lines of attack – it's all spin. Just now, it doesn't feel like spin.

Second, by bringing in former Conservative supporters, such as Digby Jones from business or Lord Stevens, who had advised Cameron on security matters, Brown shows how deeply he can reach into Tory England. Friends of Iain Duncan Smith, working on social justice for Cameron, say he too makes warm private noises about Brown's seriousness. And after the Quentin Davies coup, I'm told there are more Tory defections expected. In other words, as Cameron struggles to drag his party towards the centre, 'Tories for Brown' are peeling off round the back.

And third, the rather grimmer times play to Brown's strengths, not Cameron's. Brown may be accused of being too serious, but his calmness, his traditional view of the importance of parliament and his brooding authority, fit nervous times better than the blithe optimism and labrador-puppy skittishness of the Tory leader.

Asked yesterday about whether he was thinking of calling an early general election, our new prime minister reacted with the prim disapproval of a Victorian dowager presented with a sex toy. That was inevitable, given the backdrop – of course he had to say he was thinking only about the security threat – but the truth is that Brown's decision to lay the ground for an early election, likelier next year than this, seems sensible. The Tories have delayed their policy commissions so long that the New Labour agenda will be well understood by people before they get their messages across. On the form of his first five days, Brown is going to be far from an easy target.

Plenty, always, can go wrong. The housing market is surely on the edge of a fall, the government is heavily borrowed, the demands on spending are rising again, and genuinely tough choices (for instance about the green belt and housing) will create clusters of new hostility to a party that has already been in power a long time. Brown himself will say something, or do something, that causes howls of outrage. Prime ministers always do. He is cautious, and may lose his nerve about election timing. But so far, he has moved fast, agilely and ruthlessly. He doesn't look like a tail-end Charlie – and if I were in Conservative central office, sitting on my sacks of cash from City supporters, I'd be very worried indeed.

2 JULY 2007

The church may be struggling, but in politics its rhetoric is on the rise

MADELEINE BUNTING

New prime ministers don't get long to get their point across. Within 24 hours of his arrival at No 10, Gordon Brown was fighting for front pages with Madeleine McCann and the Spice Girls' reunion. So he kept it simple: his government was going to be about two things – competence and serious moral purpose. It's the latter that this son of the manse repeatedly emphasises as he refers back to the devout family background that provided his 'moral compass'. He is the third consecutive Labour leader to put religion at the heart of his politics, and it's not just a matter of leaders. Yet again, there are enough believers in Brown's cabinet for a decent prayer group.

It's a curious phenomenon that at a time when Christianity continues its steady decline in this country, religion has re-emerged as a central inspiration of political rhetoric – not as the flash-in-the-pan aberration of one individual but now well established as a convention of the centre ground, acknowledged by the Cameroons as much as by Labour. This strange afterlife of religious belief must be pretty galling to secularists and humanists.

It's even more evident on the other side of the Atlantic, where almost all serious contenders for political office have to go through a process of personal confession of faith, which must prompt the likes of Richard Dawkins to choke over their breakfast. Hillary

Clinton happily does God, as did her husband, as does Barack Obama, who recently was moved to confess: 'I learned that my sins could be redeemed. I learned that those things I was too weak to accomplish myself, He would accomplish with me if I placed my trust in Him.'

Obama and Brown express themselves very differently in response to their respective political cultures, but the important point is that they are both doing much the same thing – resorting to a biblical tradition of language, character and morality. It is as if with the collapse of what John Gray in his new book calls the 'political religions' – most significantly, communism – there is no effective alternative ethical language other than that of the Bible. The 20th-century traditions of humanism, secularism and even atheism have signally failed to develop a popular language of morality in which to describe moral character and the disciplines of responsibility, self-restraint and duty that are essential to democracy and social wellbeing. If you want to convince a sceptical, inattentive electorate of your moral purpose, you have to use the shorthand of faith.

It's back to the old staples – the millennia-old stories of repentance, redemption, Samaritans, eyes of needles, camels and shepherds of a Middle Eastern society. Being British we prefer these referenced rather than a sermon – a distinction Brown observes meticulously, anxious not to offend anti-religious sensibilities. But on the occasions when he lets loose, in church gatherings about global poverty for instance, he is his father's son, the preacher.

The differences with Blair's faith are striking. It's very hard to imagine Brown praying with anyone, let alone George Bush, nor is he likely to make references to God's judgment on his Iraq policy, and least likely of all is his being tempted down the path to Rome. Blair found God in emotionally charged prayer meetings in Oxford hosted by a gregarious Australian vicar. In contrast,

Brown saw faith sustaining communities through hardship in his father's ministry – he describes it as 'social Christianity'. He was not interested in theology and personal salvation in the hereafter, the hellfire and damnation side of Presbyterianism, but in how religion inspires bonds that help individuals and communities through hard times, how it provides solidarity and ensures resilience – and that still fascinates him.

No one knows if Brown is really a hand-on-heart believer. His commitment is intellectual and practical. What intrigues him is how religion is useful. Its values have historically facilitated the development of capitalism – the Protestant ethic – and democracy, and like his fellow Scot Adam Smith, he believes morality is vital to the effective functioning of both. That makes him an unusual figure in British intellectual circles, and it's to the US that he's turned for inspiration. What he's found there in a string of writers, which includes Robert Bellah (a favourite of fellow traveller Chief Rabbi Jonathan Sacks) and Robert Putnam, as well as more rightwing thinkers such as James Q Wilson and Gertrude Himmelfarb, is the anxiety about a moral and social breakdown.

The problem, said Bellah in *Habits of the Heart*, is an individualism 'which denies the basic reality of our interdependence' and identifies with the 'typical virtues of adolescence' such as independence but also the 'less savoury adulation of success, and contempt for weakness'. The consequence is a 'radical disengagement' from society. The challenge is to 'renew the cultural capacity for community and solidarity', wrote Bellah more than 20 years ago, and he suggested both 'biblical traditions and civic republicanism' could help. It's advice Brown appears to have been following since, not least in his development of the concept of Britishness.

As politics increasingly moves into a territory of personal behaviour – how do you persuade people to forgo consumer goodies to save for pension provision and to eat healthily to avoid obesity, the respect agenda, parenting (it's significant that many of these issues have landed in the lap of his closest associate, Ed Balls) – Brown is increasingly going to find that his Kirkcaldy religious DNA comes into conflict with his faith in the free markets and their promotion of a voracious consumer culture. Put crudely, how can the state hope to inculcate an ethic of responsibility into its citizens regarding eating and spending in a culture that urges fast food and is saturated with cheap credit? It's a bit like putting a bottle of whisky in front of an alcoholic and asking them to kick the habit.

Much of Brown's political career has been clarifying the relationship between the market and the state. What lies ahead is an even more demanding task: how to resolve the conflict between personal freedom, the market and the morality he believes must underpin both of them. Feeding the hungry and clothing the naked is the easier part, but his manse morality is going to take him into much more difficult waters.

2 JULY 2007

A new dawn after 13 years

ROY HATTERSLEY

It has been a good five days, made even better by the slice of luck with which Gordon Brown's premiership began. Inside the cabinet, Paddy Ashdown – obliged to argue for Liberal policies – would have been a grain of sand that irritated without becoming a pearl. By declining Brown's offer, he spared the cabinet hours of tedium and made his party look more interested in confrontation than in compromise.

Some Labour party members will regard Brown's ecumenical initiative as proof that he is not genuine Labour. But, tribal politician though I am, and despite my instinctive distaste for turncoats, I cannot see why it is wrong to enlist new adherents to the government's cause. All prime ministers hope to attract high-profile recruits. Alun Chalfont, the *Times*'s defence correspondent who joined Harold Wilson's Foreign Office, was said to have become a peer, a privy councillor, a minister and a member of the Labour party in one afternoon. If Lord Digby Jones assists in the pursuit of a genuine Labour industrial policy, I do not care how he would have voted at the next election had his peerage not prevented him from voting at all. It is the policies that matter, and on the evidence of the past five days, the policies are going to improve.

When Alan Johnson announced that hard-working doctors and nurses had to be convinced that their skills and dedication were properly valued and respected, he was gently breaking the news that the days of oppressive health service targets were over. In the speech with which Brown accepted the Labour leadership, he was explicit that local authorities and housing associations were essential allies in the drive to build affordable houses for rent as well as sale. The doctrinaire reliance on speculative building that has left Britain scandalously short of low-cost accommodation has been rejected at last. The changes in health and housing policy are no more than common sense. But social democracy and common sense often go hand in hand. Almost everything Brown did last week – what he said and how he said it – suggests that common sense is on the way in and celebrity politics on the way out.

Of course, the prime minister has already said and done some things of which most Labour party members disapprove. Labour prime ministers always do. There will be almost universal disappointment that he has endorsed the city academy programme by reappointing Andrew Adonis as schools minister.

But I served happily, and with a clear conscience, in Jim Callaghan's cabinet for two years after his notorious Ruskin speech had begun the counter-revolution against the comprehensive system. In politics you can rarely have it all your own way. The best we can do is hope to identify shared aims. Brown's policies would undoubtedly reduce the inequalities that scar our society. If he chooses to call them 'modernisation', egalitarians should not choke on the word.

Thirty years ago (when 'modernisation' was called 'revisionism') we Croslandites argued that change was essential to achieve our goals. The problem arises when, instead of looking for a new and improved version of social democracy, we search for an alternative. Charles Leadbeater, once an adviser to Tony Blair, said the problem with New Labour was that it was neither new enough nor Labour enough. Brown shows every sign of remedying both mistakes.

The paradox of Brown's success last week was the way in which he managed, despite the appointment of half a dozen Liberal advisers, to remain undisputedly Labour. That was immensely reassuring to more people than the tightly knit group of politically motivated men and women who regarded Blair as an apostate. The continuing commitment to long-held principles gives a politician 'bottom', while ideologically footloose ministers encourage the question: 'Do they really believe in anything except winning the next election?'

Therein lies the second paradox. By demonstrating that there is more to politics than winning, Brown is making winning more likely. So, I feel more content with the political prospect than at any time since, 13 years ago, I spent the evening with John Smith after telling him I was leaving parliament. That night it seemed that a genuine Labour prime minister would soon form a proper Labour government – cautious, moderate but essentially radical. That hope was extinguished on the following Friday. Today it is alive again.

7 JULY 2007

Floods

The prime minister, Gordon Brown, will visit areas devastated by the flooding today as insurers said the crisis would cost them £1.5bn and civic leaders warned that some people may not be able to move back into their homes until 2009.

Brown promised a 'comprehensive' programme not just to help the hundreds of people who are still unable to return to their homes but to help communities recover.

The prime minister's spokesman denied the government had been slow to react. 'The prime minister spoke directly to the local authority leaders involved some days ago. We've been looking at financial assistance and what we can do to follow on from that in the last week or so.'

12 JULY 2007

Good sense but no surprises

LEADER

Gordon Brown brought a small constitutional novelty to parliament yesterday: an early sniff of the Queen's speech that formalised his enthusiasm for announcing policies several times over. The most telling thing about the statement was not the programme Mr Brown set out but the emphasis he chose to put upon its various parts. Nothing in it was fully new, but by talking much more about some issues (housing) than others (crime) Mr Brown underscored his desire to take the government down fresh paths.

One of those – let slip at prime minister's questions – was his decision to bring into doubt plans for new supercasinos. The folly of gambling liberalisation has already caused the government much misery, not just in the choice of Manchester as the site of the first gambling palace, which infuriated Labour MPs, but from the very start, eating up parliamentary time and political credibility. The case for the large-scale expansion of casinos has always been thin, and the case for a network of supercasinos even thinner. It is too late for Mr Brown – who was closely involved in the initial decision to change the law – to extricate himself from the whole Gambling Act. But if he pulls the plug on supercasinos, as he now seems likely to do, he will have done something to mitigate its worst effects. Manchester will not be happy, but retreat is the right course.

If Tony Blair had been in charge of yesterday's summer statement, it would surely have been dominated by Home Office legislation on crime and terrorism; the hyperbole of fear and the so-called respect agenda. Now that Mr Blair and John Reid have gone, the mood has changed. Not completely – Mr Brown did confirm that there will be a further push to raise the 28-day limit under which terrorist suspects can be held without charge. But the new prime minister mentioned the terror bill almost in passing, way down a list of legislation that gave priority to housing, a topic that did not much interest Mr Blair, at least not until he realised the cost of his new home in Connaught Square.

In part, this may just be a smart recognition on Mr Brown's part of the potential political cost of high property prices and climbing interest rates. But he is right to put his energies into the issue. Labour's record in office has not kept pace with the rhetoric: John Prescott, in charge of housing for most of a decade that saw the issue shunted between four departments, repeatedly promised a great expansion of low-cost social housing. But the reality is that fewer such homes were built than under the Tories.

Over the past year social landlords completed 21,892 new homes in England. In 1996-7 they built 24,630.

Turning this round will be difficult, not least because the price of land keeps climbing. There are no cheap sites on which to build new property. That is why the government is keen to change planning laws, to allow new sites to be found and to stop local objections delaying development. Mr Brown yesterday tried to reassure MPs that he wanted to see brownfield sites developed, protecting green belt land. But it is hard to see the government's previous target of 200,000 new homes a year by 2016, let alone Mr Brown's expanded one of 240,000, set yesterday, being met without using sites that were once protected. That worries environmental groups. But it also leaves Mr Brown with a challenge. He promised new developments of eco-towns, but if he insists (as he should) on high standards, costs will rise and targets will be missed.

Not a Queen's speech – not even a little princess's speech – yesterday's statement was still a decent use of parliamentary time, a step away from a ritual that saw the monarch announce a democratic government's agenda. The tone was refreshing, the content, on examination, much less new. As such, it gave an accurate description of the Brown government.

19 JULY 2007

This isn't like 1997's euphoria at all. And what a relief that is

JOHN HARRIS

With today's byelections in Ealing Southall and Sedgefield likely to provide sound electoral proof of the much-discussed Brown bounce, it's not only the usual cheerleaders who are brimming with Labour's new sense of hope. Within a week of the handover at the top, one backbencher – hardly a member of the awkward squad but a little too left-leaning to have ever been a paid-up New Labourite – found herself so full of good cheer that she could not hold it in. 'It's just like 1997 again, isn't it?' she asked one of her colleagues, a claim that should probably not be taken entirely seriously, though it highlights the outlook of a party that recently looked as if it had succumbed to a gloomy fatalism.

In keeping with the new mood, those of us who have held out the hope of a social-democratic revival unquestionably feel lifted. Some, like our backbench friend, are getting carried away. Others are trying to square renewed faith with the deepseated ambivalence that Gordon Brown often seems almost to encourage. Still, there are reasons to be cheerful, many of which boil down to the difference between Labour's recent history and what looks like its immediate future.

Last month I sat in Manchester's Bridgewater Hall and heard a Gordon Brown speech peppered with themes you would not have heard from any Blairite – a turning-up of the volume on child poverty and acknowledgement of the insecurity and vulnerability that has come with globalisation. In its wake there have been equally heartening shifts. To a strangely muted fanfare, the government appears to have waved goodbye to the old Blairite dream of the NHS being reinvented as a mere commissioner of contracted-out care, and embraced a vision outlined by the Brown camp in 2003-4: private providers being used to plug gaps, but – for reasons as much pragmatic as ideological – being kept out of core services. The housing green paper may not contain the revival of old-style council housing, but its proposals for a big role for local authorities would have been unthinkable a few months ago. Ditto the noises about ramping up the role of education authorities in the academies programme, and emphasising the involvement of universities rather than tycoons.

At that point, we should stop and consider the inevitable downside, embodied by the arrival in government of that renowned progressive Digby Jones. No matter that the cosy position of the super-rich is being questioned by even the *Daily Mail*, and that huge coverage of Tuesday's Joseph Rowntree Foundation report turned up the heat on inequality yet further. In his first couple of interviews as chancellor, Alistair Darling has sounded mealy mouthed about private equity tax breaks and apparently unconcerned about the slack cut to those Learjet commuters who enjoy non-domicile status.

That there has been no kerfuffle about Darling's stance says a great deal about Labour's present mood. It would be naive not to acknowledge that Brown's dangling of a snap election has conveniently firmed up the party's optimism with an injection of discipline. In time, however, debate and dissent will return. Over the next year, pay close attention to the coalition of trade unions, MPs and activists that backed Jon Cruddas's admirable run for the deputy leadership. Let us not forget that Cruddas won the single biggest number of first-preference votes, and knocked out three members of the cabinet. Having turned down a minor party post and the offer of a junior ministerial job in Hazel Blears's Department of Communities and Local Government, he is currently taking stock; but he and his allies are set on developing their influential ideas about modern inequality and insecurity – it was partly thanks to the Cruddas campaign, for instance, that Labour belatedly embraced the housing issue – and approaching the new government as candid friends. In essence, they cleave to the old soft-left idea that being radical need not tip into hostile oppositionism.

Some will see that as the stuff of hopeless compromise, but the alternatives are unappealing. By way of research, I had a quick look at the website run by that righteous parliamentary rump the Campaign Group of Labour MPs, and was instantly confronted with comfy nostalgia and the politics of the shopping list: demands for student grants for all, renationalisation of the railways, the rolling back of Tory union legislation, and all the other hard-left shibboleths that have been in place since the early 1990s.

For those whose views are a little more nuanced, there is one particularly important consideration. For all the talk of the Brownite-Blairite wars being brought to a close, many of those who were recently equating the prospect of a Brown premiership with political disaster have only provisionally gone quiet. Make no mistake: should Labour lose the next election, it is in Brown's moves away from eye-watering Blairism and his gentle encouragement of Labour's social-democratic instincts that they will locate his failure, doubtless cheered on by the same media voices who still cannot quite believe that Brown won out. To be blunt, if he goes down, the serious Labour left goes with him.

So, welcome to the new era of high stakes and inevitable disappointments, but an optimism that may just turn out to have a much firmer foundation than that of the fizzy euphoria of a decade ago. To answer the question posed by the aforementioned backbencher, it is not like 1997 at all. And you know what? Thank God for that.

20 JULY 2007

Brown gains double win in first poll test

TANIA BRANIGAN

Conservative hopes of ending the Brown bounce suffered a setback early this morning, as the party came third in two high-profile byelections despite a push spearheaded by David Cameron. Voters gave Gordon Brown a cautious endorsement in his first electoral test as prime minister, when Labour held on to both Ealing Southall and Tony Blair's former seat of Sedgefield, albeit with much-reduced majorities.

The results raise questions about the Tories' ability to recover from the boost the government has enjoyed since the handover at No 10 and, perhaps more damagingly, about Cameron's changes to the party. Many saw the decision to parachute a charismatic political novice into Southall as evidence of the Tories' tendency to put spin ahead of substance.

23 JULY 2007

The signals say no to a snap election: The Brown bounce points to an early poll but don't be fooled

LARRY ELLIOTT

Less than three months ago the mood inside the government was gloomy. The Conservatives were riding high in the polls and Labour took a dreadful hammering in the local elections. Now it's the Tories who are depressed after two third places in last week's byelections.

The Westminster gossip now is that Gordon Brown may call a snap October election, which would not only exploit Labour's bounce since he became leader but would provide him with his own mandate. Although nothing would give the prime minister greater pleasure than giving David Cameron a good going over, a snap election still seems unlikely.

In part, that's the result of Brown's overall approach to politics, which has always tended to be long term. He doesn't do snap anything. He may consider, for example, how voters – who seem generally happy under Brown so far – would respond to an election they might not consider necessary with Labour only just over two years into a five-year term. It's also the case that the party is skint. That, after all, was what cash for honours was all about.

The most telling reason for caution about an autumn election, however, is that by the time people come back after their summer holidays, the economy may not look quite so clever from Labour's point of view.

That may sound counterintuitive. After all, did not the latest growth figures on Friday show that Britain has just completed 15 straight years of economic expansion? Is it not the case that growth is steaming along at 3 per cent, providing Labour with the perfect platform for an election campaign: everything's fine, so don't let the Tories mess it up?

Given the momentum behind the economy it would be daft to imagine that it will have fallen off a cliff within three months. Yet, the economic mood is set to darken.

25 JULY 2007

Brown fails to banish Blairism from No 10

TOM CLARK

At his party's 2003 conference, Gordon Brown bellowed: 'We ... are at our best when we are Labour,' pointedly omitting the prefix 'new'. Aides quipped that concerns about the word count had forced the three-letter adjective out. But the real purpose was suggesting a future Brown government would provide a break with Tony Blair's New Labour policies. Tomorrow, parliament goes into recess, after a busy four weeks since the handover. Glancing over the end-of-first-term report card, how much has changed?

There are new priorities – particularly housing, in which Blair never showed much interest. Equally significant, however, are changes in attitude that cut across departments. The government is still keen to be close to business, but seems willing to maintain a little more distance when it comes to social questions. That has been seen, for example, in the move to ditch the supercasino. It is seen, too, in the NHS. Under Blair, 'diversity of supply' became a goal in itself, but the new health secretary, Alan Johnson, instead suggests that the private sector should be used only where it adds to, rather than replaces, publicly provided services. In housing, where the private sector and third sector have long been the only games in town, councils look set for an enhanced role – even though, as I write, it is unclear how far the financial rules that have hindered council-house building are really being relaxed.

Blair famously boasted of the 'scars on his back' incurred in scraps with public sector workers. Brown, however, seems keen to show professionals that he will listen. The Treasury chief secretary, Andy Burnham, told the *Guardian* last week that he would slash the tally of targets – which so tie the hands of public servants – from 110 to 30. The schools secretary, Ed Balls, meanwhile, has moved to mend broken bridges with the National Union of Teachers, and seized on the launch of a slimmed-down curriculum to stress the importance of teachers enjoying autonomy.

Crackdown politics, such a feature of the Blair years, are now less in evidence. Where last summer's terror alert was tackled with high drama, the botched bomb plot that emerged in Brown's first days was met with calm resolve. Under Blair, tough talk on crime went alongside legislation that created new offences at the rate of one a day. Yet when Brown set out his plans for the coming parliamentary session there was no suggestion of a new criminal justice bill. And the new justice secretary has suggested that non-custodial sentences, rather than jail-building, are the way out of the prisons crisis.

A healthy distance from business, a new respect for the professionals, and more liberal justice policies ... and I've not even mentioned John Denham's increased student grants. Have progressives finally got the Labour government that they dreamed of back in 1997? Not quite. The same political pressures that shaped Blair's agenda are now ensuring that Brown will offer more continuity than change.

When at the Treasury, Brown fought off the get-tough policies on single mothers that were regularly cooked up in No 10. It may seem perverse, then, that one of the first acts of his government has been to propose forcing lone parents to sign on to the inflexible jobseekers allowance. But that is what the new PM feels that the taxpayers who foot the welfare bill demand. While the drive to privatise may have cooled in health, a welfare green paper last week proposed contracting out work from jobcentres, without any clear rationale. And an enlightened approach to crime still seems a long way off – Brown last week set a ball rolling that could see possession of cannabis again become an offence carrying a five-year jail term.

You can take Blair out of Downing Street, but, given the pressures on the government – from business, the media and much of the electorate – evicting Blairism from No 10 will not be quite so easy.

25 JULY 2007

It's been an intense initiation, but people are listening to Labour again

JONATHAN FREEDLAND

He's endured trial by fire and trial by water, and he's still standing. Today marks four weeks in the job for Gordon Brown, an initiation more intense than anyone could have anticipated. The attempted terror attacks on London and Glasgow came within his first 72 hours inside No 10; now he contends with the worst floods in modern British history. One cabinet colleague concedes that had Brown 'dropped the ball' in handling either crisis – and, remember, the flood menace has not yet receded – it might already be over for him. If Brown had faltered or panicked, voters would have formed an early, fatal impression.

Even before those twin disasters struck, the stakes were always going to be high for this July. Brown won't even have the luxury of FDR's 100 days to prove himself. He can't do anything in August, a political non-month. He knew when he took office on 27 June that the public view of him would congeal in these first four weeks, a time when people are already disengaging, preparing to go on holiday or watching the sport on TV. There was little room for error.

How has he done? There have been some stumbles. He was shaky in his first prime minister's questions and he patently has none of his predecessor's gifts for conveying the apparently spontaneous, empathetic remark. He could find no such language to convey what he had seen in submerged Gloucestershire on

Monday, for instance. And some of the non-politician 'talents' he has brought into his government have strayed badly off-message.

But set aside those relatively minor glitches and Brown's first month looks like a striking success. Last week, Labour won two byelections – despite being in mid-term in its 11th year in office. The national polls record a predictable Brown bounce, but also a warm personal reception. Today's *Guardian* survey shows not only a six-point Labour lead but also nearly a quarter of Tory voters conceding that their opinion of Brown has risen since he became prime minister. You pick up the same impression anecdotally, as those who do not follow politics obsessively describe the new prime minister as solid, reliable and grown-up. The word 'gravitas' comes up a lot.

In conversations this week with several senior cabinet ministers, it's clear that the Brown command view all this with pleasure but not much surprise. They had, after all, planned meticulously for this period and knew what they had to do. First, they wanted to sear into the public mind the notion that there had been a change of government. They knew the voters were tired of them and that the Tories' best shot was 'time for a change' – so change, they resolved, is what the voters would get.

That meant Brown repeating the word nearly a dozen times outside No 10 on his first day, but also signalling that everything – or at least those things the public did not like – would be different from now on. So the presidential style of Tony Blair has been replaced by the much-heralded return of cabinet government, with two-hour discussions on constitutional reform, for instance, which – brace yourself – actually alter government policy.

Brown sent the collegial message even more directly by dispatching Jacqui Smith to speak first on the attempted London terror attacks, and by having Hilary Benn at his side when briefing on the floods. Privately, Brown says there are two approaches to his job. One is to walk into the room and say, 'Right, I'll do everything' and make yourself the focus of activity. (I can't imagine who he has in mind.) And the other is to delegate and then make sure everybody else is doing their job properly.

But there's been more than a change in political process. The new prime minister has rapidly chucked overboard those items of Blair baggage the public disliked. The ditching of the supercasino, the likely reclassification of cannabis and a retreat on 24-hour drinking have won expected plaudits from the social conservatives of the *Daily Mail*, but not only from them. The supercasino had become the symbol of an aspect of the Blair era – the materialism, the worship of bling – which clearly made many Britons uncomfortable. Downing Street has been struck by how few people have mourned the roulette wheel's passing. In this context, Brown's dourness, his repeated references to his upbringing in the manse, reinforce the point. Eventually, people may tire of it, even feeling vaguely judged by the puritan in No 10. But for now, and given what's gone before, the roundhead Brown fits the moment.

He's also used July to signal that his priorities will be domestic. The word Brown picked up on his pre-prime ministerial tour of Britain was that voters wanted the government to 'come back home'. They'd had enough of the strutting on the global stage, and wanted ministers to return to British bread and butter. Brown has acted on that, ensuring his lightning visits to Paris and Berlin were so quick they were barely noticed. He'll go to Washington next week, but you detect little of his predecessor's enthusiasm for that aspect of the job.

He had one last objective for July. Assembling the New Labour coalition in 1997 was easy: all you had to do was unite everyone who opposed the Tories. It's binding purpose was essentially negative. Brown's task in 2007 is harder, to supply positive reasons for people still to support Labour. That's why he's so proud of his recruitment of a former head of the navy, Lord West, or a business chieftain such as Digby Jones: they suggest that Labour offers a positive project people want to join.

One astute shadow cabinet member suggests that if Brown is presenting himself as the candidate of change, he'll have to go for an election soon: he won't look much like change when he's been in power for 18 months. The polls must make that tempting. A cabinet colleague adds that Brown's driving goal is to win his own mandate, that everything we see now is preparation for that.

And yet Brown's caution will surely prevail. He might cite the historical precedents for a change of prime minister without an election, and insist that it would look like careerist opportunism to trigger an early poll, but it is surely fear of failure that will hold him back. He doesn't want to be remembered as the shortest-serving prime minister in history.

Besides, his offer to the electorate will not be 'change' anyway. Marking a break from the Blair past was just a necessary first step – like 'meeting a hygiene standard', according to one ally – in order to get the public to listen to Labour again. Once they are, there will be more to say. And that work will begin in September.

CHAPTER TWO

GORDON'S MISSED MOMENT

Gordon's pushing ahead in the polls, the voters look friendly, the commentators are all treating him kindly. Natural, then, that the Westminster village should immediately start contemplating the possibility of an election. As it turned out, a (thankfully) quickly shut down security threat, followed by a thoughtfully handled flood crisis, were only minor tests of the new Brown premiership. The real test for the leader, still only weeks in, would prove to be a purely political one; not 'events, dear boy', but a self-conjured crisis over when, whether, how, he should seek a direct mandate. And this scenario played into all the best and all the worst of Brown: the need to make a precise judgment call over an issue that only strictly matters as an indicator of his own political skills. If he calls a snap election, will it seem opportunistic? Are the polls solid enough? If he waits, will he risk what he (and the party) have in the short-term won by changing their leader?

As the story unfolds, it's clear that the decision is far from being an easy one to make. The psephology is not emphatically supportive one way or the other. The hints and signals of voter mood are ambiguous. But in this process of making the decision, really only one thing matters – that he makes it clearly, and resolutely, and then moves on. And that's the one thing that didn't happen.

5 AUGUST 2007

You can rely on Gordon for loos, but for an election?

ANDREW RAWNSLEY

When the floods were inundating his new realm, Gordon Brown almost found himself in the shit. Touring drowned areas of England, he asked those handling that emergency what they most needed. He was disturbed to learn that there was a problem with sanitation that was threatening to go critical. Soon afterwards, the chairman of the civil contingencies committee back in London found he had the prime minister on the phone growling at him to get 900 Portaloos to Tewkesbury.

A few days after sorting out lavatories for distressed voters, Brown was on a plane to the United States for talks about Afghanistan, Darfur and Iraq. This weekend, he's in London, rushing back from his broken holiday in Dorset for crisis conferences about the outbreak of foot and mouth. It's debatable how much difference will be made to the handling of that by Gordon Brown's physical presence in Downing Street. But, for him, it is not enough to be in charge. He needs to be seen to be in charge. It's a bit reminiscent of Margaret Thatcher, another workaholic prime minister, who so hated taking holidays that she spent them longing for a problem that would give her an excuse to go back to work early.

One day, it's war. Another day, it's Portaloos. Next, it's cattle disease. That is the life of the modern prime minister, as Gordon Brown has been discovering during his first frantic five weeks in No 10.

I make you this bet. No one in Team Brown had the foresight to write emergency loos into the original masterplan for his First Hundred Days in power. Nor was an outbreak of foot and mouth factored into Gordon's grid. While they might have guessed there would be a terror alert, they could not have planned for the car bomb plots either.

Gordon Brown has always been known as a great planner. And yet it is the unplanned that has worked out to his advantage. Harold Macmillan was only half-right when he talked about 'events, dear boy, events'. It is not the events themselves that define a leader; it is how he responds to those events. Brown's performance in a crisis was one of the apprehensions about him before he moved into No 10. Tony Blair's fear on that score was one of the reasons he was doubtful about his successor. The general judgment is that Brown has responded well in an emergency. Overall, he has had a better start at No 10 than either his enemies – or indeed many of his friends – anticipated. So much so that it is exciting speculation that he might be tempted to call an early election.

About that, let me make a confession. After intensive research into the question and following many conversations with people at the most senior level in both the government and the opposition parties, I still don't have a clue when Gordon Brown is going to call a general election.

Let me reveal something else to you: everyone else who is speculating about his intentions doesn't have the foggiest whether he will go to the country this autumn, next spring, the year after or the year after that. The cabinet does not know. Ed Miliband, who is putting together Labour's next manifesto, doesn't know. Douglas Alexander, who is in charge of planning the election campaign, doesn't know.

What I do know is this. Before he got to No 10, the working assumption of Brown and his inner circle was that the government was so damaged that it would take a lot of time to win back the confidence of the voters. The earliest they expected to be able to call an election with any confidence of winning was in the spring of 2009.

Those assumptions are certainly being recalibrated. One reason is the surge in the opinion polls. In the six months before Gordon Brown moved into No 10, Labour was behind the Tories in all but one poll. Since he moved into Downing Street, Labour has been ahead in every single poll.

Labour MPs who once despaired of keeping their seats are now much more upbeat; Tories who once thought they were finally on their way back to power are now much more downcast.

Talk of an early election adds to the panic attack afflicting the Conservatives after David Cameron's most torrid period as their leader. Which is why it suits Labour to excite speculation by dropping hints that the manifesto is already in production and putting Labour MPs 'on alert' to start campaigning in September. The possibility of a snap poll helps Brown impose unity and discipline on his party while destabilising the Tories. It is an encouragement to Labour supporters to start writing cheques for their penniless party. It puts pressure on Cameron to rush into policy commitments earlier than he might otherwise have done and sooner than might be clever if an election turns out to be two or more years away.

The truth about Gordon Brown is that, like any sensible politician in his position, he is trying to keep his options open and his cards close to his chest. I've little doubt that a large part of him would love to go to the country early. As one member of the cabinet puts it: 'Gordon wants his own mandate.' He may have had a much better start than many of the sceptics in Labour's ranks had anticipated. But in one crucial respect, he remains in the shadow of his predecessor. Tony Blair won three elections in a row; Gordon

Brown has yet to win one election on his own. If he could be sure of victory, he'd obviously announce a general election tomorrow.

His trouble is that he cannot be sure. And there is an enormous penalty for calling this wrong and chucking away a perfectly good majority by going to the polls sooner than he had to. Brown knows he would look like one of the greatest fools ever to occupy No 10 if he called an early election and wound up with an emaciated majority. It would be worse still if he lost all his majority and found himself trying to negotiate an extended lease on power courtesy of Sir Menzies Campbell.

Were he to lose altogether, he would become one of the shortest-serving prime ministers of all time, forever ridiculed by historians and condemned by his party. It is with good reason that people have always called this the loneliest decision that a prime minister ever has to make.

The first question nagging him is whether the 'Brown bounce' is merely that. Does it signal the beginning of an improvement in the government's fortunes that will prove durable or is this just an upwards blip that will soon fade away? In conversation about election timing with close allies, Brown has been heard to remark that modern voters are 'volatile'. He has taken an interest in the fate of Shinzo Abe, the Japanese PM. After taking over from a charismatic and combative predecessor of the same party, his honeymoon with the voters proved to be short. His poll ratings crashed, and he has just been humiliated at the ballot box.

Brown's inner circle are palpably unsure how to read the public mind and wary of over-interpreting these opening weeks of his premiership. That caution was expressed publicly by Ed Miliband when he remarked the other day: 'It's important not to get carried away by opinion polls.' As this key ally of the prime minister went on to say: 'We've got a big job to do to earn people's trust.'

Would people trust an early election? Sure, most respondents tell pollsters that's what they want. But voters don't always react well to being given something just because they have asked for it. Brown is being sold as a serious leader for serious times. The initiatives, plans and reviews that he has announced since he arrived at No 10 are designed to establish him as a leader with a long-term project for Britain. An early election could be read as a sign that he hasn't got confidence about the future. The Tories would cry that he is cutting and running early because he knows there are bad things just around the corner. They would not be deterred from saying that simply because they had previously urged an immediate election.

Brown will also want to have a much more precise idea about the nature of his support than you get from the headline figures of the polls. It will not look good for his prospects if Labour is piling up more votes in places where its seats are already safe, but is still in trouble in the southern marginals that he has to win to secure a fourth term.

If he reads the detailed data from the polls – and, of course, he pores over the fine print – he will know that many of the public haven't yet come to a firm conclusion about him. He is on probation. Those expressing satisfaction with him exceed those saying they are dissatisfied, but the biggest group of voters are those who do not express an opinion one way or another. About four in 10 people are reserving judgment on their new prime minister. Which is another good reason for him to reserve his judgment about when to ask the people to give their verdict in the ballot boxes.

Gordon Brown hasn't even told Gordon Brown when he will call a general election. He doesn't know either.

20 SEPTEMBER 2007

Brown to keep Tories guessing on autumn poll

PATRICK WINTOUR

Cabinet members left a two-hour strategy session yesterday persuaded that Gordon Brown plans to go through next week's conference in Bournemouth keeping his options open on an autumn poll.

Senior cabinet figures said that it was quite feasible to keep the focus on the message of the conference, even with media speculation continuing on whether there will be a snap election. Brown could leave it until the following week, on the final day of the Tories' conference and the day of David Cameron's speech, to call an 25 October poll.

One senior cabinet minister said after yesterday's session, largely dedicated to the party conference themes, that they had personally switched to believing that the prime minister would hold an autumn poll. The arguments in favour are for Brown to seek a personal mandate, and a fear that Cameron is gradually building a substantial war chest of party funds. But another minister argued the party simply does not have the regional organisation in place at the moment to contest an election.

The mood in the cabinet is volatile, and the *Guardian*/ICM opinion poll showing Labour's lead has increased to eight points has strengthened the hands of those calling for an early election.

It is thought the chancellor, Alistair Darling, is advising against, even though it appears the government has not been damaged by the Northern Rock crisis.

Speaking after the meeting, Douglas Alexander, the election co-ordinator, set out Labour's conference aim: 'Over the next few days we've got to show that we have the vision to change the country for the better.'

24 SEPTEMBER 2007

Election fever

LEADER

Gordon Brown has managed to say almost nothing of interest in the past few days, a fact that will surely please him. The prime minister's robotic interview in the *Sunday Times* and his less-than-specific breakfast television chat to Andrew Marr have brought the current political guessing game about a snap election to boiling point. So have nods, winks and real confusion inside Mr Brown's team about what he intends to do. Yesterday, as Labour's annual conference got under way, delegates, MPs and journalists dashed about Bournemouth asking each other whether there would be an election in October, or November, or not at all. Conservatives, forced to plan both a party conference and an emergency campaign warbook, are asking themselves the same thing. From his suite in the Highcliff Hotel, Mr Brown has managed the mystery, confining himself to a few enigmatic lines: 'getting on with the job'; 'clear choice'; 'when the time comes'. These could point to an immediate poll, or no poll at all – which is all part of the game.

Today, however, Mr Brown will have to say something when he speaks to his party for the first time as its leader. Not necessarily about an election, or even the absence of one, although if the prime minister really has no intention of holding a contest it would do both him and democracy good if he said as much. As things stand, Mr Brown risks being seen as a man who wanted to go to the country, but decided not to: 'Gordon's missed moment' is a phrase that could come back to bother him.

Much more than this, though, the prime minister's speech is important because it offers him a chance to clear up a greater mystery: what does Mr Brown intend to do in government? This might seem an odd question. In fewer than 100 days as leader he has taken Labour to a point where it expects to win, which is a brilliant achievement. He has given an impression of change – and used that word often. He has opened the door to some potentially significant changes of policy – in terms of relations with the United States, the constitution, perhaps public services. The scent of renewal and progress is everywhere. Like a skilled aromatherapist, Mr Brown has conjured up a relaxing environment, soothing away many of the stresses left by Tony Blair.

But this does not yet amount to anything specific. His government is still one of imagined possibilities. This is not Mr Brown's fault: not long in the job, he has ruled so far in a period in which parliament and politics have mostly been in recess. His predecessor was much criticised for doing too much, too fast. He has been right to bide his time.

Today's speech, however, is the moment to move from generalities to specifics. If he does not intend to call an election – and the odds are surely still against one – then Mr Brown must instead put solid meat on the bones of government. He needs to move from the sort of language that has carried him along so far – largely optimistic banalities to which no one can object – to a challenging and authentic description of his priorities for government.

Interviewed yesterday, Ed Balls – as close as anyone to the prime minister – promised that he would offer 'vision' today. But Mr Brown would do well to narrow his field of view. He says he wants world-class public services, but spray-on solutions, such as his promise to deep-clean all hospitals, are no way to get them. What, too, does he intend to do in Iraq? Or on climate change, Crossrail, financial regulation, the consequences of devolution – the intricacies, big and small, of administration.

Election fever has proved to be as infectious as the diseases now sadly affecting British farming. But a snap election held on political momentum and no sort of explanation is not a mandate for government. Today Mr Brown should offer detail and not just vision, whether or not he intends to go to the polls.

25 SEPTEMBER 2007

'I will not let Britain down': Brown sets out plans to dominate centre ground

PATRICK WINTOUR

Gordon Brown yesterday used his first conference speech as Labour party leader to make a direct appeal to the conservative instincts of middle Britain, vowing to create an aspirational society based on the foundations of duty, respect and responsibility.

In an unusually personal hour-long speech, shorn of any direct reference to David Cameron or the possibility of an imminent general election, Brown promised not just to occupy but to 'expand and reshape the centre ground of politics'.

He also set out a raft of often-symbolic new policies on crime, education and the health service that repeatedly emphasised the virtues of discipline, Britishness and an explicitly biblical morality.

In his most personal passage he admitted: 'Sometimes people say I am too serious, and that I fight too hard,' conceding that the accusation might be true. But he countered he was a 'conviction politician', adding: 'Families all across Britain know that things don't come easy and that there are things worth fighting for.'

Apart from emphasising his seriousness of character, the speech's purpose, his aides suggested, was to sketch out Brown's progressive agenda, which will deprive David Cameron of political oxygen, squeezing him further and further from the centre ground. The aim, aides revealed, was to build a movement of 'Brown Conservatives' modelled on the Reagan Democrats.

He received a warm four-minute ovation from a party that seemed to be relieved to have a rest from the oratorical brilliance of his predecessor.

In a series of lightly sketched new policy directions designed to associate him with middle Britain, he urged the police to use new stop-and-search powers to defeat gun-wielding gangs. Police will also be given 10,000 handheld computers to cut bureaucracy and paper-based form-filling. He also promised to strip licences from shops that repeatedly sell alcohol to those who are underage. Parents who fail to supervise their children will be fined, and teachers will be given support to exclude disruptive and bullying children.

On crime, he promised: 'Any newcomer to Britain who is caught selling drugs or using guns will be thrown out. No one who sells drugs to our children or uses guns has the right to stay in our country.'

Turning to the health service, he drew on his own experience as a teenager who almost lost his sight after a rugby ground accident. He promised a check-up on the NHS every year and a more personalised service. In a passage warmly applauded by the union delegates as a warning to private contractors, he promised: 'Matrons will have the power to order additional cleaning of wards, and send out a message – meet the highest standards of cleanliness or lose your contract.'

On education, he said too much talent was wasted through the curse of the poverty of aspiration, promising to offer every secondary pupil a personal tutor through their school years. He hinted that he would raise the target for reducing CO_2 emissions in the climate change bill, as well as promising to double the number of planned eco towns from five to ten.

As expected he made no reference to the possibility of calling a snap election, though he did tease Bournemouth delegates by saying he was often asked whether he could recommend the job of prime minister to anyone. He said he always replied: 'Not yet'.

He mentioned Britain or Britishness no fewer than 80 times, often tracing his patriotic and moral roots back to his father's sermons. And in an opening eulogy to the strengths of the British character he spoke of this summer's tests, of terrorism, the financial turmoil at Northern Rock, foot- and-mouth, and floods, which he said had revealed an indestructible spirit.

'There is no weakness in Britain today that cannot be overcome by the strengths of the British people. Don't let anyone tell us the British people that this country of ours, which has over the centuries given so much to the world, has ever been broken by anything,' he said.

In a passage that was much discussed in advance by his team, he said he was seeking to create an aspirational Britain, 'a Britain of all talents where all are encouraged to aim high and all by their effort can rise'.

The Conservatives dismissed the speech as full of reheated policies and lacking any overall inspiration. Cameron said: 'After that uninspiring speech, it is clear that Gordon Brown has no answers to Britain's problems. That is why we have all along called for a general election and continue to do so today. We are ready and waiting.'

25 SEPTEMBER 2007

A conviction politician, but where, Gordon, is the edge?

POLLY TOYNBEE

The conference banners proclaimed 'Strength to Change Britain'. The speech would tell what change Labour's next decade would bring. The answer? The man himself is that change.

He might have reminded us of Gandhi's famous exhortation, 'We must be the change we wish to see'. Leaders these days, as ever following American political fashions, must now be the embodiment of the policies they stand for. Their life stories must be the living parable that tells the people where they come from, drawing from their past a graphic narrative of where they are going. Identity and authenticity must personify their ideas.

Where did Brown's conviction and moral compass come from? Out came the old family tales of Kirkaldy, the values of his father's sermons enjoining him to 'treat everyone equally, with respect' and his father's favourite parable of the talents. Picture the humble local state primary and the bus up the hill to secondary school with the friends who have shared the good times and the bad, some who made it and some left behind through lack of opportunity. There too was the tragedy of nearly losing his sight, with the tender love and care from NHS doctors and nurses that makes him the services passionate defender. For a man they said could never do modern, touchy-feely politics, he does it well and the story does indeed resonate with his policies. So now his story is the nation's own narrative too.

Nothing so vulgar as 'Match that, Eton boy!' passed his lips.

Indeed, no politics, no parties, no cheap jibes or squalid election-eering interrupted this solemn Father of the Nation oration, despite the fevered speculation in the hall.

If turning a complicated life into a celebrity story makes toes curl and teeth grind at something plainly out of character, these days politics is personal. They take a risk in making cerebral, seri-ous Gordon Brown what he isn't. Hiring Saatchi & Saatchi to produce 'Not Flash – Just Gordon' might devalue that very currency of honesty he stands for. Beware the image-makers. Beware too the verge of jingoism in his old-world Britishness riff.

So how much change will the Brown era bring? Nothing in this speech signalled significant policy shift, only a change in empha-sis. It was almost vegetarian in its lack of new beef, with not one bold stride into bullish new territory. This was more a steam-cleaning of New Labour policies, renewing what worked, building on went before – with many salutary reminders of how much good there is to be built on. His genuine passion to see every child gets a fair chance in life wasn't the usual perfunctory couple of paragraphs, now obligatory for Tories too, but his own solid core underpinning everything else he said. He left no doubt that this is his purpose and how he will judge himself in the end, a Labour passion that always came more naturally to him than Blair.

But this is an odd time and this was an odd event, less a confer-ence than an election rally. There never was in living memory a conference for any party of such strange unity, almost unnerving, defying all the natural rules of politics. Can there be no glimmer of a cabal or caucus anywhere, a leader complete master of all he surveys? Mrs Thatcher had her wets, Blair had his Brown. Brown will find grit in his oyster too.

Experience says it can't last long. No doubt he read with quiet satisfaction the latest Populus poll showing 73 per cent agree that he has represented no lurch to the left and that 'the Labour party is never going to return to old Labour'. Indeed this is not a hall full of old Labour lurchers but earnest activists yearning to win again.

Nonetheless, if in his listening mode he were to take note of what gets claps and cheers at packed fringe meetings, he would hear a party that yearns too for more radicalism. Surely Labour has earned it after three wins in a row? There was applause at any mention of gross boardroom excess and alarm at the widening wealth gap. There was enthusiastic praise for Brown's poverty programmes at home and abroad – but a strong sense too that politically that doesn't grip public imagination without a critique of greed. Brown's solitary reference to this was shamefully cowardly: 'The right of company boards to make their own decisions, but obligations to the rest of society too,' was all he said.

Opposition to faith schools draws another cheer: what is Labour doing increasing them? There was a chorus of concern about low pay and women's pay. He should listen too to the claps at mentions of eroded civil liberties. There were sighs and head shakings over the money wasted on Trident. These are not old fellow-travellers but those who know how miserably tight the spending round will be. Stop and talk to these delegates and every one of them is engaged professionally or as volunteers in good works of all varieties, needing funds for all that is still to be done. But there is not, say Brown's people, any intention of raising taxes when spending shrinks.

These are totemic Labour questions, things that define why people join, why they trudge about the streets whenever an election summons them, why they bother to meet on wet Thursdays in winter. They liked the mood music, they like the man, they think he's their winner, but even as they cheered him before he began to speak, many wistfully missed that extra edge, the sharper blade to fight the battle ahead.

But commentators do well to remember how easy it is to stand on the sidelines and urge Labour to be braver and more radical, when no one knows how far it's safe to go. Incremental improvement may be all the country wants, not excitement and political panache. Focus groups and polls will always warn Labour to stay rooted to the centre ground. Giving conviction free rein might be a sign of great leadership, but then it might take the party galloping over the precipice again.

Brown belongs to the scarred generation, seared by 18 years of failure: hubris will never be his failing, but caution might. However, at meetings round the conference there were plenty of reminders that now at the cabinet table sits the new generation who say they would and could be bolder in future, who see the missed opportunities and the mistakes of the last decade. One said with glee that another election victory would banish the old fears and 'finally, once and for all, see off the *Daily Mail* and all it stands for'. But will that be the boss's view? Probably not.

7 OCTOBER 2007

'I'm not persuaded' – why Brown ducked the election

NICHOLAS WATT, JO REVILL
AND NED TEMKO, THE *OBSERVER*

Dressed in a casual dark blue shirt, David Cameron looked a relaxed figure when he walked into the driveway of his Oxfordshire home early yesterday evening to respond to Gordon Brown's announcement. The leader stepped across to the waiting television cameras and proceeded to tear into the prime minister for his 'humiliating retreat'.

In remarks carried live on Sky News, the Tory leader said: 'The prime minister has shown great weakness and indecision and it is quite clear he has not been focused on running the country these last few months. He has been trying to spin his way into a general election campaign and now has had to make this humiliating retreat.'

Cameron's sharply worded attack showed he believes the climb-down marks the end of Brown's honeymoon and gives the Conservatives a chance to launch an all-out assault.

The Tory leader, who will take to the airwaves again today, will note the revelation in today's *Observer* that strong support for the party's pledge on inheritance tax played a major role in forcing the prime minister's hand. Labour's private polling showed that the party's support had started to plunge in marginal seats after George Osborne, the shadow chancellor, said a Tory government would exempt houses worth less than £1m from the tax.

The grim poll figures set the scene for Brown's dramatic decision, which he announced to his inner circle in Downing Street last Friday evening. Accustomed to issuing crisp instructions to officials, Brown uttered just a few words to inform them that he had abandoned plans for an early election. 'I am not persuaded,' the prime minister told aides after a day of ad hoc meetings to decide whether to take the gamble of his political life and call an election next month.

With many in his camp determined that Brown should hold an election – and some ministers assuming they would be hitting the campaign trail within days – the prime minister agreed to sleep on the matter before finally making up his mind. 'I will think about it overnight,' Brown said as he headed up to his flat above 11 Downing Street after a long week that included a day trip to Iraq.

Waking yesterday at his usual early hour to catch BBC Radio 5 Live's early morning news bulletins, Brown signalled to aides that his decision was final. An early election would be a grave mistake after devastating feedback from Labour's 'super-marginals', passed on by Brown's pollster, Deborah Mattinson.

The prime minister's announcement today is his first serious setback since he entered No 10 more than 100 days ago. Matters were not helped when news of his BBC interview was leaked yesterday afternoon to the Conservative home website, allowing Cameron to appear on television before Brown is able to explain himself fully to the nation this morning. 'There has been a degree of clumsiness,' one minister told the *Observer*. 'But I am sure we can shake off the criticism by Christmas.' One well-placed figure involved in preparing for a possible poll said: 'You don't march your troops up the hill and march them down again.'

A senior Labour figure was blunter: 'What a complete mess. We have got ourselves into this. We should have dampened it down much earlier. Instead, we have handed the initiative to the Tories.'

Brown is furious at the way in which the Tories have accused him of manipulating the political process by using one of the prime minister's most powerful weapons – the timing of an election – to destabilise his opponents. But he knows he will struggle to blame others for fuelling speculation about an early poll because senior ministers, including his closest allies, Ed Balls and Douglas Alexander, openly floated the idea.

Such remarks show that Brown knows he will take a big hit after appearing to clear the decks for an early election by embarking on a trip to Iraq during the Tory conference and putting together two major economic statements to the Commons on Tuesday. But holding an early election would have dealt a far greater blow, as the Tories could have taken a significant, though possibly by no means fatal, chunk out of Labour's 66-seat majority.

Osborne homed in on Labour's super-marginals, according to Labour's polling, with his inheritance tax cut. 'If you look closely at the marginals, you will see that the inheritance tax is cutting through,' one Labour source said of the 44 seats Labour would lose on a swing of 5 per cent or less. Sixteen of the seats are in London and the south-east, where property prices have tripled.

'Gordon was told he would win the election and he would have a comfortable majority,' the Labour source said. 'But we are dealing with many constituencies where Labour would be in a difficult situation in the long term. There are lots of constituencies that are on a knife edge and ... could be lost next time.'

Labour officials, who were still consulting MPs in marginal constituencies about an early election as late as Friday morning, were told to back off. Dr Howard Stoate, MP for Labour's 13th most marginal seat in Dartford in Kent, which he holds with a majority of just 583, told the *Observer*: 'My own view is that there is no particular need for an election at the moment.

'We've got a good working majority in the Commons and the polls show that people like what we're doing. There is no major burning issue on which people are demanding to go to the polls.'

Downing Street officials, who appreciate that Labour's pro-election camp may have overreached itself, concede they would struggle to overturn the growing support for a change to inheritance tax during a three-week election campaign. But No 10 is convinced it will be able to unpick the 'unrealistic' Tory costings of the plan over the next seven to 18 months when a general election is likely to be held. One senior Labour source outlined the thinking: 'Microwaving someone or pickling them over time, that's the difference. At all the best restaurants, the food is cooked slowly.' Ministers will trawl through the Tory plans to fund their tax cut with a flat-rate charge of £25,000 on all 'non-domiciled' residents.

Brown believes the Tory pledge was superficially attractive because Osborne delighted Middle England voters. But Downing Street believes it will be able to convince those same voters that Tory plans to fund the scheme, which are based on estimates on the numbers and wealth of 'non-domiciled' foreigners residents in Britain, are flaky. This uncertainty was borne out by a senior Tory who said: 'We are absolutely confident of our figures, but do admit there is a debate about whether they all add up.'

A Labour source said: 'You need a few months to persuade people that the Tory plan on inheritance tax is not credible. When you get to a point where that is steeped in the public mood, there will be a pretty big public backlash. That will hang round their neck for some time.'

On a balmy late July afternoon, ministers were in buoyant mood as they met at Chequers for a special 'political' cabinet. An early Brown bounce in the polls had convinced the prime minister to ask Douglas Alexander, his election co-ordinator, to place Labour on an election footing.

The 26 July meeting was the first time that ministers discussed what then seemed an extraordinary proposition: to exploit the 'Brown bounce' in the polls by holding the first autumn election in 33 years. Brown was against a snap poll, on the grounds that Labour had to do more than promise change; it had to deliver it. Within weeks, as the bounce endured, he had instructed Labour officials to draw up plans for an autumn election, though he always remained sceptical. What transpired will serve as a reminder of the dangers of underestimating the Tories and the potentially fatal mistake of 'toying' with the electorate, as David Blunkett warned during the Labour conference a fortnight ago.

Younger members of the cabinet, led by Balls and Alexander, were last night being criticised for leading the charge for an early poll with the aim of wounding the Tories in a fourth successive defeat.

Alexander, a normally cautious figure who is one of a handful of under-40s in the cabinet, let it be known that an early poll would 'close the deal'. This was Labour-speak for finishing off Cameron in what would be a major blow to the Tories, who would have failed under both traditionalist and modernising leaders. Balls was equally keen, though he warned at the conference that the new government might need more time to show it could deliver change.

Brown was attracted by the idea of floating the possibility of a snap election to destabilise the Tories. His gamble paid off at one level: the Tories were panicked into releasing tax-cutting pledges, which Downing Street believes will unravel.

But some cabinet ministers believe a high price has been paid. Talk of an election killed off whisperings against Cameron among senior Tories and also gave John Major a chance to hint yesterday that Brown had behaved improperly, because a November election would raise 'serious constitutional issues'. Senior Labour figures also believe that a serious mistake was made the moment a November poll was floated on the eve of the Labour conference. This was designed to allow the prospect of an election to hang over the Tory conference last week. 'If we had shut this down a week ago, it would have been fine,' one source said. 'Instead, we have handed the initiative to the Tories. I hate to say it, but Cameron and Osborne have played a blinder in the past week.'

Others offered support for Brown. 'You have to remember that Gordon is very cautious man, a consummate strategist, and he won't have taken any decision without having looked at every possible implication,' one member of his circle said. 'But it is also about trust. Before the leadership election, and during it, he talked again and again about the need to win the public's trust, almost before he could do anything else. I think the polls do now show that he has won their trust, and what he won't do is squander that by appearing opportunistic. There's clearly a worry that this is how an early election might appear to some voters.'

As he settled down to watch England beat Australia in the Rugby World Cup yesterday afternoon, Brown knew the stakes were high. But his aides, who have been cautious about an early election even when the speculation was intense, insist that the prime minister genuinely felt it may have been right – and indeed humble – to submit himself to the British people to win his own mandate.

'Gordon has not been tearing himself in knots over this,' a well-placed source said. 'He always needed to be convinced. He is sanguine; it is a weight off his mind.'

9 OCTOBER 2007

Lies, damned lies and a vision of the future

SIMON HOGGART

Gordon Brown wanted to tell his press conference that he hadn't called off the election merely because the polls were against him. It must be ghastly to say something when you know that every one of the 100 or so people listening have decided you are fibbing.

Seriously fibbing. Lies, whoppers and porkies! Pants ablaze, nose growing so long you could have used it to peg out next week's washing.

There's a psychological condition called Munchausen's syndrome by proxy. But this was Munchausen unplugged, unchained, in his own right. It was Billy Bunter saying: 'Ouch, yaroo! I didn't steal your cake, and anyway it tasted horrid.' It would have been more embarrassing if it hadn't been so funny, and it would have been funnier if it hadn't been so painful for the poor fellow.

Mind you, he probably didn't think he was fibbing. Politicians have a gift for convincing themselves of what they say. You can fool some of the people some of the time, but you can usually fool yourself whenever you want.

This was his case. Yes, he had contemplated an election. But his 'instinct' had been against it. What he really wanted to do was to put his 'vision of the future' before the people of Britain. He used the word 'vision' over and over again, though I stopped counting at 30.

Why had he not told us about the vision thing before? Because of the party conferences. He had always planned to wait until after they were over.

As for the notion that the Tory lead in the polls had anything to with it, heavens to Murgatroyd! (I paraphrase.) How could it have been a factor, when Labour was going to win whenever the vote was held? Why, candidates in marginal seats had been begging him to call an election!

Foot and mouth, floods, terrorism and Northern Rock had all stopped him from presenting his vision in the summer. Now at last he could! The debate he had started was 'stepping up to a new level'. There were commissions, citizens' juries, and deliberative assemblies, he said. If Gordon Brown ever sees a child drowning in a boating lake, he will leap into action and set up a committee to consider the whole question of boating lake safety.

You could tell how rattled he was by the great waves of cynicism billowing towards him that he repeated himself. He 'relished the chance' to debate the Tory tax cuts, and would 'relish' telling the electorate why they wouldn't work. 'I would relish the chance for a forensic examination!'

Someone else asked, incredulously: 'Are you saying that your decision had absolutely nothing to do with the state of the opinion polls?'

'Yeah,' he said curtly, his voice tailing away. 'I saw the opinion polls, and the many seats we would have won ... but I returned to my first instinct, to give time for our vision to be realised, to implement our vision.' People, he added, would 'relish' the debate! He made politics sound like a cheese sandwich slathered with chutney.

Had he just been frightened? No, the public would judge in the end his strength, the ability to take difficult decisions, and being brave about the right things, he said, trying to look strong and brave about everything.

But I doubt anyone was convinced. Was he a ditherer? He went off on to a ramble about how 'I did the right thing [in 1994] when I said I wanted Tony Blair to be leader of the Labour party, and that was the right decision!'

At which point, had he been hooked up to a polygraph, it would have exploded in a mighty shower of sparks.

11 OCTOBER 2007

Brown faces first cabinet criticism as Johnson attacks election dithering

WILL WOODWARD

The first public cabinet criticism of Gordon Brown's handling of the decision to rule out an election emerged last night as the health secretary, Alan Johnson, blamed the prime minister for the government's rocky start to the new parliamentary term.

'I'm not saying we are blameless ... if he [Mr Brown] had thought it through and decided a weekend earlier, we wouldn't be having all of this,' Johnson told the BBC after David Cameron routed Brown at prime minister's question time. The prime minister had 'not had the best of weeks', Johnson said.

On Monday Brown admitted to reporters: 'Your weekend has been better than mine,' two days after he announced that he would not be holding a snap election after all. 'I could have made it earlier, perhaps I should have made it earlier.'

Johnson's admission shows how much ministers have been rattled by the fallout from Brown's decision not to go to the polls, taken at the end of the Conservatives' successful annual conference and as the Tories surged back in the opinion polls.

Yesterday, Cameron delighted Tory MPs by ridiculing Brown's claim that he would have delayed the election even if the polls had shown he would win with a majority of 100. 'Never have the British people been treated with such cynicism. For 10 years you have plotted and schemed to have this job – and for what? No conviction, just calculation. No vision, just a vacuum. Last week you lost your political authority. This week you are losing your moral authority,' the Conservative leader said.

28 OCTOBER 2007

Brown is back – and this time it's personal

NICHOLAS WATT, THE *OBSERVER*

With the days growing shorter, cabinet ministers are learning to sound bright and alert on cold dark mornings as the rest of the world sleeps. 'Hello, this is Gordon; what line are you taking on the story?' are the words ministers can expect to hear down the phone at 6am as the prime minister ensures the government has prepared its 'lines to take' for the morning news.

While ministers stand to attention in their dressing gowns, Gordon Brown is fully dressed in shirt and tie as he directs operations from his first-floor office in Downing Street, known as the Thatcher Room. A large plasma television screen, which shows *GMTV* or plays *Wake Up to Money* on BBC Radio 5 Live, places Brown a step ahead of his bleary-eyed cabinet colleagues as he issues directions for the day ahead.

To the odd wag who mutters that the early-morning calls are the telltale sign of a political obsessive, Downing Street retorts that Brown is reviving the spirit of July when he stamped his mark on No 10 the moment he succeeded Tony Blair. A 'long campaign' until the next general election, not expected until the summer of 2009 at the earliest, has now been launched after the most lacklustre phase of the Brown premiership in the wake of his non-election announcement three weeks ago.

Ministers are hoping this will give the government a renewed sense of purpose to replace the gloomy mood that settled over Downing Street after the Tories' successful conference, when they pledged to slash inheritance tax. The Queen's speech on Tuesday week, when the legislative programme for the next year will be set out, is being held up as the moment for Brown to signal his vision for the future.

It cannot come a moment too soon for many ministers, who wondered whether the government had lost its touch after they returned from the conference season to find there was hardly anything to do in parliament. 'We've had Downing Street on the phone asking us to do statements when we haven't really got anything to say,' one cabinet minister told the *Observer*.

Brown's friends say it is no surprise that parliament has been quiet during the 'overspill' period between its return from the long summer recess in early October and the Queen's speech a month later. But they admit that the prime minister took a severe knock when he abandoned plans for an election in the wake of the warm response to the Tory tax plans. 'We can recover, but we can't afford another mistake like that,' one senior source said.

Brown, for his part, believes he has suffered – and the Tories have benefited – from something that never afflicted Tony Blair: the absence of a Labour rival. When Blair passed through a difficult period, Brown's stock rose. This ensured that the main political battle remained within the Labour party, leaving the Tories as spectators. In recent months, it has been the Tories who have benefited when Brown suffered.

Downing Street says Brown has now put the gloomy period behind him and even feels a 'sense of relief' that he can return to his original plan of waiting before holding an election. If Brown has a renewed spring in his step as he phones ministers early in the morning or cajoles officials over the bacon sandwiches, there is one dark element. His loathing for David Cameron, apparent to MPs during their increasingly testy exchanges in the Commons, is deepening.

The prime minister has barely spoken in private to Cameron since he lost his cool with the Conservative leader in early September. Brown abruptly ended a telephone conversation with Cameron, while he was explaining the second outbreak of foot and mouth, because he saw the Tory leader pop up on television lambasting the government in a pre-recorded interview.

Brown and Cameron were never likely to develop the easy relationship that Blair enjoyed with his opponents. Brown can barely pass the time of day with Tory leaders because he believes that, for all their talk of modernisation, the Tories will always return to what he regards as their comfort zone: cutting taxes and public services. This is hardly helped by Cameron's Etonian schooling.

But the animosity has become personal. Brown has not forgiven Cameron for referring, in what he regarded as mawkish tones to the prime minister's second son, Fraser.

Cameron, who speaks openly about his disabled son, Ivan, offered warm words for Brown and his wife, Sarah, when Fraser was diagnosed with cystic fibrosis shortly after his birth last year. Cameron expressed 'huge sympathy' for the Browns in a television interview in July, a move that upset Brown. MPs have heard the prime minister say words to the effect that Cameron can talk about his own kids all he wants, but he's got no right to talk about Brown's.

His anger shows how relations between the two men are now beyond repair. Cameron meant his remarks to be a friendly word of support from one father to another (his own life was transformed by the birth of his profoundly disabled son in 2002). But Brown winced at the mention of Fraser on television because he barely mentions his son in public.

The different approaches to their children underlines the differences between the two. Cameron speaks openly about Ivan, who was born with Ohtahara syndrome, which has left him unable to walk, talk or feed himself.

Friends say that Ivan's early days, when the Camerons took it in turns to sleep beside him on hospital floors, was a life-altering experience that made the Tory leader a different man and a different politician. Brown, by contrast, will not discuss details of Fraser's condition in public.

Amid this background, the atmosphere between the two men is souring. Brown regards their weekly encounter across the dispatch box as an important part of making him accountable to parliament. But Cameron's theatrical success is not impressing Brown, who believes the Tory leader is failing on substance. Downing Street believes this was illustrated last week when Cameron ploughed on and condemned the government for planning to claw back schools' budget surpluses after Brown had said he was reviewing the issue.

Brown has said to MPs: 'The guy reads out a script, with a studio audience behind him. And it's the same script and the same response, no matter what answer you give him. It's not parliamentary debate: it's just soap opera and soundbites. I'm not going to do that rubbish.'

The poor relations between Brown and Cameron show that one thing is certain as the political classes brace themselves for the 'long campaign' ahead: not since the days of Margaret Thatcher and Neil Kinnock have the leaders of the two main parties held each other in such contempt. Labour MPs hope that the party will soon turn a corner ahead of what promises to be a bitter political battle between Brown and Cameron for supremacy on the centre ground, where the next election will be won.

CHAPTER THREE

A DESPERATELY FLAWED HERO

Brown spent the winter of 2007-8 with his head down, battered by the growing doubts of many within his own party. Emerging into the spring, it seemed as if the great strategist lacked the main quality that his advocates had always lauded him for: a sense of big picture, a grand strategy, a clear and convincing game plan that would bolster faith and generate a sense of direction and confidence. Those on the left who had hoped for a radical shift under Brown were disappointed that so little seemed to have changed; even 'old' Labour loyalists started to feel anxious. And once the doubts arose, it became rapidly harder and harder for Gordon to reclaim his reputation.

6 MARCH 2008

Gordon Brown's age of ambition is actually one of rising anxiety

JOHN HARRIS

No matter that the economy is headed for a slowdown and hard-working families are anxiously eyeing the future: according to Gordon Brown's speech at last weekend's Labour spring conference, we're now living in the 'age of ambition'. He and his people seem to have clumsily had a go at cribbing from Barack Obama. The language verges on the nonsensical, but you get the idea: Brown is now aiming for 'a Britain where every parent of every child born today can watch them as they sleep and dare to believe that nothing is beyond them realising their potential'.

Meanwhile, factional tensions rumble on. Those on the left who once thought that – to paraphrase an Obama-ism – Brown might be what they had been waiting for, are downcast and depressed. According to some rumblings, even influential Brown allies have been dismayed by his cave-in to ministers who want to maintain a Blairite direction. Insiders reckon the loss of Peter Hain has contributed to a change of weather. The zealous James Purnell has been given his head at the Department for Work and Pensions; Caroline Flint and Andy Burnham have been shoved up the ministerial rankings; good old Hazel Blears is reportedly joining them in pushing the PM rightwards. Their agenda boils down as follows: continue the pro-private sector and 'choice'-driven approach to the public services, attempt to out-nasty the Tories on crime and immigration, maintain the idea that an emphasis on 'aspiration' (or 'ambition') should sit at the heart of your armoury – and reject anything proposed by the unions or the Labour left as an old-fashioned irrelevance.

What is ironic is that it is this strand of the party that is singing tired old tunes. In the latest issue of the avowedly Blairite journal *Progress*, three articles go back to Southern Discomfort, a 1992 pamphlet by the Labour grandee Giles Radice. Back then, he urged Labour to get its head around 'underlying shifts in popular attitudes' that had taken root in the south-east and spread, and the song remains the same: Labour, he says in a new piece, 'must show that it understands the concerns of aspirant voters and has answers to their problems'. The key to winning in the south, says the surrounding coverage, is a 'broad-based message' on crime, 'improving and reforming public services', and 'addressing the social and economic pressures which accompany mass migration'. Not many people would argue with that, but by way of revealing what they really mean, there are withering references to people supposedly in danger of ignoring 'the lessons of the 1980s' and thinking that Labour 'simply has to renew its appeal to its disaffected and traditional supporters'. In other words, ignore just about everyone other than Blairite believers, or you face electoral wipe-out.

Such is the sound of generals fighting the last war. At its heart is the idea that Labour must speak with two voices, dishing out scraps of old-time religion to its heartlands, and spinning a very different line in the marginals. Close by, you find a self-serving cartoon of the left, in which deluded nostalgists gather round picket-line braziers and long for the thrilling days of Arthur Scargill. Worse still, the argument is absurd: that when the government is simply updating the mantras of the 1990s and so struggling in the polls that scores of MPs fear for their seats, the solution is Blairite business as usual.

Where to even start? While disciples of the ex-PM fixate on what Blair once called 'a few hundred or a few thousand votes' in southern marginals, research by the Labour MP Jon Trickett reveals a more complex picture. Given looming boundary changes, the party establishment has been talking up the importance of such seats as Croydon Central – where plenty of people might be included in the same social categories as Mondeo Man and Worcester Woman, but there are also 9,400 public sector workers, around 32,500 blue-collar employees, and nearly 16,000 voters drawn from what policy wonks call mosaic group E (aka 'urban intellectuals'). In ultra-tight Harlow, currently held by Labour with a majority of 97, blue-collar voters total 37,000, and there are 5,700 public sector employees. Across the country, it's these groups that account for masses of the 4m-plus votes Labour lost between 1997 and 2005, precious few of which went to the Tories. To point that out isn't to indulge in blinkered core-votery; it simply underlines the sorry electoral pass to which Blair and his ideas came.

The most important argument, though, is this. Whereas there was once a divergence of big issues between the heartlands and marginals – essentially, one group of concerns around post-industrial decline, bumping up against another founded on burgeoning popular affluence – the themes Labour should now be stressing apply to both. Some of this, undoubtedly, is down to 10 years of prosperity, and the fact that many of the blighted badlands of the 1980s have belatedly caught up. But much of the new agenda surrounds its flipside, and very modern concerns that have reared up in our enthusiastic embrace of globalisation, and been pointed up by those supposed dinosaurs on the left.

Here again the Blairite position teeters into ludicrousness. *Progress*'s articles cite last year's deputy leadership election as the moment when the party began to entertain potentially suicidal thinking. In fact, thanks to the left-leaning outsider, Jon Cruddas – and, to some extent, Hain and Harriet Harman – the meatiest parts of the campaign pushed it towards the political cutting-edge, and such issues as debt, affordable housing and insecurity at work, none of which were on the New Labour radar. Look, for example, at the list of Labour MPs who recently defied the government and voted for new protection for agency workers, an issue that under-lies tensions around immigration all over Britain. Among them were MPs representing such seats as Ealing Southall, Oxford East, Hendon and Great Yarmouth. Why do you suppose that was?

Blairism – even without Blair – still seems to be awkwardly poised between naive optimism and an unbecoming nastiness. Contrary to Brown's rhetoric, this feels less like an age of ambition than an era of rising anxiety – and it's the people to his left making most of the intellectual running. Moreover, lurking within their take on new times is something close to a revelation – that the same messages can be rolled out in Purley and Pontypridd, Grimsby and Guildford, and it need not involve Labour losing what remains of its social democratic soul. Relative to the political contortions of the 1990s, I'd call that progress.

12 APRIL 2008

Labour's best way to recover might be for Brown to go

MARTIN KETTLE

A spectre is haunting the Labour party – the spectre of Gordon Brown's failure. Questions about Brown abound in Labour ranks. The concern is not, as far as I can tell from many conversations this week, primarily about Brown's policies or about the changes at No 10. The question is mainly about him. Right now, the problem is Brown himself.

Don't doubt for a second that ministers and backbenchers are very rattled about their leader. Ask a Labour MP about almost any current question – the 10p tax rate, post office closures, embryology, 42-day detention, the Olympic torch, BAE Systems – and the anxieties about Brown pour out with almost indecent haste. This is not got up by the press. It is happening and it is serious. Oddly, it's the senior Blairites, once so critical, who are often the most restrained.

The more accounts one hears about Brown's meeting with his backbenchers last week the worse it sounds, and the more it appears to have been a tipping point among the previously undecided. Fisticuffs? I don't think so. But 'fevered' – the word of a senior cabinet minister – absolutely. Old hands say they have never seen a party leader lose it the way Brown did last week. Heckled by his own troops over the 10p tax rate abolition, he literally put his hands up and asked MPs to write to him with suggestions. It was a pitiful performance, some witnesses say. Others reserve their contempt for the current febrile backbench mood. 'What a bunch of knicker-wetters,' says a veteran ex-minister.

Part of this – don't overlook it – is the shock of the new. Labour's fortysomethings aren't used to bad news. All they have ever known in politics is Labour ascendant. Anger on the doorstep – especially strong over cutting the 10p tax band, ministers report – is a new experience. The younger generation are predisposed to think that this is temporary. Yes, things are bad, they say, but this the equivalent of the Conservatives in 1986. Defeat is unthinkable.

Older heads offer darker comparisons. They say defeat is very thinkable. Here, gallows humour abounds. It feels like 1978, says one. Gordon lost it with the aborted election, has been defined by the episode as indecisive, and continues to indulge in confirmatory behaviour. Another delves further back. Remember 1968, he says – but for its elections, not the street fighting. In London Labour lost every single borough bar Tower Hamlets. Two years later Labour nearly won the general election. Yes, but you lost it, is the unspoken rejoinder.

A frequent complaint, not least from people who thought they were confidants, is that we never get to see Brown now. Unfair, of course; Brown has a big job to do, but it feeds the sense of distance between party and PM into which rumour rushes. Psychologically, Brown is brooding in a very bleak place, says one MP. He's clinically depressed, opines another. The old demons that warned him he might not be up to the job are gnawing at him again, says a third. And so it goes on. He feels remorse and guilt that he has messed it up so badly. He thinks the public have turned against him. He's haunted by going down in history as Labour's worst prime minister. It's Kinnock all over again. All this in the past 24 hours.

It is hard to say how much of this is true. Some of it surely is. This much, though, is certain: Brown is not ready to give up, but nor is he confident he can win the public's support back. For whatever reason, he lacks the certainty of his predecessor. Even when Blair was wrong, he was clear about where he was heading. But Brown lacks Blair's confidence – and this is now corrosive. 'The challenge is primarily psychological,' says a senior minister, 'It's about being confident.' 'He simply doesn't know what to do,' responds a senior backbencher. 'There's no sense of direction whatever. There's nothing there.'

What can Brown do about this mood? Helpfully meant suggestions abound – be more radical, be more centrist, be yourself, be someone else, get a speechwriter, get a haircut – yet most of these miss the point. Guys of 57 don't change much. The way people have behaved in the past, a wise minister observed this week, is still the best guide to the way they will behave in the future. A large amount of the wishful-thinking school of commentary on the Labour government's predicament persistently overlooks this obvious point. There isn't an Attlee or Roosevelt lurking inside the prime minister. There's just the same old Gordon with the same old strengths and weaknesses.

A lot is written about the growing fatalism in Labour ranks. It exists, but don't exaggerate it. There is also still a hunger for re-election, especially among younger MPs. That enduring hunger is, in my view, the real reason why Brown is under such criticism. 'If David Cameron was way out ahead in the way Blair was before 1997 then people would say there's nothing much we can do about it,' says another ex-minister. 'But that isn't the case. People are saying Cameron can't nail it with the voters. The election is still up for grabs – but it's Gordon who is losing it for us.'

If that becomes a widely shared view – and there is some evidence that it is happening – then Labour faces a deeply uncomfortable choice. If Labour is to win the next election, then either Brown changes, which seems unlikely, or he goes, which is currently in the realm of fantasy. Yet not quite. There is positioning for the succession going on among younger cabinet ministers. And on the backbenches there is some talk – but it is only early talk – about how Brown might be ousted. A deputy leadership contest has been mooted as one proxy option. So has a stalking-horse challenge against Brown himself, of the sort that Anthony Meyer mounted against Margaret Thatcher. There has even been some discussion about a full-on leadership contest this summer.

Common sense scoffs at such possibilities. So do those who might benefit from them. 'No chance. Gordon is secure. Labour doesn't work like that,' says a minister who is sometimes mentioned as a possible alternative leader. Yet Labour has never been in this position either. If the spring elections go badly, and maybe even if they aren't a complete disaster, then stand by for surprises. I believe Brown has every reason to feel under greater pressure right now than he has ever known before.

14 APRIL 2008

He may be disappointing, but Brown isn't a disaster

JACKIE ASHLEY

Here are a few truths about Gordon Brown as prime minister. He has failed to project a clear sense of purpose. He has taken some decisions, such as abolishing the 10p income tax rate, pressing on with 42-day detention, and receiving the Olympic torch, that seem perverse. He doesn't radiate optimism: in fact, he doesn't radiate. He is, without doubt, Scottish. As we hit economic storms, he is unpopular. He is probably pretty frustrated.

Here are some things about Brown that are not true. He isn't responsible for 'destroying the economy': for 10 years under him, it did pretty well. He isn't clinically depressed. He isn't bereft of ideas – in fact, he has far too many ideas. And while it looks likely that Labour will lose the next election, it isn't all his fault, nor is it inevitable.

I read that Brown has been supported for years by a vast conspiratorial regiment of press allies. I put my hand up as someone who has written enthusiastically about him for years. It didn't feel like much of a regiment. We felt like a very small platoon, particularly in the heyday of Blairism. As the Iraq adventure came apart, and with Blair rubbing Labour's nose in his enthusiasm for the super-rich, it seemed to some of us that the party needed a new start and a new leader. Brown found new friends flocking round him.

Am I disappointed? Do I feel I helped sell the country a false bill of goods? For the little that it is worth, for we columnists are just fleas on the body politic, of course I feel disappointed. Blair had to go. But as this column has made clear, Brown has got it wrong on civil liberty issues, on some aspects of tax and the environment, and on the lack of a European treaty referendum. I thought he'd be clearer about his political direction. As I argued last week, he should spend less time munching on big abstract ideas with other world leaders and more thinking about hard-pressed, worried Labour voters.

But there is a bullying, vengeful hysteria suddenly erupting around Brown. It is reflected in the polls. Yesterday's *Sunday Times* told us that his personal rating has fallen to minus 37 from plus 48 last August, and added: 'The collapse is the most dramatic of any modern-day prime minister, worse even than Neville Chamberlain, who in 1940 dropped from plus 21 to minus 27 after Hitler's invasion of Norway.' I know the Brown record hasn't been spotless, but opening the gate to Nazi invaders and a row over the 10p tax rate aren't quite in the same league, are they?

There's something distasteful in backing a man, and then, when things turn wrong, instantly joining the chorus of jeering. The first thing this debate needs is a sense of proportion, even a whiff of basic fairness. Brown may have been disappointing. But he isn't a disaster. He has been too timid. But that doesn't mean he is a 'coward'. And most of those who have turned on him have their own axes to grind.

Murdoch journalists have been at the forefront of those suggesting that Brown is clinically depressed, on the edge of resignation, and in general a loathsome Caledonian vacuum. Most are long-time, enthusiastic Conservatives. Those who are not simply want a new story to report. Brown, like Blair, spent too long oiling up to Rupert Murdoch and therefore probably deserves everything he gets. But let's just recall that Cameron's Tories have now promised not only a referendum on the European constitution, but also to allow a version of the politically loaded *Fox News* into Britain, both policies designed to appease Murdoch. Ask then, whether the gleeful hostility of Murdoch's journalists towards Brown is entirely surprising? Then there are all those in other parts of the media who adored Blair and have simply been biding their time to stick the knife into Brown. There's nothing wrong with Tories being Tory and Blairites being Blairy. But let's not be naive.

So the 'next story' that the media are now assiduously promoting is that Brown will be challenged by panicking Labour MPs to stand down before the election; and that, if necessary, a stalking-horse candidate will be put up against him to force a contest. So far as I can tell, even the key Blairites in the government regard this with horror. Rightly so. If there was one, obviously outstanding, prime minister in waiting who would without doubt turn the fortunes of the party around, then there might be a case for a change.

But it ain't so. There are a clutch of bright and ambitious people who would fight for the prize – none stands head and shoulders above the rest. It won't even be simply David Miliband v Ed Balls – New Labour v Old Labour, as some, wrongly, like to characterise them. Even if Brown suddenly announced that he was off, Labour would be plunged into a fratricidal feud. As house prices tumble and family budgets contract, who thinks the country would be pleased and edified by the party in power turning its attention instead to whether David, Ed, James, Jack or whoever, should move into No 10?

Instead of calculating who will replace Brown and when, or elbowing one another, ministers should be asking themselves why they are not making a better fist of defending the government as a whole. There has been little plain speaking and a lot of hiding under the sofa. The curse of pseudo-presidential politics is that everything, good and bad, is loaded on to one person, while the rest of the government act like commentators, not the players they really are. Whether or not Labour loses power at the next election, there's a good year and more still to go, and a lot of governing to do. Obsessing about the general election is a bit like concluding that because you're going to die, it isn't worth bothering with the last 20 years of life.

As Margaret Thatcher and John Major found, and even Blair up to a point, the malign downward spiral of hostile press coverage, bad polls and panicky backbenchers is hard to arrest, let alone reverse. It may already be too late for Brown. Maybe the country has had enough of him, though I suspect it remains a slightly fairer-minded place than the current hysteria suggests. In any event, the sensible thing for Labour is to stop this public feuding. The dignified thing for Brown is to refocus on the issues that matter to people, confront problems like the 10p tax rate and the recent immigration report, and plug gamely on. Brown has been indecisive, but I don't think he's a coward. At the very least, a display of grit and stoicism would remind people why so recently they found much to admire in this complex, struggling man.

16 APRIL 2008

This man of hidden shallows is alienating millions of voters

JENNI RUSSELL

'Last week,' said a friend of mine, 'I read a list of the issues that Brown plans to take up after the May elections, so that he can seize the political initiative. And do you know what they were? Britishness and constitutional reform. I mean, my mortgage is going up, and I can't afford my petrol bills – for God's sake, what planet is the man on? What's that got to do with my life?'

As Labour slumps in the polls it's apparent there is a dangerous disconnection between the issues that concern voters and those the government thinks they should be worried about. This week, for instance, the government will be trying to push through 42-day detention for terror suspects, and combating a rebellion over the doubling of 10p tax. Meanwhile, election canvassers report that the biggest issues on the doorstep are post office closures, the loss of the 10p band, and the economy. Yet it was only on Monday that

Gordon Brown finally managed to sound as if he understood he was meant to empathise with people's fears about the coming economic storm. The week before, in an impatient interview with Nick Robinson on the BBC, he had managed to convey only a resentful irritation with the electorate for being so anxious and irrational.

For the past six months, ever since the leadership election that never was, commentators have been warning uneasily that Brown needed to establish a connection with the voters by making it clear what he stood for, and what his government wanted to achieve. For the most part, that argument has had little traction. Brown has been able to shrug off complaints about his remoteness, his indecisiveness, or the political incoherence of decisions like the doubling of inheritance-tax thresholds, because the polls kept showing the Tories were unable to open up a substantial lead over Labour. The global financial earthquake has changed all that. Labour's last trump card was economic stability. Now voters are looking at the party with a much more unforgiving eye.

Labour's support has always been drawn from two key groups. One votes chiefly from self-interest – the party's policies match its social and economic needs. The second votes largely as an expression of values. It is drawn to Labour rather than the Tories because it believes that the party stands for a fairer society and a more rounded, generous view of what it means to be a human being. Brown's government is in trouble because both groups are becoming increasingly disenchanted.

MPs for marginal constituencies have been acutely aware of the party's vulnerability for some time. One minister I spoke to was frank about the tactics that are being adopted. Labour's national message was now so muddled, and its priorities so unlike voters' own, that some MPs were no longer selling the party's brand on the doorstep. 'It wouldn't work. What people want to know is, what can you deliver for them in their daily lives? You can't knock on the door and give them some vague slogan dreamed up in Downing Street, "Hello, I'm here to unlock your talent." Instead I'm selling my own brand. I ask people, "What are the issues that matter to you locally?" And they want a CCTV camera, or a hospital to stay open, or their daughter to move up a housing list. And you act on it, and it's hugely time-consuming. But that's what people want. And it's only at the end that you say, we're just collecting some details here – and you say you're from the party.'

The minister says about a dozen MPs have adopted the same personal approach to their constituencies, because trying to defend national policies is not what's going to get them re-elected. People are too confused and disillusioned. 'We've created an ideological vacuum. All major political parties have abandoned ideology. The Tories have done the same; they've abandoned tax cuts. Then, when Brown came in and talked about his moral compass, you thought ideology might be coming back. But it wasn't. His actions don't fit his words – inheritance tax, ending the 10p rate. So you can't argue, this is what we stand for.'

It is the disjunction between values and actions that is so damaging for Brown. He claims to believe in social justice, economic prudence and individual liberties, yet his record shows remarkable inconsistencies on all three. He presided over a boom based on cheap credit and mega City bonuses, while inflicting the giant mortgage on the nation that is the private finance initiative. His final budget snatched money from the poorest purely in order to score a quick hit against the Tories, but he never had the courage to bring in higher taxes at the top. His government found billions to bail out Northern Rock, but refused to find the £40m to refund the struggling families who had saved for Christmas clubs through Farepak.

As for freedoms, his instincts lead him to favour intrusion, oversight and control. Not only is he pushing ID cards and detention without trial, but his government has given councils and 318 other bodies unprecedented powers to spy on citizens suspected of the most minor offences. Even his introduction of tax credits to help working families has been fatally flawed, because the process of claiming them has been made so bureaucratic, punitive, intrusive and censorious that many of those who go through it end up hating the government and its agents.

This record in itself is enough to alienate millions of voters. It is made worse because although Brown is drawn to abstract ideas, he thinks public services should only be judged by outcomes that can be costed or measured. That obsession prevents him understanding the real impact on ordinary lives of so many official decisions, from shutting post offices to closing swimming pools or forcing people to go to giant GPs' surgeries. He doesn't grasp the fact that economic efficiency is not always people's overriding concern – that in their search for good lives, people expect that to be just one of the factors involved in making a political choice.

What Brown's supporters still maintain is that the man must be given more time and opportunities to set out his stall. That's no longer a credible stance. Brown has had well over a year to make an impact since Tony Blair announced his departure, and he has to be judged on his record. Reluctantly, those of us who hoped that the man had hidden depths have had to conclude that he's a man of hidden shallows. It's not a question of, as one MP put it, letting the nation see who he really is. We've seen it – the flickers of grim worthiness beneath the nervous, bumbling, indecisive arrogance – and on the whole we're not impressed. But as Brown is neither likely to acquire a new personality nor to be replaced unless the electorate throws him out, the only question is whether the party and the cabinet have got the guts or the mechanisms to push him into making the coherent and worthwhile decisions that will resonate with both the party and the voters.

Labour's chief politicians are currently divided between those who are pouring their energies into plotting their own paths to power, and those who are transfixed in the headlights of the impending disaster. The onus is now on them to start making collective decisions on Labour's future before they find that there isn't much of one left.

19 APRIL 2008

Running scared

TOM CLARK

When Gordon Brown used to hold meetings at the Treasury, coffee would be served with the milk already added. I always thought that summed up his style. Such was his eagerness to get on to business that he had no time for the 20 seconds it would take to pass round the jug and the biscuits, a ritual that broke the ice across the rest of Whitehall. The intriguing question was always where the extraordinary work ethic came from: commitment or fear?

For four years I was a special adviser, of the distinctly nerdy variety. Appointed as a social security expert without political experience, the job provided a ringside seat at the heart of the government, including occasional attendance at small No 10 meetings where Tony Blair would lock horns with his chancellor. I moved departments, but always worked in the economic sphere where Chancellor Brown's writ rivalled that of the prime minister. As criticism of Brown has grown increasingly strident, I've been thinking back to the days when I watched him at close range, trying to work out whether there is truth in the fashionable charge that than there is no more to him than empty ambition.

Certainly, the man I saw was not one who was drawn to the trappings of office. During the 2005 election, I would sometimes see him typing away at an anonymous desk in the hideous call centre that was Labour HQ. Party staff said that, unlike several colleagues, he only ever asked for second-class tickets. Blair may have swooned over rich businessmen, but the time I saw Brown most animated in private he was chatting away with a representative of underpaid shop workers. The slogan from last year – 'Not flash, just Gordon' – worked (for a time) because it was true.

Since becoming prime minister, Brown has failed to come up with a convincing mission statement, but everything I saw inside Whitehall suggests he does have strongly held values. One old hand in the civil service I knew advised me that the key to getting a policy cleared by the chancellor was sticking a graph on the top showing how the poorest stood to gain most. When Blair came up with a reactionary gimmick; docking child benefit for truants, for example; Brown would be on the phone to our department to get it stopped, booming: 'What kind of party are we becoming?'

Round a small table with Brown, I saw him consider the warnings of Treasury officials, and of Tony Blair, who argued child poverty was proving so costly to tackle that the statistical goalposts ought to be shifted. Brown understood that a tough long-term target would prove a rod for his own back as prime minister, but he was adamant. The Polish thinker Leszek Kołakowski defined social democracy as 'an obstinate will to erode by inches the conditions which produce avoidable suffering'. That is a fitting description of the grinding way that Brown worked as chancellor, using every budget to dish out a little more cash to hard-up families.

Over the decade, what Brown gave to the poor compares with what Thatcher directly gave to the rich, although it certainly doesn't feel that way. Part of the reason is that Brown was never straightforward about what he was doing, talking only in terms of rewarding hard work, and never redistribution.

This was not the only sense in which Brown struck me as less than straightforward. Late one night at Labour's 2003 conference, I found myself bolted up in the hotel room of an old backbench friend of the chancellor. Watching the news report of Brown's speech, my companion was thrilled, reading the chancellor's booming peroration – 'at our best when we are Labour' – as a promise to call time on the aberration of Blairite New Labour. He was not the only one to see it that way. An orchestrated effort by Brown allies to make noise about everything from pensions to top-up fees had ensured the bars were buzzing with anticipation. But when I looked back over the speech in the cold light of day, he seemed to have said very little.

It was not that he could not articulate his vision – at a private Labour meeting in 2004 I heard him give as articulate an account of the party's purpose as any I have heard. Rather, he was pro-foundly pessimistic about what the voters would tolerate – and as a result said almost nothing in public that he thought might offend anyone. Not trusting others to share his instincts, his aides would talk about securing 'rightwing cover' before signing up to any radical policy. There was an interesting contrast with Blair here, even though the latter was just as convinced of voters' reactionary impulses. Brown contorted himself around these, regarding them as constraints, a pose that makes him look calcu-lating. Blair, by contrast, was mostly content to adopt these impulses as his own, thus preserving the appearance of sincerity.

Brown was unendingly anxious about losing control of the detail. It sometimes felt as though his aides expected to clear every page of virtually every document I worked on, no matter how triv-ial. While some retained a sunny disposition, others would explode over a trifle. After signalling a vague interest in a No 10 plan for some sort of a review, I was rung up and told: 'You have committed an act of war.' Another evening I was watching David Attenborough when a different aide rang on the mobile. 'How are you?' I said. The reply came: 'Pissed off'. The subsequent shouting was so loud I had to wrestle away my partner as she tried to grab the phone and intervene. All that anxiety was about nothing more than a note I had written rubbishing an opposition policy. The fury arose, not over the substance, but because I forgot to clear it with Team Brown. I always suspected the rough treatment they meted out to me mirrored the way in which the chancellor treated them. I never saw him explode myself, although he did once come close, railing at me about my former employer – a thinktank that had been making some politically inconvenient points about the economy.

Any decisions of significance, and many of none, would await a meeting with Brown himself. Scribbling notes to himself in a thick felt pen and chewing on his nails, Brown would run these encounters by asking quick-fire questions of whoever made a proposal until they could no longer answer. He was rightly concerned to ensure plans were thought through. More than anything, though, he was playing for time. If, as rarely happened, his battery of questions was exhausted, he would ask instead: 'Why do we need to say this now?'

A decade of nodding and winking in different directions encouraged everyone to see in Brown whatever they wanted. But that useful ambiguity was never going to survive the move into No 10, although it is not clear that Brown has understood this. The sense of drift currently besetting the government comes from a mismatch between what Brown would like to do – and in some cases is actually doing – and what he is prepared to defend. In health, for example, there has been a marked change for the better. The government has strong-armed GPs into working more hours – while pulling the plug on overpriced private treatment centres. That change accords exactly with what Brown had previously hinted at, but, terrified of being painted as Old Labour, he does not explain how the direction has changed.

In education there has also been progress, with a serious drive to stamp out the bias against poor children in the scramble for school places. Brown, we may assume, is behind these, because they are being driven by his closest political friend Ed Balls. But while Balls makes the running, Brown keeps his head down for fear of upsetting middle-class voters. The anguished need to placate middle England led to last year's wheeze of cutting the main rate of tax by abolishing the 10p band. Characteristically, Brown took care to limit the losses faced by the poor, and the real impact will be small. The problem with such sorcery, however, is that it leaves the party and the public confused. If they believe he has given up on the poor, then they may ask: what is the prime minister for? Brown's job was always going to be tougher than Blair's. Taking over an administration battered by a decade in office is inevitably harder than sweeping fresh into power. And a cautious reading of what the voters want is the inevitable price for power. The alternative stance – no compromise with the electorate! – is the shortest route to oblivion. Nor is the tendency to postpone decisions, and to agonise over them, always a weakness – despite the spectacular own-goal of last year's election that wasn't. Brown's great talent for spotting what might go wrong explains how he pulled off the extraordinary feat of surviving a full decade as leader-in-waiting. And Blair's stock might have been far higher – and the world a better place – had he displayed similar regard for analysis before invading Iraq.

But Brown's fear of open political conflict is dangerous. When I saw him in meetings with Blair where the two disagreed, the pattern would be for Blair to ask animated questions, and for

Brown to refuse to answer them, looking downwards and saying, 'It is not an issue for today.' Managing to fight for the leadership unchallenged, Brown has got to the top without having to confront anyone.

There are times when a prime minister is put on the spot, and he has to decide in an instant which side he is on. Surrounded by Chinese security guards recently, Brown stood next to the Olympic torch but refused to actually hold it, a scene that made plain that the frontman part of the job is better done by intuition than calculation. Such ineptitude could be forgiven if Brown were prepared to stand up and fight for the policies he believes in. But less than a year into his premiership I am starting to worry that the fog of fear has thickened to the point where he could struggle to chart a course through it. To quote another of his favourite lines for closing meetings, 'I'm afraid it's all very difficult.'

19 April 2008

Brown did well in Boston, but must avoid the Blair delusion

MARTIN KETTLE

If ever a moment perfectly embodied the current calamity of Gordon Brown's premiership, it came at the White House on Thursday afternoon. On the one hand, the power and pomp of a summit with the US president to discuss mighty global issues. On the other, the decision to interrupt the schedule to make a pleading phone call to Sheffield to prevent the resignation of just about the most minor office-holder in the government. Sorry, Mr

President, it's more important for Britain that I talk to Angela Smith about tax right now.

It is hard to imagine a more exquisite example of the sometimes brutal mismatch between outward pretension and inner turmoil in Brown's existence than this abject prime ministerial phone call from the White House to talk Smith down off the political window-ledge. It is not good for Brown and it is definitely not good for Britain. It is true that this duality has always been deep within Brown and that he probably cannot change it. Even in the good times Brown has always been an unusually striking combination of vaulting global visionary and obsessive domestic operator cohabiting inside the same rumpled suit. However on this trip to the United States the two Browns have been compelled to parade in the public spotlight together – and it is a demeaning sight in a prime minister.

Washington is a place that exposes the tensions between aspiration and reality more pitilessly than any other. Even if the Americans didn't keep talking to him about Churchill all the time, it would be hard for any visiting British prime minister not to feel puffed up by a sense of history and by a feeling of walking in hallowed footsteps. But the immanence of American hyperpower can be daunting too. Washington makes visiting prime ministers feel important but at the same time it exposes how little they really count for.

Brown being Brown – congenitally incapable of switching off from managing the domestic political process – the contrast has been greatly intensified this week by the rapid drain of authority at home. While one part of Brown's sleepless brain continued to engage with pressing issues such as the credit crunch and epochal challenges like reform of the global institutions, on which he made a significant speech in Boston yesterday, the other part stayed down and dirty in the British political bearpit.

Fixing Smith's wobbly was the most dramatic example of this rear-view mirror fixation. But in Washington Brown was also fighting Frank Field's revolt over the 10p tax rate abolition, fulminating against Lord Desai and the former minister Brian Wilson for their brutal press comments, and fretting about the local elections. As well he might – especially if he studied the latest straw in the wind of Labour's southern discomfort. In a Suffolk county council byelection on Thursday, Labour's share of the vote slumped from 33 per cent in 2005 (which wasn't itself a great Labour year) to an 8.8 per cent fourth place behind even the Greens. With Gwyneth Dunwoody's death, there is now also a Westminster byelection in Crewe and Nantwich to worry about, one that Labour cannot afford to lose.

It is always tempting for both politicians and media to regard these sweaty battles as a much more real and vivid dimension of politics than a speech about the reform of international institutions in an age of globalisation. It's tempting because partly true. After all, who's really interested in another speech when the prime minister is a wounded animal? And which of us needs reminding that Brown is a past master at trying to distract the public from his embarrassments and failures? As one senior Labour figure put it to me this week: 'You can always tell things are going wrong at home when Gordon presses the button marked Africa.'

Even so, politics always was about abstract nouns as well as concrete nouns. Moreover most politicians – and Brown typifies this – are in public life to do good as well as to make a name. And anyway it is difficult to argue, in the face of climate change, nuclear proliferation, Islamist terrorism, global economic failure and the damage of Iraq – and with Darfur, Palestine, Somalia, Tibet and Zimbabwe, among others, unresolved – that the world would not benefit from better international processes and institutions. We must not hide behind an ineffective United Nations.

So Brown did some good work in Boston yesterday. But there remains a danger that he will dissipate his effectiveness by deluding himself, as Tony Blair did, into believing that he is uniquely able to shape American global thinking. He is not. Americans are capable of working out their own interests. Brown is not and never will be the author of American foreign policy. His priority ought to be to get Britain's own story straight – a story in which engagement in Europe, the British military effort, nuclear non-proliferation and climate change are the crucial unwritten chapters. It would be nice to believe that Brown shares the strategic view of these issues that David Miliband has begun to set out at the Foreign Office. But Brown still needs to prove that global institutional reform, like Africa perhaps, is not a button that he likes to press when things are getting out of control at home.

21 APRIL 2008

Brown to woo Labour MPs
over 10p tax rate cut

Gordon Brown is expected to address a parliamentary meeting this afternoon to try to woo Labour MPs threatening to rebel against the budget as David Cameron promised to attempt to 'stop the government in its tracks'.

On the BBC Breakfast TV programme this morning, Cameron called the 5.3 million 'very hard-working people on low incomes' affected by the change in the tax rate the 'losers' of the 2007 budget.

The scrapping of the 10p tax rate, announced last year but put into effect this month with the new fiscal year, has resulted in 70

Labour MPs and half a dozen ministerial aides publicly voicing their concerns. The debate over the new tax rate system has reached new heights a week before parliament is due to start voting on the finance bill.

But sources close to the chancellor, Alistair Darling, said that he would not rewrite the budget, echoing statements made by Darling himself yesterday.

'There's no quick fix to these plans, because it's a tax change. It's a complicated problem,' the source said.

29 APRIL 2008

Brown, like Blair, has come to office at the wrong time

ANTHONY SELDON

'What I've done is listen and made the right long-term decision.' 'The issue is doing the right thing – and doing the right thing even if you were not to win a vote is far more important.' No, not words uttered by Tony Blair, but Gordon Brown, after the most turbulent week of his premiership so far. It culminated in damaging allegations from Lord Levy on Blair's doubts about his successor. Levy was never – despite claims – a confidant, but Blair did doubt Brown, profoundly so in the final months. Only when Brown won his spurs by convincing Blair he would not unpick his agenda did Blair decide to back his leadership bid. It was a close-run affair. Blair certainly had his own internal mud-slinging, reversals and U-turns. But his flip-flopping came towards the end of his time in office; Brown's has happened after less than a year in No 10. The tragedy that is Brown's premiership – for such it is – is unfolding before our eyes.

The one important question about Brown is what would have happened if he had become party leader in July 1994 and prime minister in 1997, rather than Blair. Whoever succeeded at that point would have been able to reap the harvest of those glorious early years of New Labour in power – and, let's face it, the achievements of the first term were far more Brown's than Blair's. Had he taken over at that point, Brown's personal peculiarities (which recall Anthony Eden with his petulance and anger, and Edward Heath with his egocentricity and sulkiness) would have proved less of an obstacle.

Personalities of Brown's introverted type flourish when things go well, but find it hard to cope in adversity. Many prime ministers, like Churchill, have had their own 'psychological flaws' and yet have served with distinction. Blair's own extrovert and optimistic personality would have been better suited to the adverse conditions that bedevil any long-serving administration. But the combination of his immaturity and Pollyanna mindset was fatal when mixed with the euphoria of those early years in power, when it was inevitable that only flim-flam emerged from No 10.

Brown's seriousness would have made a much better fist of it. He had the makings of becoming a considerable prime minister, especially if he had then stood down for Blair before 2003, as Blair initially intended to do for Brown. But the dinner discussion at Granita went the other way, so we shall never know how Brown might have fared if he had jinked ahead.

Brown's golden period as chancellor lasted from 1997 to 2001, but then he made a serious mistake. Instead of preparing for office – building alliances across the party, assessing who should fill his government, and deciding what he wanted to do with power – he went into sulk mode. Brown's sense of grievance and injustice got the better of him, and he descended into a deep despair, where his actions and bad language, his bullying and secrecy, were unbecoming of a chancellor, let alone a prime minister in waiting.

Levy's claim that he was told by Blair that Blair thought Brown 'a liar' in denying any involvement in the plotting of 2006 seems wide of the mark. True, Brown's henchmen were never far from the scene, but it is doubtful that Blair would confide in Levy, a figure who wasn't even in Blair's middle circle let alone his close entourage. Blair certainly wobbled over the question of Brown's succession but, in the absence of a credible leadership challenger, became convinced that Brown could rise to the job.

Brown is now reaping the results of his failing. No prime minister since Eden more than 50 years ago had more time to prepare for office. No prime minister has come to No 10 more ill-prepared for power. Unlike Blair in 1997, he is up against the six 'golden rules' that handicap many long-serving governments: longevity in office and the associated boredom of the electorate; a depleted stock of able ministers; loss of reputation for economic competence; an increasingly hostile press; internal divisions over policy and the succession; and a revived and credible opposition. In Brown's case, he has to face not only the younger David Cameron but also Nick Clegg, making him look old and out of touch and posing the difficult question: 'Why Brown?' In all these areas, Blair's lot was so much easier. Brown has also suffered from the loss of his ablest lieutenants who were close at hand from 1997: Ed Balls, Ed Miliband and Douglas Alexander. All now run departments, leaving Brown's political team a shell.

All is not lost. Brown needs to start articulating what he believes. If 2001 was one wrong turn, October 2007 was another. His indecision over the election that never was damaged his authority. But it is not too late to stop the second-guessing and fudged decisions, and start becoming the conviction politician that he is. We need to hear more on his views on poverty at home and abroad, a moral foreign policy, and how to revive his party after what are expected to be damaging election results this week. Brown may lack Blair's political touch, but he has a formidable mind and deep convictions. Let's hear them: time is running out.

8 MAY 2008

Pity the PM –
the mob are in full cry

SIMON HOGGART

It was awful, and it's getting worse. When I was at secondary school we had a temporary teacher for a term. He was hopeless. There is no group more cruel than young teenage boys, except young teenage girls, and we treated him unmercifully. At the end of term a friend and I saw him cycling down our street, and, separated from the feral pack, felt great pity. We stopped him, apologised for our class's behaviour, and said we hoped his next post would be happier. I would have told us to go to hell, but he seemed pleased, which was more than we deserved.

I haven't had that feeling since, until watching poor Gordon Brown. Fresh from the disastrous local election results, he must feel dejected, barely able to keep up an appearance of confidence, reciting by rote his government's achievements, over and over again, as if repetition might dull the jibes, deflect the barbs.

Yesterday, before prime minister's questions, there was a huge cheer when Boris Johnson walked in, and another, from Labour, when Mr Brown appeared. But it was obvious which enthusiasm was sincere. The Tories had been briefed to ask humiliating questions. As the only member with experience of unseating a sitting prime minister, asked Shailesh Vara with galumphing sarcasm, how long did he think he had got? Nigel Evans said polls showed people wanted him to step aside for a 'younger, fresher and more charismatic leader'. Even James Grey joined in: 'Does the prime minister ever wonder why on earth he took the job?'

Instead of ignoring him, Gordon piteously banged on about jobs, reducing poverty, public services, and so forth. It was the political equivalent of 'Please, will you be quiet, oh please?'

When the boys are in full mob cry, everyone joins in, even nice, obliging people like Plaid Cymru's Elfyn Llwyd. Ken Livingstone had said that he was going to do some gardening and take his children to school. 'What is the prime minister looking forward to when he leaves office?'

'I look forward to building a stronger economy and creating more jobs,' said Mr Brown, unhappily. No, that's before you retire. Afterwards you can look forward to building a stronger barbecue pit, and creating a water feature.

And David Cameron kept up his – decreasingly subtle – attempts to imply that the prime minister is going insane. He asked about the Scottish Labour plan for a referendum on independence. The prime minister implied that this might happen, but only in the distant future. 'I think,' said Mr Cameron, 'the prime minister is losing touch with reality.'

He taunted him with Charles Clarke, who has been attacking Gordon for weeks now. 'He always has something helpful to say!' the Tory leader mocked. There was a silly row about who wears more makeup on television. They both finished with weary soundbites – Cameron: 'Give up PR and start being a PM.' Brown: 'A Labour government delivers, and the Conservative party just talks.'

At last the weekly nightmare was over, and he could return to the peace of the staff room, or 'No 10' as he calls it.

15 MAY 2008

Waiting for the future

LEADER

Less than a year into his job, Gordon Brown is already on to his second draft legislative programme, even as many parts of the first one remain undigested. Some of the most significant bills announced last year have yet to leave parliament – on terror, climate change, education, employment and embryology – and a prime minister in decent political health would feel no need to add to them. The whole idea of a draft Queen's speech is anyway rather absurd, the verbal equivalent of double counting. It is an artificial attempt to feign seriousness and consultation that yesterday saw parliament go through the motions of discussing the long-term when the purpose of it all was Mr Brown's short-term survival. He came to the Commons talking of the future in an attempt to ensure that he has one.

He does at least have a strategy. This week's costly retreat on 10p tax and yesterday's premature statement have abated the storms that seemed about to pull the government apart.

Next week the Crewe and Nantwich byelection may bring back Mr Brown's troubles, but for now he is crawling from the vortex. This is despite the fact that his statement was lumpy and repetitive to listen to, and David Cameron's assured response was one of his most engaging parliamentary performances. Labour MPs will be fooling themselves if they think yesterday's statement will make much of an impression on voters, but it may change the mood inside their party, not least because many of the policies Mr Brown announced were sensible ones.

He deserves credit for resisting, as his predecessor might not have done, the lure of populist quick fixes. The emphasis was on public services and the economy, not instant tough laws on crime (although Mr Brown remains fixed as ever on ID cards and 42 days' detention). He is right to pay attention to housing and his scheme to buy unsold new homes to let to tenants is a good one, even if the £200m earmarked for it will not buy much property and is being allocated from existing budgets. It is good, too, to hear the prime minister talking of new rights for agency workers. The progressive package also included two smaller bills that deserve to find parliamentary time, after being dropped in previous years, on coroners' courts and marine protection. Like several other things mentioned yesterday, they are not new, but that does not make them any less worthwhile.

The prime minister's problem is that almost anything he announces now, after 11 years in power, stands open to two obvious criticisms. The first is to suggest that Labour is simply trying to fix a problem that it created – the case with yesterday's new banking laws. The second is to ask why now, and why not before. Promises to sort out bad schools and focus the NHS on the patients who use it are all very well, but the government has been promising to do exactly this since 1997, with mixed results. As Nick Clegg put it yesterday, 'another stir of the legislative pot won't save the prime minister'.

What might, is evidence that his government is achieving its goals. Mr Brown has never been short of ideas and ambition, but he is in charge of a government, not a thinktank. The grander his proposals, the greater the worry that they will come to nothing. In the two years before the next general election – a poll in 2009 is improbable, and the tone of yesterday's statement makes it more so – the prime minister must find ways to show he is changing Britain for the better. Draft statements and more reviews will not do that. The climate change bill, mentioned again yesterday, was announced by Tony Blair in 2006 and is still not law, even though it only sets targets. That sort of sluggishness is dispiriting. If Mr Brown wants to enliven the government, he will have to narrow his vision on to a small number of attainable things. These do not have to be modest – he has the strength to be revolutionary. But yesterday's statement did not encourage the belief that it will happen.

18 MAY 2008

Brown seen through rose-tinted spectacles

RUTH SUNDERLAND, THE *OBSERVER*

There is a notion abroad in the commentariat that Gordon Brown, though a rubbish prime minister, was a brilliant chancellor. The man himself seemed to hark back to his supposed glory days last week when he asked the electorate to judge him on the basis of his handling of the economy – brave words at a time when the governor of the Bank of England is refusing to rule out a recession and the current occupant of Number 11 is busy with yet another rewrite of the budget.

But Brown's chancellorship was never as wonderful as it looked; in reality, he was sowing the seeds for the troubles that now beset him. His claim to greatness as chancellor rests not on prudence, but on niceness. He was lucky enough to be at the helm during the decade of NICE ('non-inflationary, consistently expansionary') growth, which, as Mervyn King told a fearful nation this week, has turned nasty. Economists are busy inventing new acronyms, such as VILE (volatile inflation, less expansionary), or CRAP (close to recession, absent a policy), which is as close as they get to cracking jokes.

Early on, Brown did some very sensible things, including granting the Bank the power to set interest rates without political interference, keeping the UK out of the euro, and winning the esteem and trust of the City to an unprecedented degree for a Labour occupant of No 11. He deserves credit, too, for his largely unsung commitment to alleviating poverty in the developing world, as well as his genuine efforts to eradicate child poverty at home.

The grand illusion, though, was the belief that he had single-handedly ushered in a new era of prosperity and stability. Not so. Brown enjoyed a golden legacy from his predecessor, Kenneth Clarke, and the start of the Nice era might more fairly be dated to September 1992, when Britain came out of the European exchange rate mechanism, rather than May 1997. His reign as chancellor was also characterised by a seemingly benign world environment of low inflation and low interest rates, the opening up of former communist economies, the growing strength of emerging markets and the globalising force of the internet.

As we now know, this was not the dawning of a new golden age, but the long prelude to the catastrophic credit crunch. Brown, however, either did not recognise or deliberately declined to confront signs of danger. The flood of cheap debt enabled the housing and consumer credit boom, the rise of rapacious private equity operators and foreign takeovers, leaving us with a sinking property market and in hock to the rest of the world because we have neglected our manufacturers and exporters. The banking sector is depleted of capital and handing begging bowls to share-holders, and the stock market has been denuded of blue-chip companies such as Boots and BAA, sold off to debt-ridden corporate raiders.

Brown's love affair with the City was at first a welcome break from the Spartist tendencies of old Labour, but there was far too little challenge to monstrously bloated bonus packages and the sort of inventive banking practices that led to the Northern Rock debacle. Public spending continued apace long after the International Monetary Fund began issuing pleas for restraint. Government borrowing as a proportion of national income is now higher than that of most other G7 countries, leaving only a thin cushion against the impending economic headwinds.

The climbdown last week over the abolition of the 10p tax band is an example of a typical Brownian manoeuvre coming back to bite. Even the U-turn has been bodged; the government cannot afford to reinstate the 10p band, and its solution of increasing allowances will still leave the badly paid worse off, bizarrely allowing the Tory Bullingdonites to claim to be the party that supports the poor.

Both the Bank of England and senior investment bankers believe they can see the beginning of the end for the narrow financial-sector crisis, but the pain is only just beginning to arrive in people's homes and workplaces. But the biggest threat to Brown is not economic downturn, it is not dissidents in his own party, and it is not David Cameron. It is his continuing belief in his own myth. That seemed intact last week when he promised not only to steer the country out of its troubles, but that the nation and the government would emerge 'stronger and better'.

We have to hope he is right – if so, he truly will have performed an economic miracle.

23 MAY 2008

Brown facing meltdown as Labour crash in Crewe

NICHOLAS WATT, STEVEN MORRIS, ANDREW SPARROW

Gordon Brown is facing the gravest crisis of his premiership after David Cameron led the Tories to their first byelection gain in a quarter of a century this morning, on a 17.6 per cent swing that would sweep the party into Downing Street. In one of the most humiliating setbacks to Labour since the era of Michael Foot, it saw its majority of 7,078 at the 2005 general election wiped out as the Tories won a majority of 7,860.

The blow, delivered by an electorate unmoved by a £2.7bn tax giveaway in this month's mini-budget to solve the 10p crisis, paves the way for a bloody Labour inquest. Some cabinet ministers have warned that the prime minister will face a leadership crisis by Labour's annual conference this autumn unless he shows that he can turn the party's fortunes around.

In scenes reminiscent of New Labour's byelection successes in the 90s, jubilant Tories in Crewe and Nantwich celebrated as their candidate, Edward Timpson, won with 20,539 votes, 49 per cent. The result, on a high byelection turnout of 58.2 per cent, was particularly sweet for the public school-educated Timpson, who brushed off Labour's 'anti-toff' campaign to secure the Tories' first byelection gain since 1982.

28 MAY 2008

If I were Brown, I'd tell the whole lot of them to get lost

SIMON JENKINS

It is horrible to watch. The old chief is sick but the tribe does not gather round to help. It does not offer him dignity in his apparent demise. It kicks him, gouges him, tears at his limbs, jeers at his record, taunts him to get up and fight back. When he does stagger to his feet, the knives flash and colleagues turn away. Et tu, Brute?

The Tories used to be the nasty party. Not now. The savagery being shown to Gordon Brown by the left defies anything hurled at John Major, William Hague or Iain Duncan Smith. Even as these leaders fought against hopeless odds, they could count on a praetorian guard who understood that loyalty was all and that the party had to live to fight another day.

A year ago, Labour chose Brown to succeed Tony Blair by acclamation. Though he was little known to the public, his courtiers assured us he was so good that there need be no leadership contest, no testing of alternatives, certainly no general election. After the bling of Tony and Cherie, there would be the clunk of Gordon, substance, seriousness and an eye for the long term. Bliss was it that dawn to be alive and a Brownite.

You have to pinch yourself to read the press just a year ago to grasp this edifice of self-delusion. Here is Brown 'pulling down the curtain on celebrity politics'. Here is Brown 'at the top of his political game' as he grapples with a terrorist bomb and a flood emergency. Here is 'the mature statesman' in Washington, and here a reformer in the mould of Bagehot with his 'constitutional package'. He has 'rejuvenated Labour and sown panic in Tory ranks', said one and almost all.

Much of this was from Labour politicians eager for preferment and Labour journalists eager for access. But there was more to it than that. The accolades were apparently an honest assessment by the left that Brown was the ideal response to the missed opportunities of the Blair era. He would put ideological spine back into the New Labour project.

Now what? An unappealing gimmick of the parliamentary lobby is the anonymous derogatory quote, banned by respectable US newspapers. Copy is spattered with 'a senior cabinet minister' or 'a leading backbench MP' castigating the actions or prospects of close colleagues with no risk of self-revelation. Lobby journalists use this stylistic device without having to reveal their source – supposing there is one.

Brown has this month endured enough anonymous derogatory quotes to pass muster as St Sebastian. At least the Labour peer, Lord Desai, had the courage to attack him openly and a junior minister, Ivan Lewis, spoke of 'the beginning of the end'. Others mutter behind their hands that things must improve or there will be that most ominous of political happenings, 'rivals biding their time'.

I never thought Brown was a particularly good chancellor. He was initially lucky in his inheritance and adept at turning away blame. For 10 years, he remained near invisible in his Treasury bunker, terrified of moving even to the Foreign Office. He had no special qualities to bring to national leadership, for which he was clearly unsuited by temperament. He was tetchy, introverted and sour of countenance. His only qualification for Downing Street was his lust for it. After a sustained dose of Brown, I suggested, Blair's Britain would seem a golden age.

Labour gobbled Brown whole and is now gagging on him. It never catalysed the Thatcher revolution, as Blair and Brown were forced to do in power, and thus never fashioned a critique that might have held the two in check. The left gorged itself on power and ignored the privatisation of public investment, the growing inequality, the crazed targetry, the corruption and centralisation of the Blair/Brown era. It naively bought the line that, at the end of the day, there would be 'social justice'.

The left thought it could deplore the glitz and spin of Blairism without acknowledging that such personality projection was the 'new politics'. It then pretended that by choosing Brown it could atone for its sin in choosing Blair, as if thereby restoring some vague ideological balance. This was an epic analytical blunder and the electorate appears to have rumbled it. Labour apparatchiks can only wander in a fog, murmuring about change and delivery.

If I were Brown I would tell the whole lot of them to get lost: 'You acclaimed me, you voted for me, you wanted me and now you are going to have me, the full distance to 2010.' As Blair made Labour's leaders as impregnable as Castro, Brown's position is very strong. He has never been overly concerned by the opinions, or interests, of his colleagues, and is unlikely to start being interested now. Instead he has an ideal opportunity to practise the old Trotskyite maxim, 'weak is strong'.

The prime minister has extraordinary executive power and, on present showing, nothing to lose. Unless he needs specific legislation, he can make any decision he likes in the knowledge that, whatever else Labour MPs may do to him, they will not vote him out of power and precipitate an election.

Brown could do all the things I rather sense he would like to do. He could abandon 42-day detention, withdraw from Iraq and call the Olympians' bluff by slashing the 2012 budget. He could cancel Trident, stop ID cards and kill the NHS computer racket, saving billions. He could tax those who have grown enormously rich under his regime and give generously to the poor. He could even honour his hoary old pledge to liberate local democracy and reinvigorate civic pride.

When Michael Bloomberg became New York mayor in 2001, he said he would be happy to serve just one term if he could be remembered as doing the right thing. He tried it, and promptly became the most unpopular mayor in history. Yet by 2005, his single-mindedness was recognised and he won popular re-election.

Wild horses will be needed to deliver Brown an election victory, but all the more reason for him not to waste time courting cheap popularity, such as his recent cannabis decision. If doing what he thinks will be popular makes him unpopular, why not take a chance and do what he thinks is right? It might even prove popular.

7 JUNE 2008

Make Brown an exclusive brand

SIMON HOGGART

A few weeks ago I mentioned how really upmarket brands pay money to keep their names out of the public gaze. For instance, Pol Roger's top vintage champagne, Cuvee Sir Winston Churchill, is sold only to merchants who will make sure it never goes into clubs frequented by rock stars or footballers. If it were ever sprayed round a podium at the end of a Formula 1 race that would be regarded as a disastrous failure. The exclusivity of the brand has to be maintained.

Maybe that's the solution for Gordon Brown. Keep him out of sight. Don't have him out there commenting on everything, whether it's a byelection result or teenage knife crime. There's a clip of Clement Attlee being interviewed on live television:

'Do you have anything to say to the British people, prime minister?' asks the interviewer. Attlee's reply – 'No' – strikes me as admirable. I suppose Brown would still have to do PM's questions, though he could confine himself to curt, factual replies and avoid political point scoring, at which David Cameron is so much more nimble.

Over the months and years he would become a somewhat enigmatic presence, or rather absence, thought to be spending hours in private, working diligently and quietly for the good of the voters. That way he might even be forgiven, by some Labour voters, anyway.

18 JUNE 2008

A year in, it's clear: we got Brown wrong. He is simply not up to the job

JONATHAN FREEDLAND

Something tells me Gordon Brown won't be in a party mood next week. June 27 will mark his first anniversary inside No 10, and yet I suspect he won't be cracking open too many bottles of bubbly. He can look on the bright side, noting that he is at least still in the job. Otherwise, he will look back on a year that has been too awful to celebrate.

After the double punch meted out at the local elections and at Crewe and Nantwich in May, the talk was of giving Brown the shove. That seemed cruelly unfair. Surely a prime minister deserves at least a year in office before facing judgment.

Now that time is up. A settled view, among the electorate as well as the commentariat has formed, one that will take an earthquake to shake. I can see its distortions and exaggerations and yet, no matter how much I would like to, I cannot depart from the substance of it. I find myself in sympathy with those who admired Brown through his 10 long years as chancellor and who keenly awaited his premiership, and yet now conclude that they got Brown wrong – that, on the current evidence, he is simply not up to the job.

At its most basic, he seems to lack the skills of a man who would lead a 21st-century nation. 'He came in like an Oxford don, with a study full of files and papers on the floor,' laments one minister, who now regrets listening to the Brownites who persuaded him to back their man a year ago. 'He's a dinosaur,' the minister adds, lamenting Brown's failure to delegate, his dithering, his days that start – or end – at 4am.

The most obvious skill gap is in communication. Brown always delivered a speech like an automatic weapon, but his admirers preferred not to notice. They imagined that the wittier, thoughtful man they knew in private would somehow reveal himself to the public once he became prime minister (even if he had never broken surface before).

That has not happened. Brown still reads, rather than delivers a speech, his head down. He does not seem able to deliver three or four plain, human sentences that anyone could understand. The result is an empathy gap: he does not seem able to show any to the electorate and so they don't feel any for him.

None of this should have come as a surprise: the lack of presentational skills was visible a year ago. But plenty of us thought it might not matter. We reckoned Brown could make a virtue of his lack of glitz, offering himself as a figure of rocklike solidity in a fast and often fake world: 'Not flash, just Gordon'.

That approach could have worked. But it was fatally undermined by Brown himself. Having held back for those first three, sunny months, he fell into tricksiness and political game-playing. So he rubbished the Tories' proposed cut in inheritance tax, then copied it. He popped up in Baghdad during the Conservative party conference, promising troop withdrawals from Iraq. The effect was to show that Brown was as much of a calculating schemer as anyone else in his trade – he just wasn't very skilful or subtle at it. Not flash, just a politician.

All this came to a head of course with last autumn's phantom election. Besides the machinations clearly designed to give him a poll lead, the uncertainty created a new part of the Brown persona: that he was indecisive.

Still, it wasn't the eventual failure to call an election that did the damage. It was Brown's presentation of it, the rictus smile as he insisted that the tightening opinion polls had nothing to do with his decision. Reporters told him to come off it, snorting their derision. It was like watching a teacher lose the discipline of his class – once gone, it can never be recovered. (Even through Iraq and all the rest, such a moment never befell Tony Blair.) One minister compares it to Bill Clinton's handling of the Monica Lewinsky scandal. 'It wasn't the blowjob that did the damage; it was Clinton saying he "did not have sexual relations with that woman".' Brown could have survived ducking the election; his mistake was to be dishonest about it.

But it's not only a weakness in political warcraft that counts against him. One year on, Brown has to be judged by his record. In too many areas, he has been guilty of the very triangulation voters had grown so tired of under Blair. He drove through the abolition of the 10p tax band, seeking to win the plaudits of the tax-cutters, even at the expense of the poorest – thereby trampling on his reputation as the champion of the vulnerable. He has trashed the principle of habeas corpus in order to outflank the Tories on security, by locking people up for 42 days without telling them what they are supposed to have done.

After a hopeful start last summer, when he seemed to signal a break from his predecessor, Brown has retreated into a kind of cautious Blairism. Monday's joint press conference with George Bush was a case in point. When he first met the president last year, Brown stood a welcome arm's length away from him, frostily describing their talks as 'full and frank'. But on Monday, he was in Blair mode, lavishing praise on Bush, insisting that they were best pals with not a flicker of daylight between them. There have been similar retreats into the Blairite comfort zone, or at least indecision, on public service reform.

No less damning is the list of what Brown has not done. When caged in the Treasury, he itched to be in charge, such was the scale of his dreams for the country. Those who met him left convinced he was ready to act big. Surely he would pull all the troops out of Iraq. Or he would be ambitious on constitutional reform, driving through a fully elected second chamber or leading Britain, at long last, towards a written constitution. Others imagined that he would solve Labour's cash woes – and the party is currently too broke to fight an election – at a stroke, by introducing state funding of political parties.

None of it happened, even though his own policy team drew up radical plans. On the constitution, he offered grand rhetoric but that translated into steps such as citizens' juries that even one of his own aides admits are 'pathetic'. In this area, as in so many others, Brown has been held back by his own lack of the quality that fascinates him so much he has written a book on it – courage.

Does this mean those who backed him last year, and long before, got him wrong? Not wholly. They were right that he is a decent man, clever and phenomenally widely read; and that, even now, if he ditched the triangulation and crude stunts, pushed a programme of two or three large, bold policies, and told a convincing story about getting the country through economic turmoil – if he did all that, he could still turn things around.

But they – we – misread too much. One cabinet colleague admits mistaking Brown's tactical canniness for strategic grasp. Others failed to see his lack of bravery. One fellow minister says Labour underestimated the co-dependency of the Blair-Brown relationship. Brown needed his rival, if only to push against. Without him, he is lost.

Even the prime minister's closest allies say what has happened these past 12 months is 'tragic'. It would take a Shakespeare to do justice to a story that combines the jealousy of Othello, the ambition of Macbeth and the indecision of Hamlet. Labour's task is not simply to watch this saga play out to its bitter end, but to act – and to help this desperately flawed hero change his destiny.

26 June 2008

Gordon Brown, one year on: A huge price paid for election that never was

PATRICK WINTOUR AND NICHOLAS WATT

As journalists gathered around Team Brown on the afternoon of Sunday 24 June in the lobby of a Manchester conference centre, moments after Tony Blair had handed the Labour crown to his chancellor, a carefully planned operation swung into action.

Brown's aides moved from reporter to reporter, gently suggesting that the new leader might capitalise on his unopposed victory by staging an early election in 2008. Stories mentioning spring 2008 ran in almost every newspaper the following morning.

From then on the disastrous public debate about the election plans was under way. The election that never was – finally scrapped on a humiliating Saturday in early October – still haunts the prime minister. It has decisively shaped the media prism through which he is seen, led to a falling out within the Brown camp itself, and forced a reorganisation within No 10.

The moment of indecision has become a source of deep regret. Even now, sharply different accounts are given of the final days last autumn before it was agreed to pull back from the brink.

On one thing only is there agreement. It marked a watershed in public perceptions of Brown, and represents the biggest unforced political error in the history of New Labour.

The culture secretary, Andy Burnham, reflected in a recent interview: 'Momentum is a curious thing in politics ... Thousands of us who've worked around these jobs could sit in a room and try and work out how to get momentum and how not to lose momentum, but the truth is it hinges on the most unexpected little moments in politics – and clearly the election decision has been a key point where we did lose momentum.'

Peter Hain, now out of cabinet, is more blunt, describing the episode as a fiasco. The chief whip, Geoff Hoon, one of the 'greybeards' who counselled against the election, talks of regret. His deputy, Nick Brown, concedes speculation was allowed to get out of control. The figure driving the early election strategy from the outset was Spencer Livermore, Brown's political adviser for four years. Livermore argued that Brown needed to capitalise on his freshness, and recognise that the economy was not going to get better in 2008.

Douglas Alexander was appointed election co-ordinator to give talk of an early election substance, although he was on holiday through August in America. Ed Miliband was given the job of preparing an emergency manifesto. The political cabinet at Chequers on 15 June discussed the merits of an early election to, in the words of Alexander, 'close the deal with the electorate'. Two dates were advanced – autumn 2007, a genuine snap poll – or May 2008.

For most of the summer, the issue was pushed to the background by other events, but at the same time the polls showed Brown gradually securing a surprisingly strong bounce.

When he took over, Labour was trailing the Conservatives by 34 points to 32 in the *Guardian*/ICM poll. By 16 September the leads had reversed and Labour was ahead by 40 to 32, its biggest lead since September 2005.

Deborah Mattinson, Brown's personal pollster, and his New York-based pollster Stan Greenberg advised that the new prime minister had been established as a strong leader, a figure the electorate trusted. The post-Blair recovery had been secured far more quickly than expected and Livermore and Ed Balls, Brown's closest ally, who was promoted to the cabinet as schools secretary, urged the prime minister to put his natural caution aside.

Before Labour's party conference, though, two drawbacks to this strategy started to emerge.

The Conservatives, desperate to avoid an early poll, began suggesting that Brown would only succeed at an election if he held or increased Labour's majority. Some commentators even suggested he would be forced to resign if Labour's majority was cut. The second problem was how to establish the Labour conference in Bournemouth as an introduction to Brown's Britain, rather than one long seaside speculation about the date of the election.

Before the prime minister's conference speech an effort was made to dampen expectations. But throughout the conference week election fever grew, partly because a restriction on ministers making announcements meant there was little else to talk about. Advisers to Brown did not help by pointing to MPs in marginal seats backing an early poll. Some such as the home secretary, Jacqui Smith, in the highly marginal Midlands seat of Redditch, were strongly in favour.

But the evidence was not clear-cut. Hain recalled in a recent Channel 4 documentary: 'When I was asked by senior people very close to Gordon what my view was, I asked two questions. I said, what are the polls in the marginal seats? And I asked another question, what is the polling in London and the south, because my political antennae told me that it didn't feel very good. They didn't know. So those pressing for an early election and talking it up to journalists at the party conference did not have an answer to those two crucial questions. That worried me.'

In fact Labour did have extensive polling data in the marginals showing it was likely to win.

But mixed messages left many MPs confused. Some of the older, more sceptical cabinet voices, such as the health secretary, Alan Johnson, began to believe that the election was inevitable and that the consequences of pulling back would be worse. One minister bought a smart red winter coat as she braced herself for a cold October on constituency doorsteps. Brown himself left Bournemouth irritated that Labour's conference had been dominated by election talk. The weekend after the conference, he met his aides to decide if the election would go ahead. A decision was deferred. Planning should continue on the basis that it would go ahead, but the final decision would await the Tory conference.

Brown also met Alan Greenspan, his great mentor and former head of the US Federal Reserve Bank, at Chequers. It is likely that Greenspan warned Brown that the sub-prime housing crisis was likely to get much worse – another argument for an early poll.

David Cameron and his team prepared for the Conservative conference knowing they had possibly only a week to save themselves from a date with defeat. Opinion polls over the weekend gave Brown a double-digit lead over Cameron, which would equate to a Commons majority of more than 100.

The decision was taken at a meeting at the end of the Labour conference to activate the election plan, and work started on drafting a manifesto. The unions were ordered into action. Amicus, the single biggest union, started printing election material. Union political officers were instructed to be ready to move into the election headquarters within days. More than 200 computers were hired and 100 slots were booked at Battersea heliport. The consensus was for an election on 1 November.

As part of the preparations for the campaign, it was also agreed that the pre-budget report would have to be scrapped, although its main measures would be inserted in the manifesto as firm commitments. An interim report on the health review by the new minister, the surgeon Lord Darzi, was rushed forward, adding to the sense of momentum.

Then things started to go badly awry. The hope had been that the Conservatives would implode at their conference. But the right were on their best behaviour, containing their mutterings on the need for tax cuts to the confines of private dinners. One senior Tory said: 'The threat of the election ensured that we were disciplined and united.'

Cameron gave a nerveless performance on BBC1's *Andrew Marr Show* on Sunday morning, setting out a number of new ideas including cuts in stamp duty for first-time buyers. On Monday, the shadow chancellor, George Osborne, made his bold commitment to increase the threshold for inheritance tax to £1m.

Brown was angry, as the exact proposal had been advocated by Livermore before Brown's last budget in 2007, but withdrawn with two days to go when it seemed unaffordable.

The PM then stumbled badly. It had been decided that Brown should travel to Iraq during the Tory conference. He intended to make some measured remarks in Basra about British troops, hinting that 1,000 of them would return home by Christmas, leaving a contingent of 4,000.

His media aides out in Iraq thought the visit went well. But back in Britain it was condemned as a cheap electioneering stunt, as Liam Fox, the shadow defence secretary, pointed out that some of the troops had returned already.

The key moment came when John Major appeared on television. The former prime minister gave Brown both barrels. 'What is pretty unattractive is the nods, the winks, the hints, the cynicism, the belief that every decision is being taken because it is marching to the drumbeat of an election rather than to the drumbeat of solid, proper government. He has been letting the speculation run riot. It is clearly an attempt at destabilisation of the opposition parties.'

The mood in the cabinet had always been divided and fluid. In the no camp were veterans such as Geoff Hoon and Jack Straw, people with memories of what opposition could be like. Ed Miliband, the Cabinet Office minister and a figure close to Brown, was sceptical, as was Hazel Blears, a former party chair. Livermore was consistent. He explained the advantages and the disadvantages, but insisted that Brown would never get a better opportunity.

Peter Watt, the then Labour general secretary, who was aware of the party's dire finances, could see the advantages of a quick and cheap election.

But even advocates of an early election like Ed Balls could play devil's advocate. In some debating sessions, where there seemed a unanimous mood for an election, he would put the counter-argument.

Brown was asking for more information on which to make a decision. By the middle of the week of the Tory conference, the polling was raising serious doubts. Osborne's inheritance tax pledge had changed the political weather. Labour was struggling in some of the marginal seats in the south-east, where Tory promises to cut inheritance tax, cap immigration and crack down on crime had resonance. Alexander had seen it as his duty as election coordinator to prepare the party for an election so Brown could make his choice.

Aware that local Labour parties had few funds or activists, he had prepared a campaign heavily based on targeted direct mail. He became alarmed at the prospect of a mail strike. But he also began to wonder if he could explain to the electorate why they were being asked to go the polls now.

A small kitchen cabinet was due to meet on the morning of Friday 5 October at Downing Street, two days after David Cameron had concluded his no-notes conference speech in Blackpool with a challenge to Brown to 'call that election'. Balls left London for his constituency in Yorkshire believing the decision to go ahead had been taken. Livermore and Greenberg were clear: Labour would win, the ground would not shift in the course of the campaign, but the majority might be cut to as low as 20. Brown would have the mandate he yearned to govern for five years, but a hobbled one.

On that Friday morning it was argued in the small inner council that if Brown waited, he would have more time to persuade sceptical voters that he represented change. Bizarrely, in retrospect, it was even suggested the 2p tax cut announced in the 2007 budget would feed into voters' pockets in April 2008, so undercutting the Tory inheritance tax cut. As it happened, once the 2p tax cut arrived, voters only felt the withdrawal of the 10p tax rate.

Most cabinet ministers outside the inner circle spent Friday preparing for Brown to go to Buckingham Palace on the Tuesday after making a Commons statement on Iraq.

But as the day progressed, the prime minister, by one account, wobbled.

Word reached No 10 of a *News of the World* poll – a Tory lead of six points in 83 key marginal constituencies, meaning that almost 50 Labour MPs would lose their seats. Brown gulped – and said things did not feel right.

There was always going to be a media savaging, but arguably Labour's exit strategy was mishandled.

It was decided that the PM would do an exclusive, pre-recorded interview on Saturday afternoon for transmission on the Marr programme the following morning.

By late Friday evening selected Sunday newspaper reporters were briefed on the decision. By lunchtime on Saturday George Osborne had got wind of the announcement.

By mid-afternoon, Cameron was condemning the decision in words that still resonate: 'The prime minister has shown great weakness and indecision and it is quite clear he has not been focused on running the country these last few months. He has been trying to spin his way into a general election campaign and now has had to make this humiliating retreat.'

Instead of Downing Street controlling the announcement, the Conservatives were driving the story.

On television and at a hastily arranged press conference, Brown said he had seen the polls, but insisted that he had been guided by the need for more time to spell out his vision.

One Labour source says: 'He has faced a lot of criticism after David Cameron said he must be the first politician to call off an election that he thought he was going to win. Yes, he thought he was going to win it. But it would have been difficult for him to say publicly that he did not think he would not win it well enough. So he said he needed more time to spell out his vision.'

Brown has paid a huge personal price. Long-standing allies blamed one another for allowing speculation to get out of hand, for changing their position at the last minute and for mishandling the announcement. Alexander felt hurt that he was being blamed, and resented stories that he had been put in the political deep freeze by Brown. The fallout led to the arrival of Stephen Carter as director of strategy, and the departure of Livermore.

The Cameron circle could not believe their luck.

'If Brown had announced a snap election at the end of the summer he would have won and we would have lost,' one senior Tory said. 'David Cameron might not have survived as Tory leader.'

The events of October have changed Brown's leadership style.

One figure said: 'A lesson Gordon learnt was to trust your gut, to make decisions quickly and then to lead from the front.

'You have seen that recently over the embryology bill, where he came out and said why he supported the bill so quickly. You have seen it over 42 days, where he said he would rather lose than abandon the key element of 42 days. And you have seen it over Europe, where he has stood his ground, said what he believes and attacked David Cameron very clearly.'

But so far it has not worked.

Brown remains branded in the public mind as a disingenuous ditherer. His aides insist his fate still ultimately rests with the economy, and claim his poll decline follows the downturn in the economy, rather than his decision to skip the election.

Many ministers believe his position is irretrievable, while others believe Brown may eventually recover if voters look to the future.

One cabinet loyalist says: 'We can win the election. But we will only do that if it [the vote] is about our future. If it is a referendum on us, we can't win.'

11 July 2008

Stranded on Dithering Heights

SIMON HOGGART

Poor Gordon Brown. That 'Heathcliff' tag is going to be round his neck for a very long time. It's a little unfair. His interviewer in the *New Statesman* pointed out that he reminded some women of Emily Brontë's anti-hero.

He agreed but added 'Well, maybe an older Heathcliff, a wiser Heathcliff'. In other words, not the Heathcliff who went round hanging pet dogs, killing baby birds and thumping his wife. Though you have to remember that before Heathcliff had time to get older and wiser, he was dead.

It came on a perfect day for the Tories. The Treasury had just admitted that around 9 million drivers will have to pay £245 more in road tax, and only a small minority will benefit from the changes, contrary to what Mr Brown told us.

As even ancient second-hand cars will also attract the higher rate, it's yet another tax that is burdensome on poor people. Just the kind of fiscal disaster that gladdens the hearts of Tories and makes Labour backbenchers despair. They see their world disappearing at the next election.

They won't even be able to crawl around their towns looking for work – there are few people less employable than an unemployed MP, and not many will become peers – because the tax on an old crawling Austin Allegro with its exhaust hanging off will be higher than the value of the car.

'Everyone knows,' said George Osborne, the shadow chancellor, 'that the Labour party is sleepwalking into another 10p tax fiasco.

'Will the chancellor perform the necessary U-turn, or do we have to wait for Heathcliff to come down from Dithering Heights before they abandon this disastrous plan?'

'Dithering Heights' – it's a great line, and the fact that Alistair Darling pointed out that it must have taken ages to invent doesn't make any difference. Mind you, it could have been worse. At least he wasn't compared to Gradgrind, Wackford Squeers, or Voldemort. That's next week.

Mr Darling banged on for some time about how the British economy would cope with recession better than most, until Sir Peter Tapsell rose in his pomp.

'The pwime minister [Sir Peter has a slight speech impediment] has been boasting for months that we are especially well placed to withstand the cwisis and the credit cwunch. The opposite is the case – as is now clear to evewyone!'

Anyone could say that, but few could make it sound as if Churchill's statue in Parliament Square had come to life and given voice. It must have been like being swiped in the kisser by Heathcliff when he was feeling moody.

Moments later, the brooding brute was with us! His plane from Japan had landed at 4am, but he had conducted a cabinet meeting and was here to brief us on the G8 summit.

David Cameron was in sarcastic form. 'I speak for the whole country when I say we are pleased to see that Heathcliff has come home!'

Bit of a mistake here, I suspect. It's Cathy who came home, in phantom form, scratching at casements. The Tory leader may have been remembering not the novel, but Kate Bush's song *Wuthering Heights*. '*Heeethcleef, it's meeee, your Catheee, I've come home ... let me inna your window. Oh, whow-o-w-oh-whow.*'

Nick Clegg, the Lib Dem leader, was scathing about the G8. 'If words could transform the world, this summit would have been revolutionary.

'I hope that the G8 doesn't die a death like Heathcliff, a man ranting and raving against a world he could neither understand nor change.'

I don't think he really meant the G8, but Heathcliff himself.

CHAPTER FOUR

'THIS IS NO TIME FOR A NOVICE'

One year after the flush of optimism following Brown's entry to Number 10, Labour MPs found themselves heading off gloomily for their summer break. Responding to the swell of despondency around the premiership, David Miliband chose this moment to write a piece in the Guardian *making out a case for Labour's revival – and, perhaps, an equivalent case for his own potential succession? Certainly that's how the Brown camp read it – and the ensuing gritted-teeth commentary from Brown's camp served to demarcate this first phase of Labour dejection.*

Already, however, the single truly momentous event of Brown's premiership was about to detonate – a global downturn of epochal proportions, the worst recession for generations, dragging the world economy almost to the point of collapse. Economic disaster, of course, normally spells disaster for incumbent governments; but perhaps not this time – after all, the one strand of Gordon's reputation that appeared intact was his efficacy as an economically literate leader. Could he be the man to help lead the most economically powerful nations to a collective solution – and, at the same time, inflate his status on the domestic political scene? Surely the Conservative leadership – mostly inexperienced on economic issues – would flounder through the downturn?

31 JULY 2008

Something's got to give – will it be Brown or the party?

MARTIN KETTLE

When the opportunity of the top job comes along you have to know that you want it, have to understand what you want to do with it, have to recognise that it will change your life if you get it, and you then have to be willing to go for it, ruthlessly and intelligently. That, as far as I recall it, is a more or less verbatim summary of what Tony Blair used to say after the death of John Smith had given him his chance to become Labour leader. The rest – three general election wins later – is history.

But is that also how David Miliband now sees things today? The circumstances may be different compared with 1994, but the timing and content of yesterday's article in these pages by the foreign secretary certainly makes it look like an early leadership move of his own against Gordon Brown. Yesterday Miliband doggedly stuck to the denial that it was any such thing. I am not campaigning for the leadership, he insisted during a press conference with the Italian foreign minister – who must have felt thoroughly at home. No 10 is entirely relaxed, say Miliband's people.

Believe that if you will. But it is not just the care with which Miliband chose his verbs yesterday – Brown *can* lead Labour into the next election not Brown *will* or *should* – that gives the game away. I am clear from several conversations that Miliband has recently been putting himself through the sort of self-questioning that Blair did in 1994. And I am also clear that he has decided that he does want the job, that he has decided on what platform he will run if there is a contest, and that he has worked out what he wants to do with the prize if he wins it. The disastrous indecision that marked Miliband's conduct when Blair stepped down has gone. This time – if it comes – he is up for it.

Rest assured, too, that Miliband's article will not have been read with any generosity in sunny Southwold yesterday morning. And rightly so. For while it may not have been one of those leadership-grabbing *pronunciamentos* that were a feature of 19th-century Spanish history, it was simultaneously a lot more than just the innocent ministerial musing about Labour's need to rediscover its collective nerve that the foreign secretary pretends. Though not a call to arms, Miliband's words were the equivalent of a general order to mobilise – and we all know that mobilisation can eventually lead to conflict too.

You don't have be a paranoid inhabitant of the Brown bunker to see Miliband's article as a conscious move against the Labour leader, or to read it as an early draft of Miliband's application for the prime minister's job. I think that it is both – and No 10 is only surprised that it has taken so long to emerge. They were braced for a move of this kind after the Crewe byelection, and were disconcerted when it did not happen. Nevertheless, I would be very cautious before leaping to some of the conclusions into which some may now be tempted.

First, it is as misleading – and in some ways as mischievous – to cast Miliband as the candidate of the Labour right in any post-Brown contest as it is to cast him as the Blairite candidate. These left-versus-right and Blair-versus-Brown labels undoubtedly had some meaning in their own time. But things are more fluid and more nuanced now. Today, for instance, the labels misrepresent the emerging general consensus on the centre-left that, post-Blair and post-Brown, Labour has to more openly set out how, in a modern economy, markets must have social obligations too.

A second false conclusion is to assume that would implies will. We know now that Miliband would stand for the leadership. What we do not know is whether he will or, rather, whether he will get or make the chance. Just because as many as 90 per cent of Labour backbenchers – a figure that has been quoted to me more than once this week – now want Brown to step aside, it does not follow that he will. As the song has it, when an irresistible force – Labour dissatisfaction with Brown – meets an immovable object – Brown's apparent determination to stay – something's gotta give. But which something will it be?

Labour's current crisis remains unpredictable. Miliband has signalled his availability. But he has not called for a contest. So Brown can still rest safe on the Suffolk coast this week. His next window of vulnerability comes in September. Perhaps then the supposed majority of MPs and ministers who apparently want the prime minister to quit will make their presence felt more clearly, and on the record, than they have yet done. Yet Brown also knows that September matters. He would be a fool, if he wants to survive, not to be preparing a pre-emptive strategy of policy launches and ministerial changes that he hopes will buy him enough time to get through the conference season.

Either we must kill him or we must live with him, says one MP, in a shockingly direct phrase. Labour is not by nature a killing party. But Brown has never been weaker – and now Miliband has weakened him a bit more. It won't be long now, one way or the other.

17 SEPTEMBER 2008

How New Labour sold itself short

JEREMY SEABROOK

It is extraordinary that, in the middle of the most devastating financial crisis since the late 1920s, Labour should be struggling with the idea of whether or not to change its leader.

Whatever the failings of Gordon Brown, the last thing needed now is some sort of contest for his threadbare mantle.

It is not as though the conflict between Blairites and Brownites were a replay of wars between Guelphs and Ghibellines, factions divided by irreconcilable loyalties to pope and emperor. Quite the contrary. These are personal animosities. If they were rooted in doctrinal differences, there might be some point to the present disorder, and the possibility of a resolution. Perhaps Labour is simply mirroring the turbulence of the global economic system, which, like events in the party, seem to have outrun the capacity of mere human beings to deal with them.

Why Brown – the 'architect' of the 10 good years – is being blamed for the ending of the recent long interval of prosperity is not clear. How could he have forestalled the sub-prime mortgage crisis, or the opaque 'financial innovations' of investment banks, the mysterious world of derivatives, the selling-on of bundles of loans insured against failure, which are all now fast unwinding and revealing to the world once more what used to be called by archaic Leftists the 'true nature of capitalism'?

The hounding of Brown is irrational and punitive; a bit like the ruinous banking system – non-performing loans meet a non-performing prime minister. But what could a new leader conceivably do? What miracles would he or (less likely) she have to perform? The electoral collapse of Labour merely mimics the demolition of the financial stability on which its fragile popularity was predicated.

What we are seeing is not the recklessness of MPs, who feel the game is up and their seats already lost in an election already won by Cameron. We are witnessing a backlash against the enfeeblement of political power of those in what increasingly appears to be nominal governance, and their forfeit of the ability to intervene significantly in the affairs, not of the world, but even of our own country, buffeted as we are by the tempests of global confusion. It makes nonsense of Brown's alleged sagacious stewardship of 'our' economy: it turns out it isn't really ours at all, but a sort of outpost of somebody else's ill-managed imperium.

No wonder Brown has been at pains to resuscitate a sense of Britishness – paradoxically also inspired by America, the source and origin of all our hopes and all our woes – with the union flag fluttering from the rooftops, infants learning to lisp hymns to Britannia. This is a doomed heroic effort to reclaim territory irrecoverably lost, since it is clear we are at the mercy of forces over which we have no control at all.

We owe the 10 years of prosperity and growing disposable income to the sleight of hand of the conjurors of global financial markets, the boy-wizards of infantile omnipotence, the occultists of monetary illusion. Brown's eagerness to claim credit for that happy time stands in contrast with his desire to disclaim responsibility for the confusion for which his austere and joyless presence is – unjustly – now being blamed.

The Labour party – of all political parties – ought to have been ready with some plausible account of what has happened. It ought to have had some narrative, some fable or story of why things are falling apart. Instead, we have to read the indecipherable script of financial journalists, whose language (apart from that of a few experts in translation, such as Larry Elliot) is about as revealing as the destination of the securitised instruments in which bad loans were mysteriously whisked into outer darkness.

The Labour party ought to have stepped in with a swift forensic analysis of what needs to be done to reverse the excesses of a deregulation over which they were only too happy preside. But New Labour merged with Old Capitalism, a union in which it became not so much a sleeping as a moribund partner.

Labour, most people may have forgotten, owes its very existence to a critique of capitalism; a capacity it long ago forfeited when it decided to abrogate power in favour of the febrile unreason of markets. Labour voluntarily, of its own free will, submitted to the mutable wisdom of money and the short wit of wealth. No wonder it can do nothing but fall upon itself in impotent, fratricidal rage. Anger, once directed outwards, against injustice and exploitation, now has nowhere else to go.

Even as workers are dismissed summarily from their jobs, their monthly salary cancelled, carrying in crates the contents of their cleared desks, the small paraphernalia of abridged permanent posts, Labour is struck uncharacteristically dumb. As other people anxiously await the next shake-out of labour, the next bank failure, the collapse of their holiday firms, the inflationary bite into their small incomes, and the Liberal Democrats decide that they are the New Conservatives, Labour is powerless to provide the competent radical voice which the urgency of the hour requires.

The madness of the markets seems to have entered the soul of New Labour, faced as it is with Old Capitalism, whose nature is far less changeable than that of its sometime enemies.

If Labour cannot even tell a story any more, as Gisela Stuart says, this is because its tale has already been told. It is difficult not to see in the present convulsions of New Labour an acting out of the death-wish implicit in its abrogation of its quarrel with capitalism, a suicidal impulse given its final quietus when it called itself New, not so long ago, but in what now look like the old days.

24 September 2008

Red Gordon: The leader the party had dreamed of

JONATHAN FREEDLAND

It seems a long time ago now, back in the spring of 2007, when the Labour tribe was so certain Gordon Brown was the right man to lead them they didn't even want a contest for the top job. They had a clear image of the prime minister he would be: solid, anchored in moral purpose, a heavyweight able to punch the light out of the Tories – and with a reddish tinge which meant he stood, even if not openly, to the left of Tony Blair.

That was the Gordon Brown the Labour faithful hoped they were getting 15 months ago. In the past year, many had almost forgotten him, as a different character seemed to take up residence in Downing Street: Bottler Brown, the ditherer who ducked an election and took from the poor with a scrapped 10p tax rate, who could barely speak like a human being and who watched, paralysed, as a 12-point Labour lead turned into a 20-point deficit.

But for one sweet hour yesterday afternoon that man was banished, replaced by the Gordon Brown Labour once yearned for. In a speech performed with greater skill than any of his previous efforts – the cadences rising and falling in the right places, the high-volume, machine-gun delivery ditched – the prime minister reminded the Labour party why they had once admired him so much.

The improvement began even before he had appeared. In a surprise piece of stagecraft, his wife, Sarah, came to the podium to rapturous applause – one of several elements yesterday borrowed from the recently completed US convention season. Like Michelle

Obama or Cindy McCain, she testified to her husband's devotion to public service. Her unflashiness, the sense that she has endured tough times as well as good, threw a kind of protective layer over the PM: he gained credit by association.

Brown built on that, insisting: 'I'm serious about doing a serious job.' Riskily, given that he had just deployed his own wife, he bragged that he had not 'served up my children for spreads in the papers' – a clear dig at David Cameron, who is often photographed with his family – because 'My children aren't props; they're people.' It was a return to the message he had sought to convey in that distant summer of 2007: not flash, just Gordon.

He marched on, determined to retake the moral high ground. Speaking more personally than usual, he offered a quasi-apology for the 10p tax error, saying he was 'stung' by the accusation that he was no longer 'on the side of hard-working families', vowing that from now on 'it's the only place I ever will be'.

He borrowed a line from Barack Obama's convention speech to ram home the point: 'This job is not about me. It's about you.' More surprisingly, Brown cast himself as a Scottish Sarah Palin, adapting one of her signature lines, though with Fife in place of Alaska and Westminster in place of Washington: 'I didn't come to London because I wanted to join the establishment, but because I wanted to – and want to – change it.'

But Brown's chief effort was to push the image of himself which, during those first three months in Number 10, had begun to take root in the public mind, before it was so pushed aside. He would be 'the rock of stability'.

Brown will hope this stems the decline in his standing but that was not his primary purpose yesterday. With talk throughout the conference of a plot against him – the only issue being when, not if, he would be toppled – addressing the wider public was a luxury. He had to win over the hall.

He did that by returning to what had been old form, staking out territory to the left of the Blairite project. Never mind that he had been the co-architect of New Labour, a favourite Brown manoeuvre was always to tickle the erogenous zones of the Labour faithful, serving up some old-time religion.

Yesterday he did that by promising a 'new settlement for new times', a shift to reflect the convulsions in the world economy. Now the market would be returned to its rightful place as a servant of the people – never its master. In a sentence that delighted his audience, he declared: 'Those who argue for the dogma of unbridled free market forces have been proved wrong.'

All week, the conference fringe has hummed with similar sentiments, as Labour folk have seized on the collapse and bailout of the big banks as evidence that the neo-liberal era is over. Yesterday, Brown was keen to ride that wave.

So he spoke of freeing agency workers from 'the scourge of exploitation' and laid into the traders guilty of 'reckless speculation'.

That's not language that often passed the lips of Tony Blair. That it comes easily to Gordon Brown was one reason why he was able to remain as Labour's heir apparent for so long. Indeed, he turned to Red Gordon to get him out of trouble many times in the past and did so again yesterday.

The politics are not hard to fathom. Brown hopes that by securing his left flank, he can cast himself as the more appealing alternative to any putative rival, who would swiftly be branded as 'Blairite' and on the party's right. He knows that the trade unions are not impressed by David Miliband: in yesterday's speech Brown sent the message that in any future choice, they should stick with him.

That was not the only way in which the he pushed back at those conspiring for his removal. The public 'would not forgive us', he said, if Labour was to turn inward during the economic storm. This is proving to be one of Brown's sharpest weapons: the claim that to leave the country leaderless during such a crisis would spook the markets and anger the voters.

But the moment that caught the attention – as it was surely designed to – was a line officially directed at the Conservatives but with a handy double meaning. 'I'm all in favour of apprenticeships,' he said, 'but this is no time for a novice.' The TV cameras instantly cut to Miliband's forced smile as the Brown camp knew they would.

Not that the Tories escaped a pounding. Brown attacked them more potently than he has managed since becoming prime minister. He won gasps when he quoted George Osborne (not accurately it emerged later) declaring it was financial markets' job to make money out of the 'misery of others'.

There was still some confusion on precisely how to attack the Tories: whether to accept that they have changed, conceding that they now have genuinely progressive intentions – but are not ready to support the means to those progressive ends – or whether to argue that the change is merely cosmetic. In the end, Brown did a bit of both.

Still, this was more like the great clunking fist Brown had promised and which he had not yet bared. It gave Labour heart that, if Brown carried on like this, he might just rescue himself – and them.

There were longueurs in the speech, especially in the middle, during what even his own aides described as 'the policy slab'. And while he offered a sketch of what needed to be done to cure the global financial system, the speech was short on the domestic steps Brown plans to take. The policy proposals were all relatively small-bore: not quite lagging on pipes, but home internet and personal tutors for kids rather than an overhaul of the economy.

Still, it's not on policy proposals that a speech such as this is judged. It's on the intangible, almost emotional sense that lingers once it's over. Brown needed to leave his audience with the gut belief that he's not done for just yet, that he could still come back. He did that yesterday. But it will have been for nothing if it ends there. As one cabinet colleague said, he needs to do that 'every day, every week from now on'.

He has to kill off the man he has been for the last year – and bring back the Gordon Brown his party once dreamed of.

24 SEPTEMBER 2008

Gordon's grin:
new but not improved

SIMON HOGGART

Gordon Brown pulled off a masterstroke when he got his wife to introduce him yesterday. Poised, relaxed and good-looking, Sarah Brown was everything her husband isn't. No wonder they gave her a standing ovation just for turning up. In the tradition of political wives she gave us a moving portrait of her husband at home – 'motivated to work for the best interests of people all round the country'. No mention of hurled telephones or hands accidentally stapled to briefing papers.

Then they showed a video of Labour achievements over the past 11 years. Curiously, Tony Blair figured once, for about a second. It was the modern version of the fallen Soviet leader airbrushed out of a Kremlin salute. (He did get a single mention in the hour-long speech, but apart from that the former leader has become an unperson here.)

Bizarrely, an image of Sir Alan Sugar next appeared. For a

moment we thought he might be about to announce 'You're fired!' He didn't. But we heard from the late Jackie Wilson singing (Your Love Has Lifted Me) Higher and Higher, a piece of music as dislocated from the image of Gordon Brown as is possible to imagine. One always feels the prime minister should be greeted by a lone piper playing a tragic dirge, possibly a lament for the death of a pet otter.

The great man appeared. His ears appear to have grown bigger. He produced an all-new, different unnerving grin – the smile of someone who's nicked your sandwich and wants you to know it's not how it seems. He kicked off by saying he wanted to talk about who he was and what he believed. It turned out he believed in fairness. When politicians say they are going to rip off the facade and expose the real self, you know they are never going to say: 'I am greedy for power for its own sake. I am paranoid and vengeful, obsessed by unimportant details.'

He confessed to mistakes, though again it turned out the errors made him yet more loveable. 'What happened with the 10p [tax rate] stung me, because it really hurt that suddenly people felt that I wasn't on the side of people on middle and modest incomes.' In other words, he knew how wonderful he was, and it was a shock to find that other people didn't agree. He did admit to being unpopular, though, in a sideways sort of way.

'Understand that all the attacks, all the polls, all the headlines, all the criticism – it's worth it if in doing this job I make life better for one child, one family, one community.' It seems a modest ambition, given there are 60 million people in the country.

The big applause came for attacks on the Tories. 'We did fix the roof while the sun was shining!' he said, drawing the conference to its feet. I haven't seen so much apparently spontaneous standing since Iain Duncan Smith spoke two weeks before the Tories binned him. Then he got in a cunning 'twofer'. He said the Tories – and George Osborne in particular – couldn't be trusted to run the economy. 'I'm all in favour of apprenticeships, but let me tell you this is no time for a novice, David Miliband.' No, of course he didn't mention the foreign secretary, but he didn't need to.

Straight after the speech, a line of Labour parliamentary candidates formed outside a makeshift photo studio, looking like the queue in Red Square to see Lenin. They were all to be photographed with the leader, or possibly a cardboard cutout. I wonder how many of the resulting pictures will actually appear in election addresses.

25 SEPTEMBER 2008

Whether Brown survives, Labour has already changed

SEUMAS MILNE

Five days in Manchester may not have transformed Gordon Brown's prospects. But there's no doubting the impact that the maelstrom in the markets has had on his government, Labour and the wider mood across the political spectrum. The prime minister came to Labour's conference facing virtually open cabinet revolt, a barely concealed challenge from his foreign secretary and the expectation of a full-scale coup within the next two months.

He was last night flying out to New York with the party at least stabilised, the plotters in disorderly retreat and David Miliband bruised by a week of unflattering overexposure. Even yesterday's announcement that the transport secretary, Ruth Kelly, is planning to step down in next week's expected cabinet reshuffle arguably strengthened Brown's position. She had been identified, after all, as one of the cabinet ministers planning to co-ordinate their resignations in an attempt to force Brown out. Now she's gone, that's one less potential conspirator in play.

The shift was clinched by what must rank as the most unashamedly left-leaning speech by a British prime minister since the mid-1970s – even if the competition is admittedly not fierce. By acknowledging his abolition of the 10p tax rate as a mistake, putting 'fairness' at the centre of the government's agenda, denouncing the 'dogma of unbridled free market forces' and calling for a 'new settlement for these times' – where markets are 'servants', not 'masters' – Brown both appealed to Labour's long-stifled core instincts and signalled the essential shift towards government intervention demanded by the monumental market failure of the credit crisis.

The foreign secretary, by contrast, had arrived in Manchester on a cushion of celebratory media coverage as the undisputed heir apparent. By Tuesday, when the prime minister delivered his twin-barrelled putdown of Miliband and David Cameron – 'this is no time for a novice' – the wheels were already spinning off his bandwagon.

Fear of the return of full-blown Blairism in the shape of Miliband has been crucial in maintaining support for Brown in recent months. That was intensified at the weekend by an apparent endorsement of Miliband by the health secretary, Alan Johnson, widely regarded as the most credible 'stop Miliband' candidate. Johnson has now made it clear that he could still be in the running in a post-Brown contest. And although Miliband has made some effort to distance himself from New Labour ortho-doxy over tax, he stuck doggedly to the Blairite catechism on the conference fringe, including a hawkish, interventionist line from Afghanistan to Georgia.

That is not remotely the mood that has dominated debate in Manchester. Everywhere, fuelled by the financial crisis, there has been a thirst to discuss government intervention, equality and progressive taxation unheard of at a Labour conference for more than a decade. Ministers such as Yvette Cooper, Ed Miliband, Ed Balls and Douglas Alexander have gone out of their way to attack 'greed and excess' in the City, and call for tougher regulation and greater boldness. The influential Dagenham MP, Jon Cruddas, has been ubiquitous, arguing for Labour to opt for more radical policies and take ownership of 'the new zeitgeist' created by the crisis. Meanwhile, the Blairite irreconcilables – ministers such as John Hutton, Caroline Flint and James Purnell, who have been at the heart of the manoeuvring against Brown – are left floundering, unable to respond to the demands of the changed economic climate, still pushing the New Labour formulas of the boom years.

In crucial ways the Tories face similar problems, despite their commanding opinion poll lead. Even more than New Labour, the Conservative party has championed City deregulation and unfettered markets. The Tory shadow chancellor, George Osborne, really did say last week 'no one takes pleasure from people making money out of the misery of others, but that is a function of capitalist markets'. And with unerring timing, in the month that Northern Rock collapsed, the Conservative policy commission spelled out: 'We see no need to continue to regulate the provision of mortgage finance, as it is the lending institutions rather than the client taking the risk.' Quite how David Cameron, under pressure from his right to hold the free-market line, plans to 'share the proceeds' of nonexistent growth will presumably be revealed at his own conference in Birmingham next week.

It is there that the ranks of corporate lobbyists will be descending in force in anticipation of a transfer of power at the next election. Whether it is Brown who Cameron will face in that contest, or a new Labour leader, remains in the balance. But after this week, the chances of an internal challenge in the wake of an already-discounted Glenrothes byelection defeat in November have clearly receded. If Labour is still 20 points behind next summer, on the other hand, it's another matter.

That will depend on how long the recession and the squeeze on living standards last, as well as whether Brown is able to turn Tuesday's grand declarations into action to protect those hit hardest. The auguries are not great. When it comes to Red Gordon rhetoric which never quite makes the transition to real life, the prime minister has form stretching back years. Genuinely new policy announcements were thin on the ground in Tuesday's speech, and there was nothing remotely of the necessary scale or symbolism of, say, a windfall tax or price controls on the gas and electricity companies. Brown's pledge of fairness will be hard to stomach for millions of public service workers facing cuts in real wages while huge City bonuses continue to flow without restraint.

But Brown and Labour are fighting for their political survival and there is no other way to go. Osborne accuses the prime minister of 'retreating to the left to save his job'. In reality, it is simply a commonsense recognition that times have changed, which Osborne and Cameron have yet to make.

A first test of the prime minister's seriousness of intent will come with next week's reshuffle: a couple of significant Blairite scalps, such as the free-market enthusiast Hutton's, would be a sign that his 'new settlement' is more than a conference platform flourish. But in any case, political language creates its own momentum and expectations. Whatever happens to Brown, Labour began to change this week – and the fallout of that change is likely to be felt for years to come.

4 OCTOBER 2008

Third time lucky: Mandelson brought into Brown's economic war cabinet

PATRICK WINTOUR

Gordon Brown yesterday sought to bring fresh purpose to his premiership and tackle the global economic crisis by bringing Peter Mandelson into the government for the third time, and unveiling an economic war cabinet of businessmen and politicians at the heart of Whitehall.

Brown made his dramatic act of reconciliation to the arch-Blairite as a *Guardian*/ICM poll showed that the Conservatives had secured a post-conference fillip, boosting their lead over Labour by three points to 12 points.

However, 55 per cent of voters think the prime minister has handled the economic situation well, against only 39 per cent who say he has performed badly.

Brown hopes Mandelson's return, part of a limited but bold reshuffle, can mark a turning point in his leadership, and will be seen as confirmation of a truce between Brownites and Blairites after months of debilitating infighting.

Other key developments in the reshuffle included:

- establishment of a 19-strong national economic council, chaired by Brown, meeting twice weekly to coordinate government action to tackle the banking crisis
- creation of a Department of Energy and Climate Change under Ed Miliband

- moving Stephen Carter, director of strategy in Downing Street, to a ministerial role within the new economic 'war cabinet'

But it was Mandelson's surprise return from his job as EU trade commissioner that startled Westminster. Apart from his business brief, Mandelson will provide much-needed political strategic advice to Brown in the run-up to the next election, including trying to give him greater political definition. He will also try to tighten the Downing Street operation.

At a press briefing, Brown admitted he had had his ups and downs with Mandelson, but said 'serious times need serious people doing serious jobs'.

He added: 'If you have got someone with unrivalled experience in international business issues, someone who is respected by business for what he has done and who has built a reputation over these last few years as someone who can get things done, then if the British government can benefit from that, it's the right decision.'

Evidently astonished by the offer, Mandelson, who was only asked to return to the cabinet on Thursday, said he hoped to make it 'third time lucky'. He added that the serious economic crisis required 'all hands to the pump'.

Although he has been a divisive figure throughout his career, cabinet ministers recognise that Mandelson's appointment may pay off. One said: 'It is a bold masterstroke politically and might even work electorally.'

The Conservatives condemned Mandelson's withdrawal from Europe, saying it marked a return of the architect of spin and was a sure sign of Brown's political weakness.

Some Labour leftwingers were apoplectic. 'The vast majority of Labour MPs will think, what was Gordon Brown thinking of? He is the most divisive figure in the Labour party,' said John McDonnell, the leftwing MP for Hayes and Harlington.

The reshuffle also sees a restructuring of the much criticised Downing Street operation, with Carter leaving to become communications minister inside the economic war cabinet. He has become a peer. Damian McBride, Brown's tough but effective political spin doctor, steps back from five years' frontline briefing to work on strategic policy inside No 10. He will work closely with two Cabinet Office ministers, Tom Watson and Liam Byrne.

In a move welcomed by environmentalists, Brown has also reconfigured Whitehall so that environment and energy are married into a new department headed by Ed Miliband.

Two ministers join the cabinet for the first time: Jim Murphy is appointed Scottish secretary and Lady Royall is leader of the House of Lords.

Nick Brown, a Brown ally, becomes chief whip, replacing Geoff Hoon, who becomes transport secretary, replacing Ruth Kelly, who is standing down from politics at the next election. John Hutton, the Blairite secretary of state for business, shifts to defence, replacing Des Browne, who is leaving the government and so also relinquishes the Scottish secretaryship, his other cabinet post.

Browne was offered a variety of posts including a joint one of Northern Ireland and Scotland, but he insisted he wanted to leave frontline politics.

The *Guardian* understands that Jon Cruddas was offered the housing post at a meeting with Brown yesterday but turned it down after he was told he could not start a big council house building programme. Downing Street denies he was offered the job.

Mandelson's departure from his EU post has led Brown to send the leader of the Lords, Lady Ashton, to Europe at least until next November. Her appointment avoids a difficult byelection.

At his press conference, Brown also announced the new economic council, saying that Mandelson and 18 other ministers would meet twice a week throughout the current global crisis.

Explaining the new body, Brown said: 'Quite simply, we do not need just to change policies but the way we make decisions and the way we govern.'

He has asked Paul Myners, chairman of the Guardian Media Group, to become City spokesman, and Margaret Beckett, the former foreign secretary, to be housing spokeswoman, on the new economic council.

9 OCTOBER 2008

Staring into the abyss

ASHLEY SEAGER, JILL TREANOR AND PATRICK WINTOUR

The most concerted effort yet by global authorities to bring an end to the 14-month credit crunch, using every weapon in their arsenal, failed to restore battered confidence last night.

Stockmarkets tumbled, despite a £500bn bank rescue from the UK government and unprecedented interest rate cuts by the world's key central banks, after the International Monetary Fund warned that Britain faced its first recession in almost two decades.

Gordon Brown put his government's credibility on the line as he risked potentially vast sums of public money to save the banking system. Some estimates equated the bailout figure to £16,000 for every taxpayer in Britain.

'This is not a time for outdated thinking or conventional dogma. Extraordinary times call for bold and far-reaching solutions,' the prime minister said, promising the plan would 'show we have led the world in changing the terms and conditions on which we can help to renew the flow of money in the system'.

The plan was generally welcomed by the City, but there was concern at the lack of detail, which reflected the speed with which it had been drawn up. Investors fear that if it does not work they are staring into the abyss of a possible collapse of the banking system.

Yesterday's dramatic actions included:

- Britain pledging £50bn to buy stakes in its major banks
- A further £450bn allocated to underpin banks' finances
- Unprecedented coordinated rate cuts by central banks

The British government was forced to rush out its bank rescue yesterday morning after precipitous share falls in banks on Tuesday. Bank bosses and the chancellor, Alistair Darling, hammered out the basics overnight, but the details are not yet fully worked out.

The plan was bolder and broader than expected, extending to seven major banks as well as Nationwide building society. In return for taxpayers' money, executives will have to curb bonuses, hold back share dividends and pledge to continue lending to homeowners and small businesses.

'The co-ordinated interest rate cuts got the "thumbs down" from equity markets, suggesting we have not yet turned the corner in this crisis,' said Roger Bootle, a veteran analyst at Capital Economics. The shadow chancellor, George Osborne, demanded that the government extract promises that City bonuses would be reined in as a condition of the deal. 'There should not be rewards for failure – no bonuses for those who took their banks to the edge of bankruptcy,' he told a packed House of Commons.

The IMF warned yesterday that Britain would next year suffer its first full year of recession since 1991, as the global economy enters a 'major downturn' triggered by the most dangerous financial shock since the 1930s.

While most of the participating banks encouraged the government to produce its plan, Michael Geoghegan, chief executive of the UK's biggest bank, HSBC, warned that it set a dangerous precedent. 'I don't think it is right that the British taxpayer should need to bail out banks ... It sets a bad precedent, but the government had no alternative,' he said.

10 OCTOBER 2008

The anxiety spreads

LEADER

One question was going round markets and the media yesterday: is it working? The day after Gordon Brown launched his emergency rescue for banks, early signs were not good. The money markets, the subterranean plumbing of the financial system, remain distressed. Banks were charging each other 6.28 per cent for a three-month loan yesterday – nearly two percentage points above the Bank of England's base rate. Bankers still do not have enough confidence in each other to lend at anything less than punitive rates.

This does not mean Mr Brown's treatment has failed. Financiers need time to understand the difference the deal will make – the government guarantee on lending between banks in particular should surely have some effect soon. One fan of the British plan is the US treasury secretary, Hank Paulson, who is now talking about part-nationalising American banks too. That is quite some reversal. Still, there are two big reservations bankers surely have about the British scheme: one is the small print, the other is the big picture. The first is to do with the strings that will be attached to government help. This week's deal was hammered out in such a rush that financiers do not know the conditions the Treasury will impose on them. Instead, as each bank comes forward for its government money, it will have to haggle over what it gives up in return. Will the institutions have to clamp down on bosses' pay, or force a few executives to walk the plank? Officials would be quite justified in driving a very hard bargain and insisting that any handout has to be matched with a sharp increase in bank lending to individuals and businesses. Tighten the screws too much, however, and bank shareholders will balk, the markets will once again be roiled and the whole plan thrown up in the air. Mr Brown is surely justified in restricting dividend payments to bank shareholders which are a leakage of all-precious capital – but the very notion is bound to send shares plummeting. It would be sensible to suspend London trading in all securities tied to these distressed institutions until negotiations are closed.

It is the big picture, however, that should frighten both bankers and ministers: the bleak outlook for the UK economy, and in particular the housing market. America's banking crisis was precipitated by a slump in house prices, which led to a collapse in the value of the mortgage-based securities held by so many institutions. Britain, however, has begun the other way around. More than 14 months into the credit crunch, the UK's crisis has been concentrated in banks. The housing collapse has yet to be felt, although it is gathering pace. The Bank of England yesterday revealed a 98 per cent drop in net mortgage lending in August. As unemployment rises, the number of foreclosures and defaults on other loans is sure to rise too. The effect of that on lenders is likely to be dramatic.

When historians come to discuss the great banking crisis of this decade they may crudely split it into three parts. The first, which hit last summer, was concentrated in those banks that relied on the money markets for their funding, such as Northern Rock. We are in the second phase: a general panic about the solvency of all banks, even those previously thought to be rock-solid. And the third is likely to be driven by consumers, as more default on all those loans on homes, cars and credit cards taken out during the boom years. This paper has called before for ministers to launch an economic stimulus package. To prevent the economy going into freefall, Mr Brown will need to spend more money – but this time on keeping people in houses, helping those who have lost jobs and creating employment in the public sector (such as working on green technologies). That level of spending may be unpalatable to an indebted government already dealing with one economic firestorm. But another looks set to break, and Mr Brown must be prepared.

15 NOVEMBER 2008

Brown signals further rate cuts as G20 leaders gather

LARRY ELLIOTT AND TOBY HELM, NEW YORK

Gordon Brown arrived in Washington last night for a crisis meeting of the G20 after pledging that lower interest rates, tax breaks for the low paid and measures to make the economy greener would be at the centre of Britain's response to the global recession.

The prime minister hinted that the pre-budget report this month would make tax credits for the working poor more generous and provide cash for home insulation. Brown also said the cost of borrowing would come down, and delivered a veiled rebuke to the Bank of England for keeping interest rates too high for too long. Today's talks between the leaders of 20 major developed and developing nations are expected to endorse measures to lift the global economy out of the downturn, although some European countries are lukewarm about big expansionary packages.

Speaking to the Council on Foreign Relations, a New York-based thinktank, the prime minister said: 'We need to make monetary policy work to better effect. In the US, interest rates have been reduced to 1 per cent. The European area has been slower – rates are 3.25 per cent in the euro area and 3 per cent in the UK. There is scope, as the governor of the Bank of England says, for a further reduction in interest rates. It is an essential part of what we are doing.'

The prime minister insisted that lower interest rates needed to be accompanied by an expansionary fiscal policy – tax cuts and spending increases – and made it clear that the government wanted to avoid any financial giveaway being saved rather than spent, as happened to half the 1 per cent of GDP rebate handed to US taxpayers earlier this year.

Less well-off families are seen as more likely than rich families to raise consumption after a tax break. 'People on low incomes will have a higher propensity to spend if their credits are higher,' he said.

The prime minister said he also wanted to make sure that any fiscal boost made Britain more environmentally 'sensitive and efficient'. Measures to improve insulation and draft proofing would be part of a longer term strategy aimed at boosting green industries and technologies. 'This could be a big expanding sector. It could be for employment what IT was in the 1990s,' Brown said.

With debate raging in the US over a possible government bailout for the car industry, the prime minister made it clear that he thought the incoming president, Barack Obama, should resist protectionism.

'Restructuring of industries and services will have to take place,' Brown said . 'It's an illusion that every job will be there when this crisis is over.

'Our message should be that we can't help you keep your last job, but we can help you get the next job.'

The slump of the 1930s had been deepened, Brown said, by the lack of cooperation that prompted trade barriers to be erected. 'We have to send out a signal that protectionism is the road to ruin.' Attempts will be made today to revive the Doha round of global trade liberalisation talks, which have been stalled since the latest breakdown in the summer.

Brown said that the gap between the main protagonists in the negotiations was small, adding: 'If we could announce a world trade deal in the next few months we would get the most precious of things: confidence.'

11 DECEMBER 2008

And on Wednesday, Gordon saved the world

SIMON HOGGART

It was obviously a slip, but was it a Freudian slip? There is no way Gordon Brown would have announced during prime minister's questions yesterday that he had saved the world, like Superman recalling how he had shoved the giant meteor aside as it was about to crash into the Earth, if he'd been in full command of his brain.

But did it express some profound, half-secret feeling buried deep in his id, or ego, or wherever these things lurk? Did he really mean it, or did he just sort of mean it?

Other countries have congratulated him on the way he prevented British banks going bust. Some have followed his example. Possibly there is a small cluster of synapses which believes he really did save the world from sudden and total disaster. Perhaps the thought just popped out like champagne from a badly corked bottle. Or he could, like so many politicians, be in thrall to his own publicity. Margaret Thatcher never got over the thrill of being called the Iron Lady by the Soviets.

Here's what happened.

David Cameron was launching into his assault for the day. Putting money into the banks was all very well, but it hadn't worked. When was Gordon going to change his strategy?

He replied: 'The first point of recapitalisation was to save banks that would otherwise have collapsed.' So far, so predictable. He went on: 'We not only saved the world ...'

There was a pause, in which MPs looked at each other and wondered whether they had heard what they had heard. In that moment, the prime minister had a chance to correct himself – 'saved the banks and led the way', he said – but it was too late.

He was buried under a sudden, overwhelming, mountainous avalanche of laughter – laughter, hooting, derision, chortling, spluttering, screeching and general mayhem filled the chamber like oil in a lava lamp, bubbling and swirling.

The Tories, of course, were the most affected. Genuine hilarity mixed with the joy of seeing the hated Brown discomfited. They slapped thighs, anybody's thighs, waved their order papers, rolled around, and allowed their faces to turn a deep red colour like a Christmas glass of port.

I was more fascinated by the Labour benches. Some MPs laughed openly, mainly those who thought the whips couldn't see or didn't care what they thought. Some could be seen twitching horribly, trying to hold back their merriment. Others, such as the chief whip, Nick Brown, glowered ahead, as if the Tory laughter was as grossly inappropriate as it would be at a royal funeral.

The laughter had gone on for 21 seconds (an age in parliament) when the Speaker first said 'Order!'

When it showed no sign of dying down, he again said 'Order!'

The prime minister tried to plough his way through. But he is hopeless at snappy comebacks so, having repeated what he really meant to say, he decided to claim that the Conservative hilarity was in some way an affront. 'The opposition may not like the fact that we led the world in saving the banking system, but we did!'

21 DECEMBER 2008

Gordon Brown saved himself. Now he has to save his party

ANDREW RAWNSLEY

At a state banquet at Windsor Castle in March, someone important had gone missing when the Queen and Nicolas Sarkozy took their places at the top table. A baffled Queen inquired: 'Has the prime minister got lost?' An amused French president remarked to his wife: 'That's Gordon.'

For much of 2008, it looked as though this would be Gordon Brown's epitaph: the prime minister who got lost. There was a sequence of terrible defeats: he lost to a massive Labour backbench revolt over 10p tax; he lost to David Cameron at the Crewe and Nantwich byelection and to Boris Johnson in London; he lost to Alex Salmond in Glasgow East.

Worse still, Brown seemed at a total loss about how to rescue a premiership that increasingly appeared to have no purpose beyond survival. In the wake of the cataclysmic loss of one of

Labour's safest seats in Glasgow at the end of July, Gordon Brown made an absolutely dire speech to his party's national policy forum in which he dealt with that defeat by pretending it hadn't happened. Even ministers who were still well-disposed to him came away feeling suicidal, one groaning to me that the prime minister seemed to be in 'total denial'.

As the Tory poll lead stretched towards 20 points, the cabinet was close to what one of its members calls 'a nervous breakdown'. There were highly secretive discussions, involving some of the most senior ministers, about how they might remove him from No 10. Talking to some of his friends about that black period, some say that it would not have come to a cabinet coup. Brown, an extremely proud man and a very sensitive one, would have walked before he endured the humiliation of being putsched.

The lifebelt came in the most extraordinary form: the meltdown in the financial markets in the early autumn. The floundering, defeated prime minister was suddenly galvanised into a man of action. The Gordon Brown who had hesitated over nationalising one smallish northern bank became the leader prepared to stake eye-watering billions on saving several of them. The man who put Adam Smith on our bank notes turned into a born-again Keynesian. He would have poured even more red ink into the November crisis budget had the Treasury not resisted him.

The conventional rules of politics say that such a massive reversal of economic policy should destroy the credibility of a prime minister just as Harold Wilson's reputation never recovered from the 'pound in your pocket' devaluation of the mid-60s and John Major was wrecked by Black Wednesday in 1992. And yet orthodoxy was inverted. As the banks crashed, Brown bounced. This is partly because he has been brilliant at spinning the blame for the crisis away from himself. The international institutions failed. So said the man who had chaired the reform committee of the IMF for many years. The bubble economy in America was the culprit. So said the man who recommended an honorary knighthood for Alan Greenspan, the father of that bubble. It was down to the reckless gambling of the bankers. So said the man who indulged a lightly regulated City for a decade. The Tories howled, but largely to no avail. Polling suggests that most voters were, and still are, broadly prepared to buy the prime minister's account of the origins of the recession.

He looked confident and sounded authoritative in a crisis that allowed him to play to his strengths, expertise and international contacts. Experience has always been his best card against David Cameron and the crisis increased its potency. 'This is no time for a novice' was a line of his own invention and the best thrust of his speech to the Labour conference. David Miliband had been steeling himself to brandish the sword and was left wielding a banana.

He clawed back some respect from the voters. More importantly, he won back his self-respect. Others might laugh, especially when he inadvertently claims to have saved the planet, but he really does think that he played a decisive role in preventing a global implosion of the financial markets. Even if it turns out that he is destined to be one of those premiers who never wins an election in his own right, he will be able to say to himself that there was a great purpose to his time in No 10.

The crisis also forced Gordon Brown to reform the way he works. It is still not perfect, but most well-informed people say there have been big improvements on the chaotic management of government during his early period in No 10. 'A million times better,' remarks one minister. The national economic council, the 'economic war cabinet' he invented, has become a real centre of decision-making. He no longer spends most of his time in the small study in No 10 but works from a new open-plan office at No 12. It is more like a situation room than a bunker. Gordon Brown seems much happier in that environment where he is able to brainstorm ideas and bark orders at his key people.

Brown has also displayed an unexpected flair for political theatre. He sensationally resurrected Peter Mandelson, a figure who gives the jitters to both the Tories and his own party. Lord M has rapidly established himself as the most prominent and powerful member of the cabinet after the prime minister. 'I know it sounds strange, but Peter has made Gordon much more relaxed and confident,' says someone who has known both men for many years. 'At the same time, Peter can be blunt with Gordon about his faults in a way no one else can.'

While the media were successfully distracted by the extra-ordinary return of the Dark Prince, Gordon Brown also used that reshuffle to act ruthlessly against those whom he suspected of plotting against him. There was a purge of the ministerial allies of David Miliband and James Purnell. Nick Brown, his personal enforcer, was made chief whip. That is a corrective to the view that Gordon Brown has become a new man. He has the same virtues and vices. His staff still get bombarded with emails at all times of day and night. Sometimes the prime minister is gnawing anxiously over the next day's headlines; at other times he wants a detailed briefing on some highly technical economic point and he wants it yesterday.

Gordon Brown is what he has always been: a cross between nervy journalist and nerdy academic. He still lacks a lightness of touch. At his final news conference before Christmas, he was asked to describe his year. 'Challenging,' he replied boringly. He still struggles to do empathy, sounding hopelessly bureaucratic and inappropriately partisan when questioned by David Cameron about the tragedy of Baby P.

His character has not been transformed. What's changed is the prism through which the media and voters now view it. The crisis made his qualities – experience and seriousness – seem more important than his handicaps. Labour is still behind in the polls, but the deficit has been reduced to the sort of modest gap from which midterm governments often recover to win the next election.

Many people, both Labour ministers and their Tory opponents, think this can't be sustained: the public will turn against the government in the New Year as the recession grows more savage, business bankruptcies multiply and dole queues lengthen. That is another orthodoxy that will have to be upturned if Labour is to win a fourth term.

Gordon Brown rescued himself in 2008. The next year will test whether he can really save his party.

26 January 2009

Tories regain lost ground as ICM poll shows faith in Gordon Brown waning

Voters think that Gordon Brown's high-profile battle to turn around the economy is doomed, according to a new *Guardian*/ICM poll. Only 31 per cent think the prime minister's strategy will make things better. Most, 64 per cent, think it will either achieve nothing or even make the situation worse.

Even Labour's supporters are doubtful: only 48 per cent of people who voted for the party in 2005 believe that the government's measures will work.

The deepening crisis has left the party facing heavy defeat. Overall Conservative support is up six points since last month's *Guardian*/ICM survey. At 44 per cent it is only one point below its

25-year ICM high. Labour is on 32 per cent and the Liberal Democrats are on 16 per cent.

Today's poll, carried out after last week's second round of bank bail-outs and subsequent sharp falls in the share value of those banks, shows that public attitudes are hardening against the government. One estimate suggests that the Conservatives would win around 360 seats on today's figures, a majority of about 70. Labour could expect to win around 240, 30 more than it did at its nadir under Michael Foot in 1983.

26 MARCH 2009

Gordon Brown: A statesman abroad, under fire back home

PATRICK WINTOUR AND NICHOLAS WATT

It wasn't supposed to go like this. A week before the international summit that Downing Street hoped would cement Gordon Brown's reputation as the statesman leading the rescue of the global economy, he was to crisscross the world building an international agreement for his revival plan.

But instead of emerging as a visionary figure bestriding the world stage, the prime minister has been forced into embarrassing retreat by a coalition of an increasingly independent-minded chancellor, an uncharacteristically combative governor of the Bank of England and the cold-eyed verdict of the markets.

Gordon Brown appeared to back off pressing for a further fiscal stimulus in next month's budget after what was described, semi-mischievously, in the Commons yesterday as a coup by the governor of the Bank of England, Mervyn King. There will now be no big stimulus in the budget, if Brown had indeed ever been planning one. The failure of the government gilt sale yesterday – the first since 1995 – merely underlined this.

Vince Cable, the Liberal Democrat Treasury spokesman, was only being semi-ironic when he claimed at prime minister's questions that the governor of the Bank of England had mounted 'a very British coup d'etat by sending his tanks down the Mall, effectively seizing control of the British economy through his command of monetary policy, and putting the government under house arrest'.

Labour MPs know the past 48 hours have been bad for Brown, not only because it looks as if he has been defeated by the Treasury, but also because it fuels the impression that he is bent on spending to save his political skin.

Senior Tories were chortling yesterday at the way in which the one-time Mr Prudence was now desperately piling all his chips on red. They chortled even more when the children's secretary, Ed Balls, said in an interview in the *New Statesman*: 'Would I like to be chancellor at some point in the future? Of course I would.'

3 APRIL 2009

Gordon Brown brokers massive financial aid deal for global economy

PATRICK WINTOUR AND LARRY ELLIOTT

World leaders yesterday agreed on a $1.1tn injection of financial aid into the global economy, with Gordon Brown claiming that the grand bargain he had brokered represented 'a coming together of the world' that would speed recovery from the worst recession since 1945.

The sprawling deal set out in a nine-page communique hammered out over two days of talks in London also contains tougher-than-expected measures to tighten financial regulation, including a clampdown on tax havens, the final part of the deal to be struck, after an impassioned call for compromise by Barack Obama.

The US president said that 'the patient had stabilised and was in good care', claiming that, by any measure, the London summit was historic.

'It was historic because of the size and the scope of the challenge that we face and because of the timeliness and the magnitude of our response,' he said.

The transatlantic compromise between America and Europe led to a jump in shares in London and New York. The FTSE index closed up more than 4 per cent at 4,124.97. The deal won praise from business leaders, as well as anti-poverty campaigners, but dismayed the green lobby with its lack of measures to combat climate change.

The prime minister also won agreement from other G20 world leaders that the International Monetary Fund will monitor the existing stimulus, and that the leaders will re-examine the issue at a further summit, probably in New York or east Asia in September.

Overall, the resources of the IMF will be trebled from $250bn to $700bn, following the lifting by the US of years of opposition. In a sign of the shift in world power, China agreed to provide $40bn of the new loans given to the IMF, with more to come from Saudi Arabia.

Brown has tied his political future to the summit, and claimed: 'This is the day that the world came together, to fight back against the global recession. Not with words, but a plan for global recovery and for reform and with a clear timetable.'

He insisted the deal would save jobs in Britain. He admitted there were 'no quick fixes', but believed that as a result of the deal 'the recovery, which is much needed in every part of the world, will advance faster'. He had managed to achieve more in 10 weeks than he had previously accomplished over 10 years, he asserted.

A British cabinet member said: 'The scale of this deal will help with Gordon's underlying credibility. It will remind people what he is there for. It will be a slow burn, but the markets have jumped, and the polls will probably follow.'

3 APRIL 2009

Brown won't save our jobs. But he may save his own

LARRY ELLIOTT

Five miles of the River Thames and 11 years, 11 months in government separate Tony Blair's acclamation as Labour prime minister at the Royal Festival Hall and Gordon Brown's hosting of the G20 summit in Docklands yesterday. It is tempting to see the two events as book ends – one marking the start of an era, the other its end.

The prime minister certainly does not see it like that. For Brown it is just as appropriate to say now that 'a new day has dawned' as it was for Blair to utter those words when the sun came up on that May morning all those years ago. It was 'the day the world came together to fight back against recession'; it was the moment when the G20 made clear that 'in the new global age our prosperity is indivisible' and called time on 'the old Washington consensus'. And there was much more in the same vein.

Immediate reaction: let's all have a puff of what the PM is on because it must be good stuff. Britain under Labour has seen its manufacturing base shrivel and its trade deficit explode. Unemployment is likely to hit 3 million, while the collapse of the housing market and the humbling of the City has left the economy without any obvious sources of growth. Both the International Monetary Fund and the Organisation for Economic Co-operation and Development think the UK economy will contract by about 4 per cent this year – the biggest decline since 1945. Canary Wharf, the symbol of how unbalanced the economy has become over the past decade, loomed over yesterday's summit talks in more ways than one.

Again, that's not the way Brown sees it. He still believes – despite the evidence – that the British economy is fundamentally sound, and that yesterday's G20 deal on tax havens, extra resources for the IMF, trade credits and financial regulation will mark a turning point, not just for the global economy but for his government.

Here's how the Downing Street thinking goes. The crisis of the past 20 months is a crisis of the right, not the left; it was the fetish for deregulation and liberalisation that stripped all the controls from big finance and allowed the markets to run riot. Logically, therefore, restoring sanity to the financial markets must be a project for the left. Brown believes yesterday marks a big step forward in that process and, in fairness, there was plenty of meat in the comminique. Hedge funds will be regulated for the first time; there will be measures to limit the amount banks can lend during booms; tax havens are to be named and shamed; the Financial Stability Forum, an informal gathering of central bankers and regulators from rich countries, will have teeth to act as a global super-regulator – and part of its remit will be to look at the pay and bonuses of bankers.

These are not just substantial reforms, they are reforms that would have been impossible two years ago, in the days when the prevailing orthodoxy was that the best thing governments could do was to get out of the way and allow the private sector to make money unencumbered by red tape and 'punitive' taxes. We have heard a lot less of that sort of talk since those 'punitive' taxes started to fund welfare for Wall Street.

What's more, Brown is broadly correct to say that the right has been resistant to the more aggressive policy measures designed to mitigate the impact of the global downturn, fretting about bank bailouts and opposing the increased borrowing to pay for tax cuts and spending increases.

Germany and France effectively scuppered Brown's idea that G20 countries would launch big new rescue packages. But there is more than one way to skin a cat, so the focus has switched in recent weeks to providing a boost multilaterally, through the IMF, the World Bank and regional development banks. By the end of the day, Brown claimed he had cobbled together an additional $1.1tn that could be injected into the global economy. That comes on top of the $2tn pumped in by individual nations.

Not all this extra $1tn will be spent. Indeed, it will only be spent if the world economy continues to weaken at a precipitous rate. The IMF now sees itself as an organisation that sells insurance to countries; the extra resources will be used to underwrite those policies.

In the long term, Brown's view of the world looks distinctly Panglossian. Nothing in yesterday's summit suggested that the fundamental problem – imbalances in the global economy – is being tackled. Indeed, German and Japan, the countries suffering most in the global downturn, are those that need the strongest growth in domestic demand. Economic policy is now exceptionally loose: if the stimulus is removed too soon there will be a double-dip recession; if central banks and finance ministries wait too long there will be a dangerous burst of inflation. It is disappointing that the G20 has not explicitly linked the extra money for the IMF and the World Bank to fundamental reform of both organisations to make them representative of the global economy as it is, rather than as it was in 1944.

In the short term, though, none of that really matters. The question, for UK politics at least, is whether the benefits of cheaper money and fiscal easing will have become apparent by the spring of next year, the last possible date for a general election.

The good news for Brown yesterday was the evidence that the economy may turn more quickly than forecasters believe. The unexpected rise in house prices from the Nationwide may well be a blip, but the improvement in credit conditions for businesses reported by the Bank of England is more significant. It is evidence that the recapitalisation of the banks is starting to have an effect.

Let's be clear, none of these green shoots, if that is what they are, mean the recession is over – let alone that Brown is right in his claims about the underlying health of the economy. Any recovery will be hampered by the savage industrial recession of the past year, which has seen manufacturing output decline at a rate not seen since the early 1980s.

But the immediate outlook is improving. The economy is still contracting but the pace of decline is flattening out, and growth is likely to resume, albeit weakly, by the end of the year. If the economy is picking up, Brown thinks he is in with a fighting chance, because voters will be faced with a choice between an experienced prime minister who was brave enough to take the tough decisions and a wet-behind-the-ears opposition leader who wasn't. He could be right.

CHAPTER FIVE

SMEARS AND SMILES

Tentatively, warily, observers had begun to wonder whether Brown might have pulled it off. By standing tall on the global economy stage, it might – just might – be possible that enough gloss would rub off from the international summitry to reshine his tarnished aura. But political leaders rarely have much time to preserve such temporary lustre before the dust of daily domestic politics kicks up again. And so it proved for Brown. Even as it appeared that Gordon's economic resolve had indeed helped forestall an even deeper global slump, the combination of a Number 10 insider smear campaign, and then the horribly mishandled furore over MPs' expenses, swiftly stifled any prospect of poll recovery.

11 APRIL 2009

Damian McBride forced to quit over 'sex smear scandal'

GABY HINSLIFF

Gordon Brown is today engulfed in crisis after a key aide resigned and the Tories threatened legal action over explosive leaked emails discussing how to smear senior Conservatives, including David Cameron's wife, Samantha, with rumours about their private lives.

Damian McBride, one of the prime minister's closest advisers, quit over his exchange with the Labour blogger Derek Draper, in which the two discussed setting up a website to air scurrilous allegations about opponents, including unfounded allegations about affairs between leading opposition MPs. The idea was still being actively discussed until a fortnight ago, the *Observer* has learned.

Tom Watson, the Cabinet Office minister, was also facing questions after it emerged that McBride referred in one of the emails to Watson 'looking at other stories for Labour List', Draper's website on leftwing policy. However, Downing Street sources insisted Watson had been discussing an entirely separate announcement about Labour party staffing, which could be posted on the authorised site, rather than being involved in the gossip project nicknamed Red Rag.

Brown yesterday moved rapidly to distance himself from the affair, saying there was 'no place in politics for the dissemination or publication of material of this kind'.

Senior Tories have demanded a public apology from the PM and assurances that Watson had not been involved in dirty tricks, while the shadow home secretary accused Downing Street of descending 'into the gutter'. Charles Clarke, a former Labour cabinet minister who has always believed he was briefed against by McBride, said the official had brought 'shame' to the party.

13 APRIL 2009

Gordon's vicious side is now clear to the whole country

JACKIE ASHLEY

There's a juvenile, jeering, nasty side to Westminster politics; always has been, always will be. But it rarely hits the front pages and causes the resignation of a senior No 10 staffer. Damian McBride is not a name known to most newspaper readers but his most common nicknames, McNasty and McPoison, give an idea of his reputation since arriving in Downing Street with Gordon Brown.

Like any good villain, he's a hard man to kill off. They thought they'd got him before, when the cerebral Stephen Carter was made Brown's head of communications. McBride, a red-faced and sociable former Treasury civil servant, was shoved into a cupboard. But after months of turf wars, it was Carter who went, and McBride was re-established at the heart of Brown's media operation.

He can apparently be very good company. He is reportedly very clever, well-read and politically shrewd. But I say 'apparently' and 'reportedly' because McBride has always been a man who speaks only to a favoured cabal of Labour apparatchiks and chosen journalists. Outside the circle? He doesn't return your calls or acknowledge your presence. This has made him more enemies than friends; if you spot glee in the reporting of his fall, you're right.

Some parts of the story are absolutely familiar and should shock nobody with the haziest political memory. McBride's ruthlessly focused support for Brown, and Brown's need for McBride, has parallels with the Joe Haines operation in Harold Wilson's heyday, or Bernard Ingham's in Thatcher's, or of course the Blair operation, which Brown felt the rough edge of himself.

Almost every elected leader, surrounded by a hostile press and potential rivals, turns to the dark arts of briefers and ear-whisperers. In recent times, the sheer number of media outlets makes the favoured circle almost inevitable.

This gives the political leader 'deniability'. Ingham could use the secrecy code of the original 'no names, old boy' lobby system to denigrate ministers with whom Margaret Thatcher was exasperated – remember John Biffen being 'semi-detached' or the ruthless dispatch of Francis Pym? Thatcher could then smilingly greet her bemused and hurt ministers with an air of exasperating innocence.

In the same way, McBride used an 'inner lobby' of carefully selected reporters. The chancellor, Alistair Darling, wakes up to discover that key aspects of Treasury policy are being second-guessed in No 10 and that his decisions were really Gordon's. There are the stories, in cold black and white. But whose fingerprints are on them? They are a little too smudged to be sure. Labour's deputy leader, Harriet Harman, is rubbished as useless in stories which seem to have No 10's marks on them. But Gordon can smilingly deny any involvement.

It's not just those two. Douglas Alexander, once one of the keenest Brownites of all, discovers he's being dumped on for the shambolic 'election that wasn't called' last autumn. David Miliband is not only hung, but drawn and quartered too, for daring to put his head above the parapet with ideas about Labour's future.

A press operation can also be a silent assassination squad. All that makes this aspect of the McBride tale unusual is he has been sacked for spreading malice about Tories; as one senior Labour person put it to me, 'I could have fallen off my chair – most of his operations are against us, not them.' If there are journalists toasting McBride's fall, then there are plenty of Labour ministers and civil servants who feel the same. He was regarded as the heart of a Brownite shadow operation, based around a Wednesday afternoon meeting of just five or six people, which spent far too much energy plotting against ministers.

Some will say this gives the prime minister a chance for a fresh start, for him to shake off his enthusiasm for the black arts. I think it's too late. He could have changed his attitude to press briefing when Charlie Whelan, the first Brown attack dog, left. But he found another Charlie. He could have learned his lesson when he brought Stephen Carter in. But he couldn't quite banish McBride, which meant a succession of new press officers had no real authority.

The truth is that Brown has always been double-sided in his political personality and now the whole country knows it. The ideologically serious, morally driven statesman, whose steely determination was most recently on view in his successful handling of the G20, has lived his life with a sinister twin, spinning and dealing. McBride has been an extension of that other self.

Let's pause to consider where that's led the prime minister. McBride – Brown's man, Brown's prop, Brown's prosthetic reach – has been caught out trading in smears of the nastiest kind. These are sexual smears, tittle-tattle about alleged depression, juvenile pranks, kinky behaviour. Ring any bells? A decade ago Brown was at the receiving end of not so dissimilar smears. Surely the horrible irony strikes him?

But the truth is this stuff has become useless anyway. People aren't daft. Even his greatest supporters know that Brown has run a kind of dual premiership, partly high-minded and principled and partly vicious and tribal. Had this proposed website gone live with McBride's 'brilliant' material, the world would have shrugged, muttered 'pathetic' and thought no worse of Cameron, Osborne or the other targets. People know smears, and in general dislike smearers more than the smeared.

It's too late for the prime minister to shrug off McBride with expressions of surprise and horror, as if he'd been walking around with a portly vulture on his shoulder for years without noticing. McBride was as inner circle as it gets. If the prime minister didn't know what he was up to, he should have done.

Why do they do it? I can only suppose the rest of us underestimate the loneliness and insecurity of life at the top, and the near irresistible lure of having your own personal hitman, bodyguard, assassin and confidant. It must feel like security when it's really the opposite.

None of that adds up to an excuse. 'The Tories do it.' Yes, they do. (And here's a safe prediction: two years into a Cameron administration, there will be a Tory version of McBride, at much the same game.) But it's a sordid game, which is almost always discovered in the end, and which weakens every leader and every administration that plays it. This is a dreadful day for No 10; and they worked hard to see it dawn.

22 APRIL 2009

The YouTube moment

JEMIMA KISS

If No 10 wanted to be the centre of web attention for the day and create a viral video sensation, they may have hoped it would pan out rather better than this. Gordon Brown's latest video message to the people took politicians and pundits equally by surprise.

For the web community, the proposals were of less interest than the video itself. The three-and-a-half-minute film on No 10's website was uncomfortable viewing: restless swaying mixed with some dense policy details and a lot of forced smiling.

The *Spectator*'s Coffee House blog was quick to label it 'the funniest video ever to come out of No 10 ... Now that his dirty tricks unit has been exposed, he's trying to come across all cuddly and friendly ... he stops short of breakdancing, but only just.'

It wasn't the only site to observe that it felt as if instructions to 'smile' were being issued behind the camera.

Politics.co.uk said it was 'as adorable as it is pathetic', describing how Brown 'shrugs, with the manner of a friendly Gallic farmer, as he discusses the need to scrap the second home allowance'.

While Barack Obama and his team cleverly built on years of web campaign expertise to help the Democrats gain the US presidency last November, British political efforts have been more low-key. Obama has continued to use social media tools, distributing major speeches through YouTube, fielding questions through open forums on the White House site and spreading news through Twitter.

The difference is Brown. Mark Hanson, a social media consultant and Labour blogger, said that overall, No 10's operations were very good, with a willingness to experiment with sites and tools that opened up debate. 'But where they have fallen down is trying to rehearse him,' he said. 'We know he's not Obama, and sometimes it's best to leave people as they are. People will see that he is real and can make up their own mind.'

22 April 2009

A certain smile –
random, and a bit scary

SIMON HOGGART

Gordon Brown announced the swingeing cuts in MPs' allowances yesterday – on video. In the old days, prime ministers spoke to the Commons. But that has one huge disadvantage: MPs answer back. Viewers of YouTube don't. (But they can show their interest in other ways. For example, 'Gordon Brown picking his nose' has had more than 376,000 hits and counting.)

Anyhow, there is his latest policy pronouncement, on number10.gov.uk. What is most amazing is not the content of his statement, but the brand new smile. This smile has clearly been worked on for some time, possibly by a professional smile consultant. ('Now, Gordon, darling, lift the corners of your mouth. Let's see those incisors! No dribbling, mind!')

It cannot have been tried on a focus group, as it is quite terrifying. Think of the Joker in the Batman films. Then again it is the kind of smile you might deploy on a first date with someone you'd found in the small ads. ('Hmm. She says "GSOH essential". Maybe if I smile a lot she'll think I have one.') It's the smile a 50-year-old man might use on the parents of the 23-year-old woman he is dating, in a doomed attempt to reassure them. It's a doctor saying: 'Now this is going to hurt a teeny bit, but if you're a brave little soldier, Mummy might give you a biscuit.'

It is meant to be a friendly smile, even if it is almost as scary as anything Hannibal Lecter might come up with. I thought of a supply teacher who has to cope with the worst class in the school and imagines, poor fool, that he might win them over by sheer niceness. It's the smile a kidnap victim might try on his terrorist captors – 'Actually, I think you chaps have an awfully good case.'

But what makes it so frightening is that the smile is deployed entirely at random. 'Going round the country I have been struck by the comments of young people.' Big cheesy smile. Why? 'A detailed written statement setting out our plans will be made by Harriet Harman.' The smile is back, big time. Baffling. Does the very thought of Harriet Harman make him grin uncontrollably?

'Those ministers who live in official residences would not be entitled to this allowance.' Again, the smile leaps from the screen for no apparent reason. I began to wonder whether he was wired up to something, possibly via his underpants, the other end controlled by a four-year-old child who is having lots of fun.

'While the committee on standards in public life looks at the issue ... ' Smile! Now he is almost at the end, and able to visit his plastic surgeon for a face-drop and the opposite of a nip and tuck – a slice and stuff, perhaps.

30 APRIL 2009

Gordon Brown bruised after defeat over Gurkhas

Gordon Brown was struggling last night to shore up his authority after suffering his first Commons defeat as prime minister when MPs voted to allow all retired Gurkhas to settle in Britain.

Days after being forced to water down his plans to reform the system of MPs' expenses and allowances, Brown lost the support of 27 Labour MPs who voted with the Liberal Democrats and the Tories.

Up to 75 other Labour MPs abstained in the vote, which demanded that all former Gurkhas be allowed to live in the UK, not just those who retired after 1997 and a small proportion of the others. Stephen Pound resigned as a ministerial aide last night after joining the rebels.

The rebellion set the scene for another bruising day today when MPs vote on Brown's plans to reform MPs' allowances and expenses.

2 MAY 2009

Another bad week for Brown as his authority is challenged on all sides

PATRICK WINTOUR
AND ALLEGRA STRATTON

Prime ministers are famously supposed to be able to chew gum and walk at the same time, but when you are flying over the Hindu Kush pondering the world's most fragile democracy and the fate of 8,000 British soldiers fighting in Helmand, it is hard to focus on a Lib Dem opposition supply day in the Commons.

While Gordon Brown was over the border region of Pakistan and Afghanistan on Monday, the seeds of a terrible week were being sown at home, as the government blundered towards defeat in a vote over the rights of Gurkhas to settle in Britain. Twenty-seven Labour MPs rebelled, dozens more abstained, an emergency statement followed and the sense prevailed that Brown's authority had been critically undermined.

Miserable comparisons were made to the last days of John Major's premiership and historians noted the first government defeat in an opposition day debate since James Callaghan in 1978. A day later came further dispiriting climbdowns over MPs' expenses as the week of misjudgments dragged on.

'There should have been a figure back in London sorting this out,' said one minister involved in the setback.

It was obvious from Monday that Labour was likely to lose the vote on the Gurkhas. It had taken more than six months to get a decision out of Whitehall on what to do, ever since a court ruled in September that the government had not been fair to veterans whose cases had been settled before 1997. The delay was largely because the Ministry of Defence did not have any money to pay the potential pension costs, but also because no one gripped the issue at the centre.

One whip said: 'We thought two staged concessions, one to Martin Salter, and the other to George Howarth [both Labour MPs], might be enough to turn it round. But there were a group of MPs that were not listening. What is worrying is that the rebels and abstainers were not the usual suspects.

'We tried everything, but we were very despondent afterwards, saying the MPs were blind to argument. Some of them may have been cross about their second home allowance, but most of them just thought we had mishandled it. We could not get our message across.'

A minister said: 'One problem is that Gordon at prime minister's questions said this would cost a lot of money, but he did not say the next bit, which is that we have not got any money.'

A senior minister stood back and looked at the wider lessons of Brown's first defeat of his premiership: 'It's a cliche, but every government needs a John Prescott, or in Thatcher's case, a Willie Whitelaw, an enforcer.

'Brown needs someone to pull it all together. The obvious candidate is Ed Balls because he knows Gordon's mind, or perhaps Alan Johnson. Harriet Harman cannot do it because she is overstretched as it is. Jack Straw might have done it, but he seems to have lost his way, after the bill of rights proposals got shot down by the rest of the cabinet.'

Someone like a Prescott might have questioned the wisdom of trying to handle the MPs' expenses issue by unveiling an initiative in a YouTube video. Faced by an increasingly strident rightwing press, it is easy to see why communications gurus favour bypassing papers such as the *Daily Mail*.

Brown presumably believed he was speaking to a youthful, disenchanted public, on one of the few issues that genuinely engages and infuriates them. But after he had made his first excruciating grin to camera, a good adviser would probably have put his hand over the lens, shouted 'cut' and then binned the idea. 'Come back Damian McBride, all is forgiven,' say some, not wholly in jest.

Sometimes the medium can become the message and, ironically in the case of the supposed dinosaur Prescott, videos have worked unexpectedly well. But Brown had learnt early in his premiership to be authentically grave and his advisers have to stick to that. Even Downing Street's new speechwriter, Michael Lea from the *Daily Mail*, will have to match his metaphors to the man.

But Brown's bigger worry came in the lethal criticism from the former home secretary David Blunkett that Labour had a void where its domestic policy should be. 'Of course we will be judged by what we have done in terms of dealing with the economic crisis. But we will actually be judged on our vision for the next 10 to 15 years,' he said yesterday.

The bulk of Blunkett's speech was an attempt to fill that void with his version of community-localised politics. Many will disagree with his specific proposals, but there are many Labour MPs like Blunkett, worried that Brown's natural instinct and knowledge of economics lead him to neglect the nexus of social, moral and domestic policy issues on which elections are traditionally fought.

Another minister notes the lack of a centrally driven strategy from No 10 to get the government's message out and tell voters in a concerted way what Labour stands for and where it wants to go. 'Ministers in their departments are pushing out their stuff, working in their policy bubble, but there is little attempt to pull it together from the prime minister,' the minister said.

'What we lack is determination, willpower and organisation,' said one cabinet minister.

'He is good at economics, but not politics,' said a Labour select committee chairman.

Another former minister argued: 'The public will not thank us for what we have done in the past but on whether they judge we have any gas in the tank and some coherent ideas for the future.'

No 10 replies that last week it pushed out big policies on an equality bill, the future of primary education through the Rose review, and fresh ideas about community crime prosecutors. But these stories were drowned out by defeats in parliament, rebellious former ministers and the threat of a flu pandemic.

Apart from yet another rethink inside Downing Street, there is no sign of an attempt to push the prime minister out. Only Frank Field, brilliant, but alone, openly calls for Brown to be toppled after the European elections in June.

Backbenchers would be unlikely to be goaded into revolt even if the party came third behind the Lib Dems in terms of the share of the vote or saw its vote drop below 25 per cent. Most people feel they have been through that process last summer and, in the words of David Cameron, the party has made its strategic choice.

Cabinet ministers who are hardly supporters of Brown have this week been moved to near sympathy. One said: 'Backbenchers keep kicking the shit out of Gordon and then wondering out loud why he appears damaged.'

Another described the parliamentary Labour party as having gone 'la la'. Brown was the first PM to attempt to reform the expenses system. He said: 'You could post a video on YouTube and announce you were giving them £10,000 each and they would still be unhappy.' This cabinet minister, however, drew a line at stepping up to advise Brown.

Some ministers still insist that it is the recession alone that will determine the next general election. The stockmarket, looking at consumer confidence, may be enjoying a frisky spring but, in the real economy the news remains dire. Yet, if Brown can point to an upturn by late winter, the fate of 1,000 Gurkhas, and the second home allowance, will fade into a distant memory.

2 MAY 2009

No ideas, no fight, no breath of life

POLLY TOYNBEE

In free fall without a parachute, unassisted suicide, accelerating the wrong way down a motorway – the death metaphors are flowing in a dark torrent of despair from Labour MPs. What made Gordon Brown hurl himself on that row of Gurkha kukri knives?

Drowning at 19 per cent behind in the latest polls, few think the party will come up for air a third time. That YouTube grinning death's head is now a worldwide comic hit, while in the flesh the man looks more battered and hunted with each passing day. He suffers from tone deafness to everything.

'I don't regret anything I've done!' Gordon Brown declared at the press conference this week where he was abused for his economic policy by the impudent Polish prime minister, a man himself on his knees to the IMF. That's what happens when the mantle of authority slips. Whose bright idea was it to put out a chirpy press release this week promising a crackdown on rogue wheelclampers, echoing John Major's dying cones hotline?

Forced to retreat twice this week from his unilateral YouTube proclamation, the worst is yet to come on MPs' expenses when more shockers will emerge. All parties will be shamed, but the government will be hardest hit: some ministers will be disgraced – and Labour avarice is always more shocking.

No regrets? The 500,000 remaining low-paid losers from Brown's abolition of the 10p tax rate were not compensated in the budget. Worse is to come for them: I hear that the long-delayed announcement on the new rate for the national minimum wage gives them only 4p an hour more, rising to just £5.77 following two bad years of falling behind inflation even in the fat times. Inequality will grow unless the minimum wage rises a bit above inflation every year – yes, even in the hard years. Meanwhile, that 50p top tax rate hangs in the air as a political mystery without a strong redistributive narrative, unpegged to helping those in most need. Where are its vociferous cabinet defenders fighting off absurd threats from the rich?

Maybe Brown only regrets the loss of Damian McBride, his toxic confidant – not a one-off, but one of a thuggish tribe. How far has Labour lost touch with reality when leading figures try to shoehorn a party apparatchik's 22-year-old daughter into a safe seat? Rottenness easily feels terminal.

Self-destructive and bungled tactical ploys mark the Brown era: the attempt to secure 42-day detention without trial was the most cynical. But in the end what damages him most is the blame he bears for not only allowing, but celebrating, the great bubble in house prices, City bonuses and wild excess while many warned a bust would come.

Look back on the day he stood on the No 10 threshold: 'I will be strong in purpose, steadfast in will, resolute in action in the service of what matters to the British people.' He reprised his school motto – 'I will do my utmost' – and no doubt he did, but it hasn't been enough. After all those angry years in waiting, he should have been mindful of the old saw: be careful what you wish for. Many said he had neither the temperament nor the political skills for the top job. I was among those who hoped he had, because you have to live in hope. How Blair's people gloat – we told you so!

Labour faces such a cataclysmic defeat it could be out of power for many years. Ask the Tories how long it takes to climb back from the abyss. All Labour seats with a majority of under 8,000 are in peril. The Lib Dems may push Labour to third place in June, even to below 20 per cent. Defeatism grips the party: the middle-aged say they've had a good innings, politics goes in cycles and to everything there is a season; half their attention is directed towards a pretty comfortable semi-retirement. The thrusters concentrate on the battle in opposition over the leadership and the nature of the party itself. The young can't imagine quite how bad it will feel.

This inert fatalism won't do. Rumblings about removing Brown are wishful thinking in a party too listless to act. The dream scenario is that grey suits tell him to go, he obliges, and that nice Alan Johnson soothes the party through to at least a respectable defeat. Dream on. Brown won't go without assassination, Johnson is no killer (which is what makes him so nice), and many fear the bloody process would cost Labour its last shreds of credibility. Dire June may yet change that calculation: 100 extra Labour MPs fearing for their seats can concentrate minds wonderfully.

For now, David Blunkett is right that there are no ideas, no politics and no breath of life left. Where is the serious intellectual attack on the Conservatives? Cameron has just performed a U-turn of breathtaking dimensions. Gone are the hoodie-hugging, husky-driving, go-green and let-the-sunshine-in days, replaced by nothing but hard Thatcherite 1980s promises of austerity and cuts. Look what's coming, and be very afraid.

This week a survey on the ConservativeHome website of likely new Tory MPs was an eye-opener. They are socially conservative, anti-environment, anti-Europe, anti-abortion, anti-gay adoption, pro-hunting and strongly in favour of the married couples' allowance that redistributes tax to the middle class. Only 15 per cent see the climate as important: terrorism matters much more. Most want to cut money for Scotland: a Tory win will trigger new support for independence. They are well to the right of their leader, even his tougher guise. Lord Ashcroft, who channels money to favoured marginals, has nurtured a nest of MPs more to his own liking.

Labour needs to make sure as few of these as possible reach the Commons. Start with a scorched-earth pre-emption of all the easy cuts the Tories will promise: ID cards first, and the Trident madness, which even Tories now question. David Davis opened a debate on cutting benefits to the well-off that Labour could seize on. Now the old are less likely to be poor, savings can be made on universal payments. Transfer the money to the poorest before the Tories take it and give nothing back. Now I'm 60, why do I get free travel and winter fuel payments while still working? Get in on waste first – but earmark savings in ways the Tories never would.

Seizing the savings initiative might even avoid defeat altogether. Inside No 10 policies still revolve round dead issues – personalising public services and the like. The crash has changed everything and it needs Labour answers.

7 MAY 2009

Bully for poor Gordon Brown

SIMON HOGGART

Bears in Tudor times, supply teachers, the Elephant Man – they all got taunted dreadfully and it was an unpleasant, disconcerting sight. It isn't much prettier when it's done to Gordon Brown. If he wasn't still capable of delivering the odd cuff in retaliation, it would be even more squirm-making.

Take Stephen Crabb, the MP for Preseli Pembrokeshire. Like other Tories, he has seized happily on the reports of Brown's temper tantrums at No 10. Apparently, office equipment goes flying at frequent intervals and some of the language would bring a blush to the cheeks of a Millwall fan.

Crabb began with a seemingly innocent question about what Brown intended to do about bullying in the workplace, then added 'Given the reliable reports of a senior Whitehall boss throwing around mobile phones and printers and swearing at switchboard operators'.

The prime minister took a moment to cotton on, then he looked absolutely furious (as opposed to when he met Joanna Lumley: he apparently turned on the charm and she decided he was absolutely fabulous. It seems he threw nothing at her, expect possibly for a few smaller items such as a memory stick and a Sellotape dispenser). He scowled with rage, then grunted: 'Mr Speaker, any complaints are dealt with in the usual manner.'

What did that mean? That he is considering whether to sack himself for inappropriate behaviour? Or was it more sinister? If anyone complains that they have just got a Hewlett-Packard 4250 in the kisser, will they lose their job – or worse? But he can't really handle it: he didn't deny it and he didn't have a snappy comeback.

Earlier, it was David Cameron who had taken the opportunity to jab him with a pointed stick. The government was in terminal decline, he said. And what was Hazel Blears, who came up with the 'mocking' line 'YouTube if you want to' at the weekend, still doing in the cabinet? 'Where is she?' cried the Tories. From our corner of the press gallery we could see Miss Pepperpot hiding shyly beside the speaker's chair, like a small woodland creature who has heard the cries of the hunters and has decided to retreat to the safety of her burrow.

Cameron quoted her article at length, accompanied by a scholarly exegesis of what it actually meant. He accused the prime minister of U-turns. Brown accused him of the biggest U-turn of the lot: 'Compassionate Conservatism – it has gone, gone and gone.'

This was meant to sound devastating, but verged on the silly. 'I am sure that sounded just great in the bunker, while the mobile phones and printers were flying around the room,' said Cameron. Brown looked a very unhappy bear.

8 MAY 2009

More unequal than ever

LEADER

Like flashing blue lights, poverty indicators tend to show up in the rear-view mirror. Awareness of that must colour reading of the dreadful statistics published yesterday. For all the talk of ending poverty, the number of poor children did not fall, and, if anything, increased. Working-age adults dropped below the breadline rapidly, and pensioners – for whom the trends have been better – made no progress at all. To cap it all, Britain is more unequal than it has been at any time since records began, in 1961. Back then the Etonian Harold Macmillan was in charge. Gordon Brown has sincere egalitarian impulses and must shudder at the prospect of bequeathing a more economically polarised nation to another Etonian next year.

If and when David Cameron takes up the reins, the new figures confirm Britain will be far more unequal than it was two generations ago. Chiefly, that is due to what happened in the 1980s and 1990s. Despite yesterday's data it is still too early to tell whether Labour's three terms have made things better or worse, because the numbers are so out of date. They take months to crunch, covering the year starting in April 2007, since when a great deal has happened. Most obviously, the world economy has entered its sharpest contraction since the 1930s. Unemployment will be one major consequence, and it will indubitably deepen hardship. But the bursting of the bubble has tamed top incomes, while also curbing inflation, something which helps pensioners and benefit claimants living on fixed incomes. Past experience suggests the net effect of recession will be to dampen inequality.

Mr Brown, of course, can hardly brag about the slump. But he can take pride in measures to help parents make ends meet which should show in the poverty figures over the next couple of years. He will not get much credit, not least because the most of the money was announced on the very day he foolishly scrapped the 10p tax rate. But typical hard-up families are gaining around £500, with much more for some with high rents. Not enough to end child poverty, it should nonetheless ensure many more children get a decent start than in the 1990s. Taken together with the new super-tax the extra cash could, in principle, even start to turn the tide on overall inequality.

In principle, although sadly almost certainly not in practice. All the main parties have now committed themselves to miserly expenditure plans, and the prospective Conservative government is increasingly blunt in identifying tax credits as a potential source of savings. 2007 may have been the most unequal year ever. There could, however, very well be more unequal ones to come.

21 MAY 2009

Gordon Brown chaos theory: we might not win the election

SIMON HOGGART

Gordon Brown came up with a new constitutional principle yesterday: he can't hold an election because the wrong side might win.

Naturally all prime ministers believe that, which is why, like Jim Callaghan and John Major, they often leave it to the last minute, desperately hoping the polls will turn round.

But it's strange to hear it expressed so openly. Dictators use the same argument, though with more hope of success.

Mr Brown appeared on television yesterday morning and was asked about an election. He sounded as if a poll would be an outrage. 'Do you really want to see tomorrow, in the midst of the recession, while the government is dealing with this, the chaos of an election?'

This notion that an election was the equivalent of a football riot, or the bull-running at Pamplona, was seized by David Cameron a few hours later. (At prime minister's questions, MPs waded through many treacly tributes to the Speaker, who it turns out was the kindest, wisest, finest chairman any legislature could hope to have. So why did they sack him?)

The Tory leader leaped upon 'chaos'. 'What on earth did he mean?'

Gordon Brown replied that what would cause chaos would be if a Conservative government were elected.

Now, that is clearly not what he meant in the morning. What he meant on the *GMTV* sofa was that he was busy sorting out MPs' expenses, tackling the problems of unemployment, greed-crazed bankers and deflation, and simply could not be doing with an election at the same time.

Why, it was as if he were holding an urgent meeting with the chancellor and the governor, and his wife, Sarah, were to march in and tell him it was his turn to put the kids to bed.

Anyhow, Cameron was delighted with the reply. 'There we have it: the first admission that the prime minister thinks he is going to lose!'

Brown's only reply was to say that the Tories would bring in public spending cuts. But if that's what the voters want, shouldn't they get it? The logic was that an election might bring about a change of government, that would lead to a change of policy, and then where would we be?

Cameron pointed out that several countries, including India and the United States, had somehow contrived to hold elections in the midst of the crisis. 'Is President Obama an agent of chaos?' he demanded.

Brown replied with a long list of achievements, or rather what he hopes might be seen one day as achievements. If he's lucky.

Cameron replied again that he had called elections 'chaos – I call them change. Why can't we have one?'

He knows the answer. But it won't stop him asking the question.

A few minutes later, Hazel Blears, Mrs Pepperpot, was in Salford, not resigning, even though Gordon Brown had called her carrying-on 'totally unacceptable'.

'The people of Salford know me,' she said, 'they know the kind of person I am!' Well, they do now.

She broke away saying, 'I'll be late for the mayor-making, and that would be unforgivable!' As opposed, presumably, to the financial shenanigans, which are entirely forgivable.

CHAPTER SIX

HE DANGLES
BY A THREAD

For months – nearly a year – people would wonder privately, or semi-publicly, if Gordon's dominance could be challenged. Though patently scarred, and apparently battle-weary, few had imagined that the prime minister might come under pressure to quit. But that moment finally arrived in the early summer of 2009. Labour MPs had openly lost hope – and at last some of them attempted – and failed – to plot his removal. In the midst of the mutterings and speculation, Andy Beckett reflected at length on Gordon Brown's story, and character, in an article that neatly summarised in its headline the mood of the moment.

3 JUNE 2009

Where did it all go wrong
for Gordon Brown?

ANDY BECKETT

Less than two years ago, when Gordon Brown was in his early months as prime minister, the *Spectator* published a long article about how he was doing. The rightwing magazine had always been an immovable critic of New Labour, but now it struck a startlingly different note. 'The sense of liberation [in Brown] ..... is palpable,' wrote its editor, Matthew d'Ancona, who had accompanied Brown on a visit to the US. 'Every morning he clearly awakes and thinks ... "I am prime minister!"' D'Ancona concluded: 'This PM's greatest triumph to date has been to persuade the world that he is not an exhausted traveller, limping and grey after 10 years in office [as chancellor], but a man at the very start of a journey.'

In the summer and early autumn of 2007 such assessments were common across the political spectrum of the British press. 'Brown could be the first Labour leader since Clement Attlee to recast British society,' wrote Neal Lawson of the leftwing pressure group Compass in this newspaper. Brown's performances at prime minister's questions 'have been masterly', wrote Alice Thomson in the *Daily Telegraph*. 'Brown is wrongfooting Cameron,' wrote Fraser Nelson in the same paper. 'Brown could be a great PM,' wrote Peter Oborne in the *Daily Mail*.

Nowadays all this praise and excitement reads like something from a parallel universe. Brown is a prime minister so beleaguered, so unpopular and seemingly exhausted, so apparently luckless and unsuited to the job, that he attracts general ridicule and even pity. Parliamentary sketchwriters and political bloggers describe him as a baited bear, a human car crash, painful to watch. News of his humiliations travels the world: last month the *Tehran Times* reprinted a *New York Times* piece about the 'naked contempt' towards Brown shown by Cameron and other opposition MPs in the Commons.

'On shows like *Have I Got News for You*, you can get a cheap laugh by simply uttering the words "Gordon Brown",' says someone who has known Brown for decades, one of many people who – out of caution or compassion – would only speak to me about the prime minister off the record. Another well-connected Labour figure and former Brown fan says he has been a 'catastrophic leader'. Critics compare him as a leader to John Major, Anthony Eden, Richard Nixon: political bywords for incompetence, poor judgment, bitter failure. 'He's teetering on the brink of being the worst PM of my life-time,' says the veteran political writer and novelist Robert Harris.

Tomorrow, British voters will give their own verdict at the European and local elections. Labour's opinion poll figures are currently at an unprecedented low: between 22 per cent and 16 per cent. On Saturday, the health secretary, Alan Johnson, warned that Labour would do very badly in the elections. It is possible Labour will do so badly that in a few days or weeks, Brown might not even be PM – either through an internal coup, with Johnson the current favourite to usurp him, or, less likely but talked about by some Labour figures I interviewed, Brown's sudden resignation. If he survives, the next general election looms. It is a year away at most, with Labour requiring a near-miraculous recovery in its elec-toral standing to avoid defeat. Brown's premiership, it seems probable, will not make it past the three-year mark. Even John Major managed six and a half.

For almost a quarter of a century, from his election as a fierce young MP in 1983 to his first surefooted weeks in 10 Downing Street in 2007, Brown has been one of the most formidable British politicians, revered for his intellect and social conscience, feared for his relentlessness and behind-the-scenes manoeuvres. Why, then, has his premiership gone so badly?

Some of it has been down to circumstances. When Brown took office in 2007, Labour had already been in power for a decade, a long time in British politics. After the disasters and controver-sies of Iraq, and domestic policy disappointments from the private finance initiative to increased inequality, and with the Conservatives reviving under Cameron, Labour's popularity was on the slide. 'Blair just dumped this [political inheritance] in our lap and cleared off,' says Harris, once a keen Blair supporter. In 2007, the long economic boom that had helped keep Labour in government since 1997 also started to stall. 'Brown will be remembered,' says Harris, 'as incredibly unlucky in his timing.'

Yet the circumstances in which he became prime minister were also partly of his own making. He had not opposed the invasion of Iraq. As chancellor, as is now infamous, he had failed to deal with an unsustainable property and personal debt bubble. He had also missed opportunities to replace Blair as prime minister, in the three or four years leading up to 2007, when the economy and Labour's ratings were still relatively healthy. Exactly when and how Brown should have acted against Blair, and to what extent Blair may have deceived or outmanoeuvred him, is still a matter of debate among Westminster watchers; but most of them agree on one thing: Brown is, as one puts it, 'grossly indecisive'.

When he was chancellor, his appetite for deep reading and private pondering was often seen as a strength. 'Brown plays his cards against his chest,' a civil servant told me in 2004. 'Very important decisions won't be on an official piece of paper until days before the deadline. In Whitehall, the question "What will Gordon say?" hangs over everything.' But for a prime minister, presented daily with unexpected dilemmas, this sort of late decision-making can be disastrous. Brown's critics cite, for example, his slow response to the long-approaching storm over MPs' expenses, which has allowed a more nimble and shameless Cameron, despite the arguably worse behaviour of his MPs, to emerge with credit; the government's ponderous U-turn over the treatment of Gurkha veterans; the protracted controversy over the 10p tax band; and, above all, his dithering over calling a general election in autumn 2007, when he was enjoying his prime-ministerial honeymoon.

'Brown is a victim of his own internal contradictions, between being clever-clever and tactical, and long-term and serious,' says

Richard Reeves, director of the thinktank Demos and a former Labour policy adviser. 'As prime minister he's zigzagged between the two modes and ended up with the worst of both worlds: looking as political as Cameron with none of the charisma.'

Brown also suffers terribly, say his critics, from being reticent and stiff in public. In these stormy times, argues Reeves, his image as the 'weathered, slightly scowling captain at the helm of the battered ship' is not necessarily a bad fit, except that, 'a leader has to communicate. He's quite good on radio. He would probably have done quite well in the 19th century, making long speeches like Gladstone. But nowadays the principal medium is televisual.'

On TV these days, Brown looks tired and grey. Sometimes he has eye bags under his eye bags. His words often come in indigestible clots – 'what we are taking on the recession is action' – or prefaced by a flustered stutter. His voice is thinner, less booming than in his commanding years as chancellor. His heavy shoulders seem tense with fury when Cameron taunts him at prime minister's questions. His on-camera smile, too sudden and too wide, looks false and pleading.

'It's almost a physical discomfort to watch him,' says David Runciman, a politics lecturer at Cambridge. 'Brown is an almost pathological version of a closed-off politician. That kind of personality is clearly very good at politicking behind the scenes. Chancellors are meant to be closed off. They keep secrets from us, go into purdah – it's the least democratic office of state. But the relentless exposure of being prime minister makes that sort of closed-off politician vulnerable.'

Off-camera, in private or semi-private situations, Brown can be good company – even now. He can laugh about politics and its cruelties and ironies. He is not grand. He talks with an appealing Scottish directness and informality. But in his public pronouncements he seems to suppress this side of himself. In a *London Review of Books* article published the year before Brown became prime minister, Runciman foresaw the dangers of taking this approach in 10 Downing Street. Modern politics, he suggested, favoured leaders such as Blair and Cameron who appeared 'comfortable in [their] own skin'; Brown, with his old-fashioned notion of keeping his public and private selves separate, would come across as 'someone who is always holding something back', 'a man who was happy to conceal the true state of his feelings'. In the era of confessional web chat and tearful celebrity interviews, Runciman implied, Brown's reined-in public persona would not be acceptable to voters if he became prime minister.

As premier, his attempts to lighten up – the TV smile, the toe-curlingly 'casual' YouTube appearances – have only made matters worse. 'The greatest crime of all in the modern media age,' says Reeves, 'is being inauthentic.'

And yet, there remains something puzzling about Brown's inability to find the right tone. Because in certain contexts, he can. Two weeks ago, I watched him campaigning for the European and local elections in Tamworth near Birmingham. He was midway through another grim week: another wounding prime minister's questions, an attack on him by the Confederation of British Industry, more Labour MPs with questionable expenses. Minutes before he was due to arrive in Tamworth, for a visit to a college, the sun disappeared and a cold soaking storm blew in. One of the college staff muttered something to me about the weather being appropriate.

Then the official car pulled up, the sun almost instantly reappeared, and Brown got out. He looked a bit pale in the glare, but there was a vigour in his walk, in his barrel chest and big head – the body of an old-style Labour politician – and his short, strong legs. He made straight for a cluster of middle-aged female staff in white aprons who were standing to one side of the reception committee. As he clasped the women's hands, asked them questions and smiled sparingly but genuinely, there was an unexpected ease, almost a flirtatiousness in his manner. Afterwards, in a hot room jammed with tables of local dignatories and voters, there was more of the same comfortable charm. Brown put his hand on people's shoulders, held the backs of their chairs, moved courteously from table to table ('can I join you?'), and leaned in close to listen when people spoke.

It was a reminder that Brown had not risen up the Labour party by brainpower and bullying alone. At Tamworth station afterwards, I ran into a man who had just met Brown at the college. What had he made of the prime minister? 'He seemed relaxed,' the man said. 'You feel if he could meet everyone in the country he would be all right.' People used to say the same about John Major.

For most of Brown's career, many of the qualities now seen as his weaknesses were seen as strengths. At Edinburgh University, where he studied history, Brown was already a hard-nosed political operator. 'To be in Gordon's gang,' says one of his biographers, 'you had to declare undying loyalty. Brown has a weakness for surrounding himself with ... nasty people. It's almost as if he's convinced himself that if they're out breaking legs, it has nothing to do with him, as if he knows in his head, "I am a good man".' In fact, this April a senior Brown aide, Damian McBride, was forced to resign after it was revealed he had suggested that a Labour-supporting website mount a smear campaign against senior Conservatives.

By the age of 23, Brown was already enough of a name to be 'invited' (his word) to seek a Labour candidacy for the October 1974 general election. To his later regret, Brown decided not to stand – an early sign, perhaps, of his disabling caution – and Labour narrowly lost the Edinburgh South seat. It took Brown another nine years to get into parliament, but he used them shrewdly. He taught politics and worked as a TV producer for three years –

something that slightly undermines the notion that he has no understanding of the medium.

As an MP from 1983, he quickly became known as an agile Commons performer. His biographer Paul Routledge records the late Tory diarist Alan Clark, then employment minister, writing of a debate that December: 'I got into difficulty almost immediately. [Brown and Blair] were bobbing up all over the place, asking impossible ... questions of detail.'

As shadow chancellor in New Labour's government-in-waiting in the mid-90s, Brown's aptitude and appetite for the game of politics seemed almost limitless. In *Out of the Shadows*, the first of a pair of 1997 documentaries made by Scottish TV, his advisers deliver delighted asides to camera about the expert ambushes and harrying operations with which they are tormenting the fading Conservative government. Politics for Brown and his gang looks the best fun in the world.

'He has the biggest political brain in the Labour party,' says someone who knows him well. 'He has the ability to see where the politics of something is going. But that means he is constantly trying to trick everything to get to where he wants. All of his great virtues are the flipside of his failings.'

In *We Are the Treasury*, the second of the two documentaries, a change seems to come over Brown once he is in government. The cunning little grins are gone; instead he looks grave. The camera follows him and his aides on their first tour of 11 Downing Street. Brown's spin doctor Charlie Whelan makes a joke about selling off the pictures to raise revenues. Brown is not amused. He gazes at the grand offices with reverence.

'He's very conscious of how he's perceived,' an old friend of his told me in 2004. 'He has worked very hard to cultivate his iron chancellor image. He thinks it gives him authority. He thinks that's the way politics should be – serious politics, serious people.'

Some Brown-watchers detected a new sternness even before he entered office. 'In interviews he began to develop a relentless style,' writes James Naughtie in *The Rivals*, his book about Brown and Blair. 'In May 1993 Alan Watkins wrote that Brown had been "for some months now on a kind of automatic pilot which enables him to repeat meaningless phrases in a monotone".' Brown's favoured 90s phrases – 'prudence with a purpose', 'no return to boom and bust' – are even easier to mock in 2009. Yet for many years they fulfilled their role: to transform Labour's prospects by making its economic policies sound authoritative.

Watching Brown's budget speeches from his dominant years as chancellor again now, it is striking how imperfect his Commons persona was even then: the pallor, the eye bags, the over-reliance on preparation and inability to improvise are already in evidence. But as long as the economy was purring along, the fact that his booming rhetorical epics of statistics and jargon made most people tune out did not matter; he was like a successful chief executive addressing a shareholders' meeting, and the shareholders did not have to listen to every word, or even like him much, to feel he was doing a great job.

'He always seemed to be in complete control of the subject, with these blocks of words that just came out,' says the economist and independent peer Lord Skidelsky. 'He mastered the language of economics. [But] my hunch is that he never understood it very deeply. He had no effective counters to the dominant ideas of the day.' During Brown's time as chancellor and shadow chancellor, the dominant economic philosophy was pro-business, pro-banker and anti-regulation. In Skidelsky's view, Brown – like almost every senior British politician – 'bought it all'.

For Brown, who in 1989 had written that 'unbridled capitalism is inefficient as well as unfair', and who retained a strong commitment to reducing poverty, this conversion to free-market economics was a stretch. 'What markets do is have winners and losers,' Neal Lawson told me in 2004. 'That clearly has a conflict with a politics that is about equality. That's a contradiction in Gordon's politics.' But it is not a contradiction, reportedly, that his advisers have been keen to point out. 'Unlike Blair, Brown is not challenged by his advisers intellectually,' says Reeves. 'Brown is intellectually curious, well-read. But where are the real intellectuals in Downing Street? Gordon has filled it with apparatchiks and spinners.' One of his biographers says: 'Once he's made up his mind, he will not change it. Because he thinks he's thought through the issue much more deeply than anyone else.'

Now that 'boom and bust' has undeniably returned, and Labour's conversion to capitalism no longer looks like a vote-winner, the downsides of Brown's sense of certainty are painfully obvious. It is hard, perhaps impossible, for him to say he was wrong about the free market and how best to run the British economy. 'You can't expect a PM to repudiate his chancellorship, if he's been chancellor for 10 years,' says Skidelsky. While last autumn Brown took bold and seemingly effective action to avert a banking meltdown, and was rewarded with a revival in the polls, he has been unable to take lasting political advantage of the crisis in financial capitalism and free-market thinking, which for other left-of-centre politicians, such as Barack Obama, is proving a rare opportunity. 'The crisis has created something like a progressive consensus, but he's been unable to lead it, mould it,' says Reeves. 'The person who will probably preside over this consensus [in Britain] is David Cameron.'

During the long prelude to Brown's premiership, even his worst enemies did not predict he would preside over the deepest recession for decades. But many of his shortcomings were exhaustively discussed. He had 'psychological flaws', 'the social skills of a whelk', the doomed determination of a character in 'a Shakespearean tragedy' – such poison darts, usually fired by anonymous Blairites, landed in thousands of political columns. Sometimes even Blair himself discreetly took part. In 2006, shortly before Brown finally clambered over him to become prime minister, Blair told a journalist who prefers not to be named, 'If he [Brown] is going to make a fist of being PM, he's got to change his way of operating. Can he change? Probably not.'

In fact, these attacks probably helped Brown in his first months as prime minister, by so lowering expectations that his calm handling of 2007's floods and terrorist plots received disproportionate praise.

And despite the barbs, Brown survived as his party's heir-apparent for 13 years – far longer than politicians usually do in this perilous role. Brown's opinion poll ratings between 1994 and 2007 suffered only passing dips. It has been quickly forgotten over the last two years that, compared to Blair's chatshow fluency, Brown's stern and awkward public manner was often considered a virtue. 'A lot of the Labour tribe like closedness,' says one party insider. Brown's capture of the premiership also owed much to the lack of a serious rival; to his perceived moral authority and sheer doggedness; to his careful alliance-building – every new Labour MP after the 1997 and 2001 general elections received an invitation to 11 Downing Street; and, finally, to a fear in the party of what might happen if he did not get the leadership.

As a Brown premiership approached, senior Conservatives regarded it with an unresolved mixture of eagerness and trepidation. In 2004 a party strategist, now working for Cameron, told me: 'There's a very superficial view which is that Brown's good news for the Tories: more leftwing, more old Labour, more scary to Middle England. But he is probably the most sophisticated political operator in the country. It wouldn't surprise me if he had some plan to neutralise those perceptions. And operationally he'd be a far more effective prime minister than Blair, because of his attention to detail.'

It hasn't worked out like that. A former Labour minister who has worked for both Brown and Blair says, 'Brown tends to hunker down when things go badly. Work more. Sleep less. Spend less time with his advisers. The impact is incredibly transparent. By contrast, Tony Blair seemed almost to thrive on pressure.' The former minister cites the G20 summit as an example of the big-picture politics that Brown has done well. Yet, like his rescue of the financial system, the G20 won him acclaim and influence abroad, but only fleeting public approval at home. This says something about the attention span of British voters; but it also says something about the over-elaborate feel of the Brown government. 'There have been too many initiatives,' says the former minister. 'I don't think he has been able to plant a firm enough idea of what he stands for.'

This week, in the wake of the expenses scandal, he has announced he is considering 'a new constitutional settlement', including reducing the voting age to 16, creating a Bill of Rights and written constitution, completing the reform of the House of Lords and extending the Freedom of Information Act. Brown is full of other big ideas: that climate change and the recession require a new form of international co-operation and a new form of capitalism; that the public's involvement in British democracy needs to be rethought and renewed; that the world is living through the greatest period of change since the industrial revolution; that today is nevertheless 'a progressive age'.

When Major's administration was equally beleaguered, all it seemed to come up with was the traffic cones hotline. And yet, there is something escapist about Brown's preference for the longterm and the global when his most pressing problems are short-term and national.

Brown is by all accounts a proud, highly emotional man. Friends talk of how he fears being thought of as a bad prime minister. 'He believes in himself, even now,' says another close acquaintance. When you watch Brown campaigning, it is striking that he often mentions New Labour's achievements before he became premier – the greatly improved state provision for young children, for example. Given that under Blair, Brown was in many areas of domestic policy the de facto prime minister, this seems justified: there is a case to be made that his Downing Street career should be judged on the last 12 years, not just the last two.

Yet his critics and many voters are unlikely to see it that way. If Brown is to survive both this week's and next year's elections, he probably needs a sensational event, much more compelling than the imminent and heavily trailed cabinet reshuffle: a huge further twist in the banking and expenses crises, a freakish economic recovery, the bursting of the Cameron bubble. Before writing Brown off, it may be worth recalling that in 1991 the Major government was dismissed as 'pathetic' (the *Daily Mail*), 'exhausted' (the *Financial Times*) and 'a rabble ... [with] the look of death' (the *Independent on Sunday*). Less than a year later, Major was returned to office

But in all probability Brown will soon need a new job. For years he has expressed an interest in the workings and reform of the International Monetary Fund, a body that has long tried to recruit senior Labour politicians, and where a big strategic brain matters more than a televisual manner. Brown also has a large and justified reputation among the international anti-poverty lobby.

'He's resilient,' says an old friend from outside politics. 'Many bad things have happened to him. He lost his first child. He lost the sight of an eye. The last thing in the world Gordon wants is pity. He doesn't mind being hated. He would loathe being pitied.' The next few days may be tough.

4 JUNE 2009

The Hotmail conspiracy

ALLEGRA STRATTON, PATRICK WINTOUR AND DAVID HENCKE

The plotters have taken to quoting Trotsky's revolutionary dictum 'March separately, strike together' as the ideas that fomented for months reached their critical moment.

The judgment of the backbenchers was that they needed to operate independently of the cabinet, but hope that their own actions would prompt reaction from within the cabinet, leading to a pincer movement that would squeeze Gordon Brown out of No 10.

After the abortive coup of last summer it was also agreed that there had to be better co-ordination and planning.

So the plans to rise up started around one month ago – just after the government's shock defeat over the Gurkhas.

The first decision was that the stalking horse wasn't the right option: a stalking horse required the involvement of the national executive committee, which is run by Brown, and that was never going to happen.

The group of plotters has now grown to seven or eight individuals, but to this day, they have never all met in the same room and say they never will meet until their list has been sent to the prime minister.

Their invisibility and composition is supposed to keep together all the elements that went wrong with the plot last summer. Organisers have come from across the party.

In the words of one rebel MP: 'The last time around we felt that it had to come from the cabinet – that five cabinet members had to decide to go to Gordon, and then go and tell him. That was the method that was most respectful to the party and to cabinet. Then you also had Siobhain [McDonagh] and Joan [Ryan] doing their letter-writing campaign. But the two weren't talking to each other. That was a problem.'

So, just as Brown once knitted together different factions into one government – a government of all the talents, in a drive for harmony, now the new list is a rebellion of all the talents – 'Blairites, senior select committee chairmen, senior people from across the party, elements of the [leftwing] Compass campaign group, we've got them all,' said one.

'A rumour is being circulated this is a [socialist] Campaign group plot. Actually there's not a single Campaign group member on the list right now. They can join up once we get over 100 names.'

The next lesson to learn from last summer was the charge that any challenge to replace a prime minister took a prohibitively lengthy amount of time.

A key figure solicited the advice of recent NEC officials and received three separate endorsements that should the prime minister be removed, the process to replace him could be whittled down to just 23 days.

Officials who had been involved in the transition of power from Blair to Brown shared with them the timetable they would have used to oversee any challenge in 2007, but it was never needed.

This official had been due to go on the record earlier this week with his legal opinion – in an attempt to create a 'drumbeat' of pressure – but his wife forbade him from going public with such an attack on the prime minister.

All seemed to be running smoothly, then the plans were put in something of a cement mixer: the expenses scandal broke. 'It destabilised people,' said another rebel. 'Suddenly we didn't know which way people would go.'

Then recess loomed, and the rebels looked at the parliamentary timetable for the days following the return to Westminster and today's elections. They knew they wanted to have a challenge ready for the moment that the polls predictably brought bad results.

But another difficulty emerged. The days after recess showed only one three-line whip on the Monday which meant MPs would not necessarily be in London, but instead, with local and European elections looming, would most likely be scattered across the country.

So the plan evolved: the absence of MPs, the high-risk nature of any physical letter, and the need for cloaks of invisibility, saw them decide on an email strategy.

They decided there would be a 'tree' – a stalking herd – which would fan out across the parliamentary Labour party. Unlike previous rebellions which relied on huddles in corridors or face-to-face tearoom meetings, this would be better done virtually.

Recess came, recess went and at 10am on Monday morning a very respected select committee chairman came up to one rebel and asked for a meeting. 'Because I think we're going to go, aren't we'.

And so it was. The next day a Hotmail account was set up. The address gave nothing away: signonnow@hotmail.co.uk. The idea was that sympathetic Labour MPs would be encouraged to send an email endorsing a single sentence. This sentence would then be printed off and added to parliamentary notepaper, with a list of all those who responded to the email address listed with the two-word battlecry: 'I agree'.

One 'branch' of the tree joined the team two days ago to become an eighth member. The *Guardian* met this MP in the corner of a Pugin-decorated dining room and discussed the plot as glasses were arranged and crockery assembled for an event.

This MP has been involved in the plot for only two days and said he had been moved to get involved by Brown's behaviour over expenses and the way in which five MPs had been disciplined by the NEC's star chamber over expenses claims revealed in the media.

'A lot of us feel that Gordon Brown is taking Labour MPs outside one by one and shooting them. His already lamentable performance has just got worse in the last few days. Gordon Brown is a liability.'

Within the tree, there are concerns about the method chosen to assemble the signatories. One member said: 'One of the problems with what has come out already is that an email sounds very esoteric. We are asking MPs to send an email into the ether, which says they believe that Gordon Brown should not be the leader of the Labour party. That is very high risk. As it is, the Labour party has never sent out a group email and if it did I bet you'd get back 150 emails saying "account not recognised" or "mailbox too full". Labour MPs are not very electronic and I have to say I am worried about this method.'

The plot against the prime minister was not supposed to have emerged before Friday morning at the very earliest and Monday morning at the very latest. Then Hazel Blears resigned as communities secretary. Did this cause a problem for the rebels? 'No, Hazel is good – it makes matters unstable and that is what we want.'

One Blairite former minister told a junior minister earlier this week they were not going to accept a job Brown had offered them in the forthcoming reshuffle since they knew this plot was under way. But as the day wore on the cabinet were rallying around.

By 5pm, details of some of the plotters had been passed to Nick Brown, chief whip, one of Gordon Brown's strongest supporters, who is now planning a counterattack to isolate the group.

According to information given to him, they centred on a group nicknamed the Blearistas and some, but by no means all, members of the Campaign group.

Blears was said to have attempted to get Jacqui Smith to join the rebels last week, but she refused.

The chief whip, not averse to a bit of plotting in his day, said the ringleaders are former Blairites, joined by 'eccentric individualists'.

The plotters are said to have a list of up to 60 names of people prepared to sign the letter. The wording of that letter emerged last night: 'We are writing now because we believe that in the current political circumstances you can best serve the interests of the Labour party by stepping down as party leader and prime minister, and so allowing the party to find a new leader to take us into the next general election.'

The *Guardian* can confirm the chief whip has not correctly identified all of the ringleaders. The rebels are also insistent their numbers do not currently include members of the Campaign group – aware the government would attempt to paint the move as a 'leftwing plot of usual suspects'.

The government's counterattack last night was centred on persuading some of those who have signed to change their mind. They also could face a big backlash from loyalist Labour MPs when the list is published on Monday.

The leadership contenders David Miliband, Jon Cruddas and Alan Johnson have all been told by members of the tree, 'decide where you stand, but just remember that when people look back at this, they will want to know where you were on this'.

4 JUNE 2009

Whether Brown or Johnson, there's no New Labour fix

SEUMAS MILNE

Whatever cock-up claims could be made about Tuesday's string of ministerial walkouts, the resignation of Hazel Blears yesterday was an unmistakable act of revenge against the prime minister. Coming from the cabinet minister in charge of local government, it was also a display of contempt for her own party on the eve of today's county council and European elections. With Labour already expected to suffer its worst results since the first world war, Blears's decision to jump before the expected reshuffle can only be seen as an attempt to destabilise the government still further in preparation for a decisive push to force Gordon Brown out.

That the latest round of resignations started with the former Blairite health secretary, Patricia Hewitt – who has landed lucrative contracts with Alliance Boots and Cinven, a major private healthcare company, on the back of her previous job – and ended up with Blears, the Blairite minister with one of the most outrageous expenses records in government, gives a pretty clear idea of both the politics and ethics of the source of the latest onslaught. As one Downing Street insider said yesterday, Blears's 'disgraceful behaviour' may have even 'solidified the Labour party – for now'.

But not for long. There is bound to be a move against Brown in the coming days, at least from the Labour backbenches, where MPs are already drumming up support for a no-confidence letter aimed at pushing the cabinet to act. Everything depends on the numbers. But the fact that the plotters are discussing a truncated leadership election timetable that would cut out hundreds of thousands of affiliated union members from voting – exactly the kind of people New Labour has so disastrously lost touch with – underlines the political agenda of the planned putsch.

In fact, Labour's rules already allow the cabinet, in consultation with the national executive, to pick a new party leader when in government if he or she 'for whatever reason, becomes permanently unavailable', until an election can be held. But whether a majority can be assembled in cabinet right now to move against Brown – or whose interests it would serve – is another matter.

The prime minister seems likely to try to bind the most powerful Blairites even closer to him in the reshuffle to shore up his
defences. The current expectation is that Peter Mandelson will be
given a souped-up version of his existing job, as supremo of the
national business recovery plan; and it hardly seems in David
Miliband's interests to back a coup set to derail his own leadership ambitions in favour of Alan Johnson.

Brown is, of course, a ditherer and a half-measures merchant
who bears a heavy responsibility for New Labour's fateful embrace
of the City and corporate excess – he's still at it in his self-
defeating backing for part-privatisation of Royal Mail – and struggles to connect with his colleagues, let alone the public. But it's
also the case that his government has started to shift in a more
progressive direction since the crash of last autumn: moving to
take control of the banks, boosting spending to offset the impact
of recession and finally beginning to raise taxes for the wealthy.

So for Labour to oust him now because of the public backlash
over the MPs' expenses scandal, which has engulfed all the main
parties and is lapping at the front door of David Cameron's second
home, looks at least premature. The Labour case for Alan Johnson,
favourite to succeed Brown, would be to minimise the scale of
expected defeat at the general election, perhaps underpinned by
his commitment to a referendum on electoral reform.

That might be a stronger argument later in the year, though it
assumes a popularity that isn't yet tested. But the pressure for an
early general election in the case of a Johnson succession now
would be overwhelming; the contest would be clouded by
expenses referendums and likely to deliver a Labour meltdown.
Why should turkeys, in this case Labour MPs, vote for Christmas?
If Brown is replaced, 'we'd have to call an immediate election and
be decimated', one cabinet minister told me yesterday. 'This is a
perfect storm and we will get through it. 'Yes, Brown was a poor

communicator, but 'if you have to choose between ability to govern and communicate, governing is more important'.

The test of that will come in the next few days. But in any case, New Labour's decomposition long predates the froth of expenses scams. It is rooted in the profound deceit of the Iraq war, the party's embrace of unfettered corporate power and greed and its abandonment of core supporters – which have in turn paved the way for Cameron's Tories.

Yet while as in the rest of the Europe, the door has also been opened to the racist right, the kind of political challenge to neo-liberalism that has mushroomed in Germany, France and the Netherlands is still almost entirely absent in Britain: the product of a prostrate left and the stifling combination of the electoral system, and Labour's abandonment of internal democracy. Both in the economy and politics, this is a New Labour crisis to which there is no New Labour solution.

But it does provide the opportunity for MPs and others to nego-tiate a change of direction, whether over control of the banks, ID cards or postal privatisation – against which the government faces a huge backbench revolt and is already haggling with MPs and trade unionists. Meanwhile, in what seems like a throwback to 19th-century politics, Esther Rantzen, newly crowned queen of the political independents, has been speculating that the clearout of corrupt MPs was a chance to bring in a cohort of 'distinguished doctors' or 'well-thought-of teachers'. But as the GMB union leader, Paul Kenny, counters, it should be a 'fantastic opportunity' to bring in 30 or 40 working-class MPs, who are in much shorter supply.

The events of the past couple of days have echoes of last year's abortive attempt to oust Brown in favour of David Miliband, though the government's position is certainly now even weaker. Brown's vacillations with the Blairite irreconcilables, who are determined to keep Labour tethered to neoliberalism and break with the unions, have got him nowhere. He should have sacked Blears weeks ago. The challenge is now not simply whether Brown or Johnson should be leader, but to move beyond the failed politics of New Labour altogether.

6 JUNE 2009

The counter coup: How Mandelson got a grip on No 10's panic

NICHOLAS WATT AND PATRICK WINTOUR

If Gordon Brown survives to fight the general election as prime minister, he will look back to a few crucial hours on Thursday night as the moment when his premiership was saved.

In a stroke of good fortune for Brown, Peter Mandelson and Ed Balls were in Downing Street discussing how to relaunch his premiership when Brown learned of a grave threat to his position.

Shortly before 10pm, as the trio discussed the impending cabinet reshuffle in Brown's study, James Purnell called Downing Street to tell the prime minister that he was resigning from the cabinet after losing confidence in his leadership.

Brown, Mandelson and Balls spent the next two hours ensuring that a potential threat to Brown from the Blairite wing of the cabinet was stamped out. Brown went to bed in his flat above No 11 around midnight, though Mandelson did not leave Downing Street until 1.30am.

In the hours after Purnell's call, Mandelson called a series of Blairite cabinet ministers who may have been tempted to join the outgoing work and pensions secretary to persuade them to stay on board. His role was crucial. Mandelson is something of a father figure to the young Blairites and shares many of their concerns about Brown's struggle to connect with voters.

Mandelson's message was clear: Brown is the best person to lead Labour through the economic crisis. Replacing him now would lead to an upheaval that would guarantee even greater defeat at the next general election. 'There's nobody better out there,' one Whitehall source said. 'The alternative would be to consign Labour to massive upheaval and disruption.'

The Blairites who declined to follow Purnell's example fell into two groups: those who agreed with Mandelson, saying that Labour must stick with Brown; and those who who were prepared to follow Purnell's example, but would only do so if there were an organised campaign to unseat Brown.

David Miliband, the foreign secretary who was not invited to No 10 on Thursday night, fitted into the first category. As one of the few cabinet ministers to be brought into Purnell's confidence, Miliband had good reason to follow his old friend. Miliband's relations with Brown have become strained since his botched move against the prime minister last year. But he had a clear message. 'James did what he did, but David tried to talk him out of resigning,' one source said.

The Purnell and Miliband relationship, which dates back more than a decade to when they worked in Tony Blair's policy unit in his first term as prime minister, could be important in the future. Purnell, who could become a significant figure if Labour goes down to a heavy defeat at the next general election, would support Miliband for the leadership.

John Hutton, who stood down as defence secretary, symbolises the second set of Blairites. This group of ministers considered using their resignations to wound Brown, but were only willing to do so if there were a clear and organised campaign to replace the prime minister.

Hutton had long made clear that he wanted to resign because he would not be standing for parliament at the next election. But he stood back from attacking Brown in his resignation letter after failing to hear a strong assurance from Alan Johnson, the new home secretary, about his intentions. Johnson indicated he shared the concern about Brown, but he echoed Mandelson's warning that removing Brown would massively destabilise Labour. He also indicated he believed it wrong to make a judgment until the full outcome of Thursday's votes are known, when the results of the European parliamentary elections are announced tommorow night.

The new home secretary's support for the prime minister had firmed up by yesterday after the overnight operation involving Brown, Mandelson and Balls. Key members of the cabinet agreed to stay after winning assurances that Brown would mend his ways.

These ministers believe they have won two assurances. First, that cabinet ministers such as Alistair Darling will not again find themselves briefed against. There was deep anger in cabinet when Darling found himself being referred to in the past tense by Brown earlier in the week.

Second, ministers believe they have won assurances that Brown will make more of an effort to consult ministers and backbenchers, ensuring no repeat of the YouTube fiasco when he announced a series of unilateral proposals on expenses. 'There needs to be a completely new way of doing things,' one source said.

Nevertheless, even Brown's supporters were waiting last night to see if he could survive. 'This is the last throw of the dice,' one senior figure said. 'The jury is out as to whether it succeeds.'

6 June 2009

Gordon Brown supporters warn rebels against leadership challenge

PATRICK WINTOUR
AND DEBORAH SUMMERS

Gordon Brown's supporters today warned would-be rebels that the Labour party was in no mood for a leadership challenge, as they sought to rally around the beleaguered prime minister.

Brown, who was in Normandy for the 65th anniversary commemorations of the D-Day landings, reiterated his determination to carry on with the job, despite a fracturing of his authority and backbench calls for him to go.

'In these unprecedented times you are bound to have ups and downs in politics,' he told reporters in France. 'But you have got to stick with the policies and make sure that they come through.'

But a new poll of Labour activists brought further bad news for the prime minister, revealing that fewer than half of all party supporters want him to lead them into the next general election, with one in five urging him to quit now.

The poll of 800 party members carried out by YouGov for *Channel 4 News* found that one in three thought Labour stood no chance of winning a general election if Brown remained leader and 53 per cent thought they would be better off if Tony Blair was still in Number 10.

After one of the most chaotic cabinet reshuffles in recent political history, behind the scenes manoeuvring was continuing today as rebel MPs weighed the prospects of gathering enough support to mount a successful coup.

6 JUNE 2009

Smiling through the pain

SIMON HOGGART

Another bizarre day at Westminster, topped with a Gordon Brown press conference featuring that smile. Ministers were resigning faster than we could keep up. Meanwhile the House of Lords is beginning to look like an edition of I'm a Celebrity ... Get Me into Here!

In the morning we heard that John Hutton had quit as defence secretary. He had nothing but praise for Gordon Brown – he was the first minister to resign in support.

Next we heard that Sir Alan Sugar was being ennobled. For the next series of *The Apprentice*, 'Surallen' becomes 'Lorshugger'. Now Gordon 's strategy is revealed: we're going to solve the economic crisis by getting teams of unpleasant young people to sell bling on TV and wash cars.

Tories leapt into action, dishing out copies of a letter he wrote to the *FT* in 1992 when he was plain Mr Sugar. 'I have noted with disgust the comments of a certain Mr Gordon Brown who has accused me of doing well out of the recession ... ' he wrote. Well, at least he's got his resignation speech ready.

Just before noon we learned David Miliband and Alistair Darling were staying, even though Brown wanted them to move. This is becoming like a dinner party from hell, where guests refuse to accept the host's seating plan: 'I am not budging.

And have the butler bring in my pizza when it arrives from Domino's.'

Election results poured in. They were uniformly dreadful for Labour. Harriet Harman appeared to state that all was in hand. Her smile was as cheesy as a six-month old camembert. Alan Johnson was to be home secretary. This is a terrible revenge by Brown. Being home secretary in this government is like marrying Bluebeard – it's a poor career move. Bob Ainsworth was to replace Hutton at defence. Who? Somehow I doubt that telegrams have been sent to our armed forces around the globe announcing 'Bob is back!'

Peter Mandelson – 'first secretary of state' now, whatever that means – was asked what were the chances of Brown leading the party when the election does come. '100 per cent', he said. So he really is doomed.

Then the extraordinary press conference. The prime minister said he was going to be 'totally candid'. He accepted 'full responsibility' for a 'painful defeat'. But he didn't accept any blame. He was working on all the right measures. But outside, ministers were still resigning, and Glenys Kinnock was to be parachuted into the Lords, offering aid and comfort to the resistance.

The new cabinet was full of people of strength, experience and resilience, he said. 'They are not people who walk away when the going gets tough,' he said bitterly, a reference to certain others. Nor would he walk away. In fact, 'I never believe in walking away … I will never waver and I will never walk away.' He made it sound as if it would be an act of cowardice and he'd be shot, like someone fleeing the trenches in the first world war. Then – aargh – he smiled.

7 JUNE 2009

Why in the end the cabinet just didn't have the stomach for a kill

ANDREW RAWNSLEY

The morning after the night of his resignation, James Purnell told friends: 'I feel liberated.' During one of the most tumultuous weeks in the annals of Labour, the many members of the cabinet who jumped ship have looked happier than those who have chosen to remain lashed to the prime minister. In normal political times, it is the victims of reshuffles who look grim while it is the promoted who grin. In these strange days, it is the ex-ministers who have a spring in their step as if they have been released into fresh air after years chained in a dungeon. Those who remain in the cabinet clank from microphone to microphone to try to sustain the heroic pretence that they believe that Labour still has a fighting chance of winning the next general election.

I interviewed the former work and pensions secretary a few weeks ago. He was one of several cabinet members who talked to me for the making of *Crash Gordon*, my latest television documentary about the Blair and Brown years. Speaking in what was still then his ministerial suite, he did his professional best to stay on-message, but he was not his usual fluent self whenever we touched on the subject of Gordon Brown. After he'd self-ejected from the cabinet, Mr Purnell explained to me that the interview prompted him to look in the mirror and ask how much longer he could go on contorting himself into expressions of support for a leader in whom he had lost all confidence. If he remained, he knew he would have to join the defensive chorus line of ministers trying to explain away the devastation inflicted on Labour in the local and Euro elections. He just could not face pretending anymore.

It could have been the beginning of the end when his resignation letter, explicitly calling for the prime minister to 'stand aside', was released just as the polls closed at 10 o'clock on Thursday night. When he spoke on the phone to Gordon Brown, the prime minister was sitting in his war room in Downing Street with Peter Mandelson, once a close friend, then an arch enemy and now amazingly transformed into his most crucial ally. Both feared this was the start of a putsch that would finish Mr Brown there and then. Had other significant members of the cabinet also resigned, his premiership would have been over by midnight. 'The opportunity was handed to them on a platter,' says one of the prime minister's closest confidants. 'They did not take it.'

The fascinating question is: why not? After the obliteration inflicted on Labour in the county council elections, the party is braced for more and quite probably worse humiliation tonight when we get the results of the Euro elections. These are merely bitter appetisers before the full serving of calamity that faces Labour at the general election unless something radical happens to change the narrative. Yet there are still restraints on Labour committing an act of regicide that would have incalculable consequences.

The first is that Gordon Brown, even in such a mauled condition, remains a larger figure than anyone else in his cabinet. Since 1994, the Labour universe has been dominated by just two men. Tony Blair, who looks a luckier prime minister with every passing day, was one. Gordon Brown was the other. Many in the Labour party still find it psychologically difficult to imagine not being led by one or the other of them. Then there is the extraordinary resilience of Mr Brown.

A critical mass of his colleagues was coming to the conclusion that he was finished a year ago, only for the financial crisis to provide the opportunity for the prime minister to retrieve his position. It is still underappreciated just how close Britain came to a meltdown of its entire banking system so total that the cash machines would have stopped working. Businesses would have stopped paying their employees; parents wouldn't have been able to feed their families.

Whatever its other failings, the bank rescue plan last autumn did save Britain from that apocalypse. It also set a standard that was emulated around the world. As Sir John Gieve, who was deputy governor of the Bank of England at the time, says: 'It set a pattern which was blessed in Washington, blessed in Paris and more or less followed by the US and the rest of Europe.' The international arena also provided the brief respite for his premiership this April when Gordon Brown, in important alliance with Barack Obama, managed to corral the leaders of the G20 in London to come to a confidence-boosting agreement. Could David Cameron have rescued the banks or achieved the agreements at the G20? Could Alan Johnson? These are fair questions for Mr Brown's residual supporters to ask.

The prime minister's close and candid friend, Mark Malloch-Brown, a minister and Labour peer, praises his capacity to 'lead the world on these issues'. But then he adds the stinger that Gordon Brown doesn't have the same 'sure touch' at home and lacks the capacity to talk 'in language that ordinary folk understand' which makes him 'not the powerful communicator that some other political leaders are here and abroad'.

To that criticism are added many more by those who despair of Gordon Brown: an incoherent policy agenda and an inability to inspire; prevarication when he needs to seize the initiative and clumsiness when he finally tries; poisonous spinning against colleagues conducted by the dark side of his operation at No 10; a hopeless addiction to backfiring tactical wheezes. Giving a peerage to the gruesome Alan Sugar is the sort of frantic, misconceived stunt that is Gordon Brown at his very worst.

That all explains why he dangles by a thread. Yet so far, no one has found a knife sharp enough to cut it. The would-be assassins have proved more indecisive and chaotic than the king they would kill. The plotters only have a slogan: save our seats. They lack a manifesto, they don't have a plausible endgame and they are left without a credible challenger now that his senior colleagues have agreed to carry on serving in Mr Brown's cabinet. Because he was a protege of the last prime minister, James Purnell's resignation was initially and wrongly interpreted as the first move of a Blairite coup. To see these events through the old prism of the Blairite/Brownite split is to misjudge the gravity of Labour's situation and the complexity of its dilemma.

Some Blairites are indeed desperate to see the back of Gordon Brown. So, too, are some Labour MPs who would be thought of as Brownites as are plenty of Labour MPs of neither appellation. Other Blairites are playing a critical role in sustaining Gordon Brown. Peter Mandelson, garlanded with the baroque title of first secretary of state, is now the effective deputy prime minister. He joined the frantic ring-round of other members of the cabinet to try to establish whether James Purnell was a lone gunman or the first shot of a firing squad for Gordon Brown. We can pause for a moment to savour the irony of Lord Mandelson, whose first cabinet career was destroyed by Mr Brown and his acolytes, turning into the prime minister's life-support machine.

The Brownites are also fractured. Alistair Darling is – or, at least, was – a close friend and ally of Gordon Brown. His wife, Maggie, often helps to look after the prime minister's children. The chancellor may have had a charisma bypass, but he has kept his head when many others would have been driven insane by the combination of the worst financial crisis since the war and outrageous briefing against him by the poisoners in the prime minister's gang.

Early on Thursday evening, Mr Brown attempted to bully Mr Darling into leaving the Treasury. Then and again on Friday morning, Alistair Darling pushed back and the prime minister was finally forced to abandon the idea of installing Ed Balls at No 11. It was a retreat that made him look very weak, but by then he had no alternative. The sort of resignation speech that Alistair Darling could deliver would be fatal to Gordon Brown. The chancellor's hand was strengthened by the terror caused by the Purnell resignation, which also made it too risky to try to move David Miliband from the Foreign Office. In sacrificing his job, Purnell inadvertently helped to secure them in theirs.

The hope that the economy may be in recovery by the spring of next year is a further reason for some to pause before they drive the dagger between the prime minister's shoulder blades. Labour will have a story to tell the voters about how it took the action to alleviate recession and avoid depression while the Conservatives sneered from the sidelines and proposed policies that would have made it worse. To make that story convincing enough to win some credit from the voters, Gordon Brown would have to locate a capacity for communication.

Peter Mandelson has been promising sceptical colleagues that the prime minister has been given such a severe fright that he finally grasps that he must fundamentally change both the way he runs the government and the way he conducts himself. He understands that he has one last chance to work with and make a team of his senior colleagues, to try to restore his authority, convey a sense of purpose to the country and get some momentum back. Even his closest friends concede that this currently looks like mission near-impossible and many others will sigh that Gordon Brown has already proved himself utterly incapable of ever keeping promises to change his ways.

That makes it easy to attack Jack Straw, Alan Johnson and David Miliband as dithering cowards for not dealing the death blow to Gordon Brown when they were presented with the chance, though I can't help laughing when that charge is laid by those who recommended him to us as the messiah just two years ago.

One of the leaders of the backbench assassins says the key is 'the P45 test'. When Labour MPs have digested the local and Euro elections, they will realise that 'they don't have a hope in hell' of keeping their seats without a change of leadership. Yet if the calculus were really that straightforward the key figures in the cabinet would have moved in for the kill on Thursday night. 'The P45 test' cuts both ways. There's no good polling evidence yet that changing leader will rescue Labour from its plight. Is Alan Johnson really the man the Tories fear? Maybe he is. I wonder, though, why the Conservatives are not keeping that fear to themselves if it were entirely true.

Gordon Brown will be within his rights to fight a challenge, as did both Margaret Thatcher and John Major. Tony Blair, it is true, did buckle under the pressure of a backbench uprising and agree to resign. Since it was Gordon Brown's gang who executed that coup, it would be poetic justice for him to go the same way. But the positions are not analogous. Mr Blair had won three elections and enjoyed a decade at Number 10. That made it easier to embrace leaving, especially when he was given almost a further year to say goodbye. If Gordon Brown is defenestrated in the next few weeks, he will have been prime minister for less than two years. Not since Neville Chamberlain was toppled in 1940 after the Nazi invasion of Norway has a British prime minister been removed without being allowed to fight one general election. And it took the menace of Hitler and the availability of Churchill to do that.

'I'm not walking away,' he says, a declaration of steeliness designed to warn mutineers that they will have to break his fingers before they'll prise them off the doorknob of Number 10. To pile peril on danger on hazard, coup-minded Labour MPs cannot be certain that they will end up with the result they intended. They may set off with the goal of putting Alan Johnson into Number 10 and wake up two months later to find that they'd installed Harriet Harman.

A grisly struggle to force out Gordon Brown and an internecine war for the succession would then be followed by enormous pressure for an early election which would be a chainsaw massacre for Labour. That is why the cabinet clings on to a massively wounded prime minister – for fear of something worse.

8 JUNE 2009

Gordon Brown 'to limp on' despite voters deserting Labour

PATRICK WINTOUR, DEBORAH
SUMMERS AND MATTHEW WEAVER

Gordon Brown will limp on like a 'wounded elephant' unless Labour rebels can garner the necessary 70 signatures to force a leadership challenge today, insiders predicted as the party suffered its worst electoral result since the first world war.

In a devastating night for Labour, the party won just 15.8 per cent of the popular vote, allowing the far right British National party to clinch its first two seats in the European parliament.

Worse than expected results for the prime minister saw Labour pushed into second place by the Tories in Wales for the first time since 1918, suffering its lowest vote in Scotland since before the first world war and humiliatingly finishing third to UKIP nationally.

As Brown put the finishing touches to his cabinet reshuffle with an announcement on the lower-ranking ministerial posts, he suffered a fresh setback when he was forced to sack Jane Kennedy, the minister of state for the environment, after she refused to sign a pledge of loyalty to the prime minister. She said she had enough of 'the bullying, the threats, the intimidation'.

More backenchers today joined the growing list of MPs publicly calling for Brown to go, including former ministers Frank Field and Sally Keeble. But others broke cover to say Brown would now hang on. John Grogan, the MP for Selby, told the BBC Radio's *World at One*: 'I was the Labour backbencher who told the prime minister that he had a 50/50 chance of surviving until Tuesday. I now think he will survive and he deserves to survive.'

During a night of unremitting gloom for Downing Street, the Tories pulled more than 10 points ahead of Labour, with UKIP in second place. The BNP secured its first significant wins in British politics when its leader, Nick Griffin, became an MEP in northwest England, and Andrew Brons, a former leader of the National Front, won in Yorkshire and Humber.

The major parties blamed each other for the drift to the far right reflected in results across the country.

Labour's drubbing will lead Brown to offer concessions to his backbenchers by promising to delay plans for the part-privatisation of the Royal Mail and to bring forward proposals for an inquiry into the basis for the Iraq war. The prime minister is battling to ensure a backbench rebellion does not spread to the left of the party, or to MPs in Labour heartlands where the party fared worst last night.

Rebel leaders will meet later today in advance of a pivotal meeting of the parliamentary party at 6pm tonight to analyse the highly varied result and decide if they have enough support to mount a challenge to Brown.

A leading Labour rebel, Barry Sheerman, said last night he was prepared to meet the challenge posed by the party's chief whip, Nick Brown, to put up or shut up.

Lord Falconer, the former lord chancellor and close friend of Tony Blair, called on Brown to go, saying: 'I believe if we change leader then we can go into the next election, whenever it was, so much stronger.'

However, Labour insiders believe that the real danger point for Brown may have passed unless the rebels can today muster the 70 signatures required to force a leadership challenge.

'He will limp on like a wounded elephant,' a source said. 'The party will not allow him to take us into the next general election but after last night's results we can't risk anything that would trigger a general election now.'

8 JUNE 2009

To save Labour, Gordon, go with grace and go today

JACKIE ASHLEY

There is now only one person who can save the Labour party. And he is Gordon Brown. Only he stands between the party he loves and its utter collapse. That's the No 10 view, and I have only one, tiny, disagreement with it: to save Labour the prime minister should go, not stay. And he should do so this morning.

Labour now has the worst of all worlds. There was a coup, but it was so botched and half-cocked that it failed. The alternative leaders have damaged themselves and Brown. The Blairites are divided between stayers and goers. But the Brownites are divided too, as the man himself turns to lean on their old foes – Peter Mandelson and Shaun Woodward, a former Tory. There is no centre. There is nothing and nobody to rally around. It couldn't be more of a mess.

Yet even now, the mayhem inside the government is over-shadowed by wider politics. The local elections and the European results are catastrophic. It isn't only about personalities. It isn't only about the recession. It isn't only about the MPs' expenses scandal. It's that the party no longer knows what it is, or where it's going. And the public has noticed.

Granted, there is nothing harder for a party than to renew itself in power. The Thatcherites could not do it, nor could the Major-era Tories. Briefly, it seemed that with Tony Blair's resignation in favour of Brown, Labour had found an answer. But for that to stick, Brown would need to have changed his political style, and opened up a real conversation about political directions. He could not. This morning, as things stand, Labour has lost the initiative not just to the Tories, but to xenophobic and rightwing parties that once skulked ignored in the shadows.

Brown has proved one thing – he will be very hard to force out. His critics lack his singleminded, awesome willpower. Already the operation is in full swing to stop a backbenchers' revolt succeeding today where a cabinet revolt failed.

MPs, often sleepless with worry about their expenses and their futures, are being called up and threatened with being put in the media spotlight unless they stay loyal. Others are being offered jobs. And as we have seen, some people can be cheaply bought. As the Labour MP Siobhan McDonagh has said on television, there are some cabinet ministers pledging loyalty to Brown who certainly say the opposite in private.

Nor are many of the MPs contemplating revolt in a strong position to begin with. Brown's authority has drained away. But so has theirs. Then there is the now explicit threat to respond to any further move to depose the prime minister by calling a general election. Mandelson was quite forthright about it yesterday, and it's a potent threat. One of the significant rumours flying round yesterday was that Brown had already booked a visit to Buckingham Palace this morning, ready to resign at last on the basis of terrible European results.

That will up the jitter count. On the one hand, MPs will be seeing in cold print their own likely electoral futures as the breakdowns of the European poll are shown to them. In many cases this will cause despair, or panic, and ought to lead to a reconsideration of the leadership issue. But of course if they are then told Brown intends to call a general election now, that is even scarier. It's the difference between a potential death sentence and immediate execution.

Finally, Brown knows that almost all the possible alternatives to him have damaged themselves in the past few days. Senior Labour people are very critical of Alan Johnson's apparent decision to lead potential supporters up the hill only to march them down again, just before the polls closed last Thursday. They are more critical still of David Miliband for staying inside the tent. Yet by leaping, only to find no one following him, James Purnell has seemed isolated.

By now, readers will have spotted the central dilemma. On one hand I'm saying that Brown's leadership has failed and that if things continue this way, Labour is heading for electoral annihilation. That's obvious. On the other, I have just listed the strong, short-term reasons to think he can survive future coups, just as he survived the recent one. So the wagon is heading for the edge of the cliff, and nobody has the willpower to change direction.

That's why I go back to my opening thought. The only person who can save the situation is Brown himself. Couldn't friends talk him into it? I can confirm they are discussing that, calling him up without public fuss, keeping away from media interviews. Most of these friends, however, complain that he just refuses to listen to anyone now except Mandelson.

Why might Brown decide the game is up? Because he is actually a clever and politically well-read man. His political creed is a decent one. But he has a brutal side to him and he is brutally unsuited to the smooth media age. And the people have spoken. They won't ever warm to him, and they no longer admire him. He could still summon up a wry and regretful speech to admit what is obvious, and go with dignity. The day he does, his reputation will begin to rise again.

That day should be today. Changing leaders again is extremely dangerous and difficult – just a little less dangerous and difficult than keeping on like this. Ah, but ditching Gordon would cause rifts in the party, some protest. Hello, have they not noticed the rifts that are already there? Now it's not just Blairite against Brownite: old allegiances are being turned on their heads, and long friendships are being severed. It's certainly a rum old time in politics when the main voices speaking up in support of Brown are old Blairites plus Ken Livingstone and lefties who haven't had a good word to say about him for years.

Lord Falconer was talking the most sense yesterday: Labour needs a full leadership election, involving as many of the younger generation as possible, and yes, Alan Johnson and Harriet Harman too. It would all be over by July. The new leader could ask for enough time to have his party conference and set out his stall on reform, and promise an election in the autumn. Then Labour would really be able to leave the 'old politics' behind. Indeed, it's the only chance of looking more radical than David Cameron. And after a full and frank debate, and a vote, the party could unite behind the winner.

These are huge stakes, far bigger than any prime minister's sense of entitlement, and far more important than the hand-to-hand combat going on just now. I rather like Gordon Brown, much though I dislike some of the people around him. And I'd urge him – do it yourself, do it well and do it now.

9 JUNE 2009

Day of judgment: They banged their desks with approval

NICHOLAS WATT, ALLEGRA STRATTON AND PATRICK WINTOUR

On the dot of 6pm yesterday, a cheerful-looking Gordon Brown marched along the dimly lit committee corridor of the House of Commons to face one of the most packed meetings of the parliamentary Labour party in its history.

'Hi guys, it's a big attendance this evening,' the prime minister said to the assembled media as he walked into the large committee room, overlooking the Thames, where backbench Labour MPs were planning to attack his leadership.

As Brown made his way through to the platform, MPs clapped and banged their desks, in what No 10 will hope will be seen as a significant show of loyalty.

Latecomers, including Lady Royall, leader of the Lords, were unable to open the committee room doors for sheer weight of numbers. As four police officers stood guard outside the committee room – the highest number since the first ecstatic meeting of the PLP after Tony Blair's landslide election victory in 1997 – the veteran peer Lord Janner performed magic tricks after failing to make it inside.

Inside, a lineup of Labour heavyweights from the party's recent history were on hand to hear the prime minister. Lord Mandelson, Ed Balls, Harriet Harman and Alan Johnson headed the list of senior cabinet ministers who were joined by Lords Kinnock and Hattersley, the former leader and deputy leader.

It took a figure who first made his name in the Kinnock era to say what was on the minds of many MPs. Charles Clarke, chief of staff to the former Labour leader who went on to become home secretary under Blair, was heard in stony silence as he stood up to tell Brown that he should go. Tom Harris, a former transport minister sacked by Brown last year, joined Clarke. 'I told the prime minister the truth. With him at the top we cannot win.'

Of the 21 members of the PLP who spoke out during the 90-minute meeting, five were against Brown. Kinnock rounded off the meeting with an impassioned plea for the party to unite behind Brown, declaring: 'In politics, division carries the death penalty.'

Aware that the likes of Clarke would call for his head, the prime minister had prepared carefully for the meeting, which was held after he had led Labour to its worst performance in a national election in the modern era, when its vote collapsed to just 15.7 per cent. Brown knew that he was facing the most dangerous moment of his premiership amid a backbench rebellion from senior figures who were collecting names for a letter calling on him to stand down.

The day had not begun promisingly for Brown. Opponents of the prime minister believed their case was strengthened when Jane Kennedy, a respected environment minister, resigned after refusing to declare her loyalty. In remarks that struck a chord with Labour MPs, the MP for Liverpool Wavertree likened No 10's 'bullying' tactics to the Militant tendency on Merseyside in the 1980s. In a mid-morning interview outside her constituency office, Kennedy called on Brown to go, but said she expected him to carry on until 'the bitter end of the Labour party'.

As the PLP meeting wore on, it became clear that Brown would, as Kennedy predicted, carry on. He struck a humble, but defiant, note as he admitted he had weaknesses, but insisted he was the best man to meet the twin challenges of the recession and the expenses crisis.

The rebels made clear last night that they were throwing in the towel – for the moment at least – when they stepped back from publishing a list of between 50 to 60 supporters. 'Yes, the rebellion has peaked for now,' one source said.

But the precarious nature of Brown's position was underlined last night when the former cabinet minister Stephen Byers likened him to Michael Foot, who led Labour to a disastrous result in the 1983 general election. 'We all knew that under Michael Foot we were heading for defeat, but we did nothing about it,' Byers told a Progress rally. 'We must not repeat this mistake again.'

For the moment, though, the rebels are acknowledging one of the iron rules of British politics: that it is difficult to unseat a prime minister who retains the support of the cabinet. 'By carrying out his reshuffle on Friday – inbetween the results of the two sets of elections – Gordon has bound the cabinet to him,' one MP said.

The prime minister believes he has secured the support of the cabinet and the PLP, but he knows his position is far from secure. His allies believe that David Miliband, the foreign secretary, could still walk out on him. 'David Miliband could lead a group out of the cabinet this afternoon,' one senior figure said before the PLP. 'I do not believe it will happen, but it could.'

Such a view highlights the deep unease at senior levels in Downing Street about the dangers posed to Brown after what allies of the prime minister admitted were 'hideous' election results. One source said: 'There is no getting away from the fact that these are terrible results. It is a very risky time for Labour. We can still win [the general election]. It will depend on what happens in the next few months.'

Critics say that Brown is making the classic mistake of a beleaguered leader by retreating into an inner core, in what is being dubbed the Downing Street bunker. But as bunkers go, it is a friendly place where uncomfortable home truths are delivered to the prime minister. At the core of the new inner circle are Lord Mandelson and Ed Balls, who fell out when they took different sides in the 1994 Labour leadership contest. 'Peter and Ed have learned to tolerate each other,' said one source.

The new duo were in Downing Street from early yesterday as Brown consulted them on the immediate challenge: how to complete his ministerial reshuffle without any further damaging resignations and what to say at last night's PLP.

Both ministers believe that Brown will only move on if the Labour bickering ends and the prime minister can focus on outlining a credible vision for the future. Great hopes are being placed on the national plan next week, which will set out how the government will take Britain out of the downturn.

Brown is still on probation among both backbenchers and ministers. 'It is still not completely impossible that some ministers will talk to Gordon in private,' a senior Labour figure source said. 'It is more fluid than people think.'

But as MPs left last night's meeting it was left to a veteran of Labour's last turbulent period in office to declare that Brown was safe for the moment. Lord Donoughue, a senior adviser to the late James Callaghan, said: 'I'm afraid your lust for blood will not be satisfied.'

10 JUNE 2009

No wonder John Major is Gordon Brown's patron saint

SIMON JENKINS

Crowds are good at lying. That is why Gordon Brown did not make Margaret Thatcher's mistake when he faced his leadership crisis this week. He did not invite his cabinet colleagues one by one to his office to tell him the truth, as she did in November 1990. She discovered to her cost that such confidences can be devastating.

Instead Brown took his cause to the sweaty seats, gloomy walls and raucous mob of Commons committee room 14. This is safe territory where whips roam free and the dark arts of loyalty, mendacity and ambition hold sway. In such dark corners and sinister corridors a British prime minister can wield near limitless power. Brown knew that, and on Monday he trounced his foes.

With such enemies as the parliamentary Labour party, Brown needed no friends. Anyone wondering why Labour is so bad at government need only study the party in putsch mode. It is useless. Tories topple leaders with the facility of communards. Failed coups are embedded in Labour history, as Attlee, Gaitskell, Wilson and Blair could attest.

Last week's alleged conspiracy involving the 'rolling resignations' of Hazel Blears, James Purnell, John Hutton and Geoff Hoon was about as effective as the plot to kill Hitler. The press was primed with headlines such as CountBrown, MeltBrown, Brown Doomed and Browned Off. But the conspirators believed the press and the press believed the conspirators. It was magnificent, but ridiculous. It was not war.

In the first place, the prime minister had no intention of going. He is many things but not spineless. He was able to manipulate patronage and whipping through each day of the crisis, culminating in the nobbling by promotion of his chief rival, Alan Johnson. Such is the glamour of Westminster that its denizens, especially the press, overrate its constitutional power, while underrating that of Downing Street.

Second, while the Tory constitution enables a stalking horse to run and then give way to a cabinet big hitter on a second ballot, Labour requires the big hitter to declare public disloyalty of his or her boss from the start. To run for Labour leader, a candidate must almost certainly resign high office and be sure of support in parliament, the constituencies and unions.

None of Brown's senior colleagues, such as Alistair Darling, Jack Straw and David Miliband, were plausible successors, with a party or national following. The putative strongest candidate was the unknown Johnson. Other than James Purnell, most of the dissidents were ministers promoted beyond their talents, some because they were women. None was a 'big beast' of the sort that plagued the leadership of Wilson, early Thatcher and Major.

Nor was Brown's analysis of his electoral prospects wholly implausible. The local elections were appalling, but not uniquely so for a party long in government. The Tories never had a happy local election in 18 years of rule. As for the misreading of the Euro elections, it was classic Westminster-centric dazzle. These elections do not choose representatives, let along governors, for anywhere that matters to voters. They are part a referendum on the popularity of the European Union, part an invitation to kick conventional politics in the teeth, to the benefit of minority parties.

After the expenses scandal, this invitation was joyously accepted, to the glee of greens, little Englanders and rightwing racists. So much for proportional representation. As for the media cry of

'Wales has gone Tory' and 'Labour comes fifth in the south-west', it was rubbish. You cannot extrapolate such a poll in this way. It is more trivial even than a byelection. Every vox pop and canvas report testified to Euro elections as mischievous and eccentric.

I thought from the moment of his accession that Brown would make a disastrous prime minister, but would last the course to 2010. Not for nothing is Major the patron saint of Brown's circle – Major redux of 1992, rather than doomed of 1997. It is not unreasonable for Downing Street to gamble on a return of economic confidence by the start of next year, and not unreasonable to dream of another 'surge' – as in summer 2007, and during the G20 and credit crunch diplomacy earlier this year.

Brown was never likely to win a general election, but he might sensibly hope for an honourable defeat, like that other tail-end Charlie, Douglas-Home, in 1964. As such he may yet save the seats of dozens of MPs who have made such a hash of trying to oust him. Anyway, there is no other plausible scenario. Things could not be worse next year. The maxim holds that 'treason never prospers, for if it prospers none dare call it treason'. But when treason fails, it is in the interests of all to forget it.

Brown's chief saviour was his old rival, Blair, whose early reforms to Labour's constitution made unseating a leader near impossible. His post-1992 modernisation project devalued the role of unions, party conference and national executive. The man who 10 years earlier jeered that SDP defectors had 'isolated themselves from organised labour' did just that himself. Labour had to detoxify its electoral image from any association with a party dominated by trade unions or leftwing constituencies.

Blair all but ended the block vote, ended union dominance in choosing leaders and candidates, and ended the role of the party conference in selecting the shadow cabinet and writing the manifesto. Blair ended the supremacy of the national executive. Even after succeeding John Smith in 1994 Blair said: 'I would rather be beaten and leave politics than bend to the [Labour] party.'

Imitating Bill Clinton's success in America, Blair had to make Labour safe for charisma, preferably his own. That he made it safe for someone as uncharismatic as Brown is merely political irony. Thanks to Blair, Brown can hire and fire ministers at will. Thanks to Blair, Brown can disregard his party and its electoral fate. His sole constraint is his ability to command a parliamentary majority. It was to that majority that he appealed triumphantly on Monday night.

By then Brown had used his power of patronage to stem the flow of blood from the cabinet and to reassert the power, unique among modern democracies, that Britain's constitution vests in its executive. That power is awesome, strong enough to defy the argument of the polls, the party, the cabinet and the media that he should go. It enabled Brown to buy himself another year in Downing Street, and with ease.

10 JUNE 2009

A triumph for the left and for democracy

NIGEL WILMOTT

The last thing I would have expected a week ago was to end up defending Gordon Brown. But, if the attempted coup – for that's what it was – by irreconcilable Blairites and the media to overthrow a democratic government led by Brown had succeeded, it would have been disastrous for both the progressive left and democracy.

The people who walked out on Brown last week have been given enormous credence by the media. But outside the political-media elite, Jacqui Smith, Hazel Blears, Geoff Hoon, Tony McNulty and the rest have no real constituency of support, either in the Labour party or the wider electorate. Most people either shrugged or said good riddance. Who else would tout smug, too-clever-by-half James Purnell as a future Labour leader but a completely out of touch commentariat.

If Brown had been unseated by the actions of those unreconstructed Blairites – many, incidentally, deeply compromised over their expenses – it would have meant Labour would have been dragged back to the neoliberal agenda which has eviscerated the party and which was firmly rejected, along with Blair, two years ago. Their triumphalism would have made the crucial repositioning that Labour now needs impossible, leading either to a split or the party imploding.

The democratic issue is perhaps even more serious. What we have seen is a well-planned and executed attempt, using people's quite justifiable anger over MPs' expenses, to undermine the government in the lead-up to critical local and national elections. This was not evenhanded, as the *Telegraph* would like to pretend. It has been carefully packaged and presented to cause maximum damage to Labour.

And who is leading this crusade for transparency and to stop the taxpayer being ripped off? A newspaper owned by two secretive businessmen; tax exiles who have probably denied the taxpayer 10 times the amount of all the MPs' illegitimate expenses combined.

11 June 2009

The plot: The five-page spreadsheet that holds secrets of coup that failed

ALLEGRA STRATTON

At 3pm on Monday 8 June, 15 people met in an MP's office in the House of Commons to agree that, for the time being at least, the Hotmail Plot had failed.

Over eight days, the core team of the backbench rebel putsch to unseat Gordon Brown had doubled from seven to 15. In that time, seven ministers had left the government, including a high flyer who had launched an explicit attack on the prime minister.

Brown had been forced to back down over a planned reshuffle, leaving in place people he'd really prefer to have moved. But, though he had to come to a meeting of the parliamentary Labour party cap in hand that night, he knew – and the rebels knew – he was safe.

So how did the plot collapse? It had been a tumultuous eight days since parliament had returned from recess. In that week a senior rebel understood that the communities secretary, Hazel Blears, was preparing to resign and the pair agreed to meet in the next few days; but Blears never confirmed.

Then, on Wednesday 3 June at 10.30am, less than 24 hours before polls opened for the local and European elections, Blears resigned. That move is now regarded as one of the most damaging blows to the effort to remove the prime minister – the moment it started to go wrong.

'Hazel's resignation turned people against us,' one of the rebels said. 'Even her supporters found the timing of her resignation difficult to stomach. Especially that brooch [which sported the legend 'Rocking the boat'].

'It enabled the whips to make the argument that we were undermining campaigners at that moment knocking on doors for the Labour party, and created a sense of incompetence that we never really escaped from.'

Blears is still to explain the timing of her exit, but it was being pointed out that she was due to meet cabinet office officials at 3pm on the day of her eventual resignation for a further examination of her expenses – the departure allowed her to avoid what could have been another difficult confrontation over whether she should have paid capital gains tax or not.

The decision by Blears, a party loyalist to her fingertips and local activist in her heart, taken at such a sensitive point, probably reflects the widely held belief that Downing Street was using the expenses scandal to smear political opponents.

Whatever her motives, the rebels believe her resignation made a lot of the difference between getting 50 rebels to sign up to the plot, and the 70 they felt they needed.

Party rules say 71 MPs can force a contest if they all back the same candidate.

'The difference between getting 50 and the necessary 70 will be the disloyalty factor,' one told the *Guardian* when the plot was in full swing. The Hotmail Plot – so called because of the email address, signonnow@hotmail.co.uk, which MPs were asked to sign up to, calling for Brown to go, remained undetected for days until the Guardian revealed it at noon, shortly after Blears had resigned.

By Wednesday evening, the covert tactic unravelled as thousands of emails arrived. Apart from the odd one from genuinely sympathetic MPs, spoofs, foreign emails, and junk emails flowed in.

One rebel said: 'We got one email from brownn@parliament.uk [the email address of the chief whip]. It might be that they were hoping we'd publish a list and not notice his name was in it and then he could show all the names were ridiculous.'

Instead, the rebels adopted a tactic favoured by organised criminals and bought an untraceable pay-as-you-go mobile, encouraging sympathetic colleagues to get in touch that way. It became a text message plot.

One of the theories behind the covert backbench operation was that if they emerged without warning with a list of dozens of MPs from all wings of the party an unstoppable momentum would embolden disaffected cabinet members and drive the prime minister from office.

But by 6pm, six hours after the *Guardian* had broken news of the Hotmail Plot, the element of surprise was gone and the whips were in overdrive, terrifying potential rebels.

Nick Brown, the chief whip, produced names he said were involved in the plot. Some were inaccurate. The realpolitik of even being possibly associated with the plot was exemplified when a local news reporter rang one wrongly identified rebel, Paul Farrelly, at 2am to inform him they would be splashing on news of his disloyalty to the prime minister – the morning of polling day.

One cabinet minister due to meet a rebel for dinner had their meeting cancelled – there simply wasn't a restaurant in London discreet enough. Instead, that evening they would have the first of three phone calls. The cabinet minister was interested in the nature of names, irrespective of whether they had arrived by email, text or carrier pigeon.

On polling day, MPs were scattered around the country. But the rebels had to contend with three attacks – their timing, their lack of policy and their invisibility: were they left or right, usual suspects or unusual suspects?

That evening at 10pm events took another dramatic turn when James Purnell, the work and pensions secretary, announced he was leaving the cabinet. Had he been followed, the pressure may well have been too much for Brown. But the moment was something of a box of fireworks where only one went off: others who had been due to resign didn't.

Purnell caught the government by surprise, the news emerging in Sky television reports only moments after the man himself rang No 10.

But then Lord Mandelson, already in Downing Street advising Brown on the reshuffle, sprang to work.

He rang potentially wavering cabinet ministers to check they would remain on board, including David Miliband, who they understood had grave doubts about Brown. The foreign secretary eventually said he would remain and Purnell was not immediately accompanied by others, until a chaotic resignation the next day by Caroline Flint, the Europe minister.

She left with a vicious attack on Brown's style hours after she had given a public display of loyalty. 'You can put Hazel and Caroline's departure in the category of the Anarchic Departures,' a rebel said.

This rebel regards Miliband's failure to resign as the moment the plot failed.

Throughout the saga, the left was mainly silent. Jon Cruddas, the influential backbencher, was taking calls from rebels trying to recruit him to the cause, and also from elements of the soft left persuading him not to be a 'cheap date'.

He told them he continued to consider his position but the next day he wrote an article for the *Sunday Mirror* that appeared to back Brown – though his aides sent corrective text messages afterwards saying that was not the gist of his piece.

At some point during the weekend, a rumour emerged that Brown had scheduled a meeting with the Queen – a rumour rebels attributed to Downing Street ('this isn't something I blame Brown for, it's what any Downing Street operation would do when the prime minister is under attack from backbenchers').

For wavering rebels terrified about losing their seat in an instant election, the rumour may have been enough.

On Sunday night, the European election results were truly terrible for Labour: Wales lost, Scotland lost, fifth in the south-east. Though Brown had Mandelson and Ed Balls with him in the Downing Street bunker they knew he was still vulnerable.

Around this time a supplementary counter-argument did the rounds to further upset those pro-European Labour MPs already licking their wounds: if there were to be a general election it would come before the Irish referendum on the Lisbon treaty and the Tories would then truly be able to withdraw from Europe with great ease.

These were tactical counter-arguments made by a quick-witted government which the rebels should have foreseen. Though the invisibility of the plot was tacticaly clever, there were obvious flaws: there was a perception of being too rightwing; co-ordination with a disgruntled cabinet was poor; fear grew in the lower ranks of the parliamentary party that if a new leader was brought in a general election would simply have to be allowed.

The rebels knew they didn't have the numbers and decided to meet together, for the first time.

On Monday at 3pm the rebels met. All their info was collated on a five-page spreadsheet across which names, mobile phone numbers, 'other telephone numbers' and personal non-parliamentary email addresses were set out horizontally along with the initials of the rebel MP who had brought them on board and vouched for them.

Zealots who wanted Brown out were given the number zero and those newly persuaded the number one. Zero zealots made up most of the first page; ones extended on to the second and together they came to 54. Short of the 71 crucial figure but over the 50 they had briefed journalists would trigger publication.

But they decided that evening to perform a U-turn and announced they would not go public.

All that was left to do was go to the parliamentary Labour party meeting. The rebels say the PLP assumed import mostly because of serendipity rather than the suitability of occasion, since it came at the end of the first Monday back after the European elections. PLPs are always intimidating affairs and though seven rebels spoke, including Charles Clarke and Fiona MacTaggart, the plot flopped.

But there were other categories on that spreadsheet. Number four indicated friends of Brown and category three were people whose opinions were not known.

The category that was by far the longest, stretching to about 120 was number two (yesterday one rebel rang to say: 'I've just seen that two of our number twos have got jobs with the government. Patronage is a big problem for plots'.) The number two denoted: 'Possibles, if ...'

The 'If' being David Miliband, the foreign secretary. Something that many got wrong this week, including media commentators, is that the majority of Labour MPs on the list wanted Alan Johnson to take over. David Miliband would have been closer to the truth.

13 JUNE 2009

Miliband: Yes, I thought about resigning. Now I want to help save party

NICHOLAS WATT AND PATRICK WINTOUR

In the space of a few short hours on the night of Thursday 4 June David Miliband held the fate of Gordon Brown in his hands. When James Purnell, an old friend from the early years of Tony Blair's Downing Street, resigned from the cabinet, Miliband could have provoked a bloodbath in the Labour party if he had followed his example. But in a brief phone conversation with Lord Mandelson, who was in No 10 discussing the imminent cabinet reshuffle, Miliband confirmed he would be staying.

A week after the late night call, Miliband laughs at the irony that a man who became Brown's great enemy, Peter Mandelson, was asking him to save the PM.

'The government is much stronger for Peter at the heart of it,' the foreign secretary says as he recalls his conversation with Mandelson, who was awarded the title of first secretary of state after saving the Brown premiership. 'I'm not going to go into [our conversation], but we didn't sort of talk about the weather.'

But he confirms for the first time that he did seriously consider resigning from the cabinet. 'I'd made my decision on Thursday,' he tells the *Guardian*, saying he tried to persuade Purnell not to resign on the night of the local and European parliamentary elections.

'Sometimes you can make your decisions with great planning and calculation and sometimes you have to make them rather more quickly.'

While Miliband and Purnell made different choices – he admits those on either side of the divide feel 'passionately' – the foreign secretary still has the greatest respect for his old friend, who was strongly criticised by No 10 for notifying Brown minutes before his resignation was announced on TV. 'Look, James is a good friend, he has good talent. He was a very, very good minister. It is important to say that. He had the respect of his staff, he had good ideas for the future, he was good on detail and was a very good colleague. He contributed to cabinet. He is a loss. But he's not dead. He can contribute. Whether you are inside the government or outside, we've got to make a go of this party of ours.'

Such views will not be shared by Brown, who believes Purnell behaved in a discourteous manner. The prime minister is also wary of Miliband, though No 10 breathed a collective sigh of relief when he announced he would be staying.

The foreign secretary makes clear he too has changed: he feels liberated, as he knows he is virtually unsackable. The ex-head of Blair's policy unit, who has assumed a lower domestic profile since his call in the *Guardian* last summer for a 'radical new phase' of New Labour and his unfortunate appearance with a banana at the Labour conference, shows all the enthusiasm of a former think-tank warrior as he makes clear he will spend the next months outlining a vision to save his party.

This will involve uncomfortable truths about the challenges and a bleak assessment of the party's failings. 'We have all had a very, very cold, electoral shower. You have to take very, very seriously the scale of the rebuff ... My generation in the Labour party know what a privilege it is to be in government, because we saw enough of opposition and we saw how many good people it destroyed to know the utter futility. We also know from the seats we represent that my generation cannot afford to let that happen again.'

Sitting at a large wooden table in the foreign secretary's grand room in Whitehall, Miliband says he has thought very carefully about a 'route map' for Labour. Looking fresh after a three-hour 'political' cabinet meeting in No 10, discussing public service reform, Miliband says Labour must pass what he calls three tests.

'I was thinking really hard about this overnight – what is the route map?' he says as he outlines the tests Labour must pass: providing a period of competent and stable government; resetting its political compass; ensuring it is at the 'cutting edge' of policy making.

The challenge is formidable because Labour has woefully failed voters. 'We did very badly and we have to take collective responsibility for that.' The party that once embodied the values of Middle Britain has lost touch with its former supporters to such an extent that nobody knows what it stands for. 'I know what our instincts are, but the voters don't.'

But Labour has not sunk to the low of the Tories in the mid-1990s. 'John Major was down to the cones hotline at his conference in 1996. We are not down to the cones hotline. Our curse is not to have a lack of policy. If we have any curse it is that we have more policy than we know what to do with. What we have got to do is decide what are the high-impact policies for the new political landscape.'

Miliband's remarks show the essential dilemma facing young supporters of Blair who believe the intellectual argument is on the side of the centre-left. Today's challenges – climate change, terrorism and the worst recession since the war – cry out for an active state, they say. But Blairites believe it has been all but impossible to articulate this with a PM who struggles to express himself in a warm and human way. Having made his decision to stay, Miliband now praises Brown for being the right man to lead during the economic crisis.

Choosing his language with care, to avoid talk of the green shoots of recovery, he indicates the worst of the recession may soon be over. 'Let us just remember that if this does turn out to be one of the industrialised [world's] shortest recessions, shallowest recessions, fastest recoveries out of recession, that is a remarkable achievement. That is not about minimising the depths of the recession. It is about building a different sort of economy out of it.'

Amid this background, Labour must prepare for an election that will challenge to all the parties. 'The next general election will be the first of the global age. There is a new political landscape, people feel more free, but less secure; people feel there is a greater need for social justice, for economic and social stability. But they know it cannot be achieved in one nation.'

Labour will have to deliver fresh ideas on crime, antisocial behaviour, housing and public services. There will also be a renewed push on creating a mainly elected upper house in parliament, and on electoral reform, as Labour responds to the expenses crisis by embracing ideas that have been gathering momentum.

'Why should not every MP in their constituency be able to say 50 per cent in my constituency voted for me? That is what AV [alternative vote] does. Now that is not going to be for the next election. But it is part of the political class being less comfortable about saying, "things have always been like this and let us leave it".'

Miliband believes the Tories are vulnerable as they opposed the economic rescue plan and appear to be preparing the ground for cuts in public services. 'Every single action we have taken they have opposed. It is not just that they have got a vacuum elsewhere. On the defining crisis of this time, they have been profoundly wrong.'

18 JUNE 2009

Brown sacks minister over tax claims

PATRICK WINTOUR AND NICHOLAS WATT

Gordon Brown received a blow on the eve of the publication of MPs' expenses when he was forced last night to sack Kitty Ussher as a junior Treasury minister in the face of evidence that she 'flipped' her homes for a month to avoid paying thousands of pounds in capital gains tax.

As demoralised MPs brace themselves for another blow to their battered reputation today, the prime minister told Ussher she would have to stand down as exchequer secretary after the *Daily Telegraph* revealed an accountant had advised her how to avoid paying the tax.

In 2007 Ussher changed the designation of her main home for one month from her south London property to her house in her Burnley constituency. This meant she avoided paying the tax, which is liable on second properties, when she sold her Burnley home for a £40,000 profit in March 2007.

The *Telegraph* informed Ussher that it would publish a letter today from her accountant advising her that changing the designation of her homes would allow her to avoid paying capital gains tax. A principal home does not attract the tax while MPs can only attract Commons allowances on second homes.

Ussher contacted Brown who informed her that receiving such tax advice made it impossible for her to continue as a Treasury minister. Downing Street accepts Ussher acted legally and within the Commons rules.

The departure of Ussher, who announced last night that she would also be standing down as MP for Burnley at the next election for family reasons, may add to criticisms of parliament today when full details of MPs' expenses are released. A series of ministers have recently faced claims they 'flipped' their homes to avoid paying CGT. Hazel Blears, who resigned as communities secretary, paid back £13,332 in CGT after 'flipping'.

Ussher said she had done nothing wrong, but said she had decided to resign to avoid causing embarrassment to Brown. In her resignation letter she wrote: 'I do not want to cause you or the government any embarrassment. I did not do anything wrong. At all times my actions have been in line with HM Revenue and Customs guidance and based on the advice of a reputable firm of accountants who in turn were recommended to me by the House of Commons fees office. Neither have I abused the allowance system of the House of Commons in any way.'

MPs are today likely to face charges of a cover-up as the Commons authorities finally officially publish 1m expenses claims and receipts covering the past four years, but censor some of the most damaging information. The online publication will exclude all rejected claims and their addresses, disguising the extent to which politicians used the 'flipping' tactic to redesignate their second homes so they maximised their income.

The long-awaited publication, the result of a year-long court battle, came as the Speaker, Michael Martin, made a farewell address in which he fired a blistering parting shot at the party leaders, especially Gordon Brown, for failing to show leadership by backing his package of reforms to MPs' expenses last year.

In a bitter final speech, he accused MPs of 'passing up the opportunity' to clean up the expenses system last year. Martin, effectively the first Speaker to be ejected from office for nearly 300 years, rounded on MPs, describing their response to his own package of reforms as 'deeply disappointing'.

He said: 'I wish with all my heart that that package of recommendations had won the confidence of the house last July. And I wish that party leaders had shown then some of the leadership they have shown now.'

In reality, David Cameron whipped his shadow cabinet to support the package, and much of the resistance was organised by Labour backbenchers. Brown himself did not vote and 33 ministers voted for the status quo.

19 JUNE 2009

MPs' expenses: Gordon Brown, prime minister

Arranged for brother Andrew to pay someone to clean his London flat.

Strong defence from No 10, which released cleaner's contract showing paid holidays, NI contributions and pay rises – all on the instructions of the future PM.

Cleaning and laundry bills for his London flat. Charged £57.50 for laundry but lost the receipt. Charged £1,157.50 for garden maintenance. Charged £352.50 for 'six-part treatment and inspection for mice' at his London flat in May 2006. Same problem in Scotland. Charged £88.13 in 2007: 'Cleared choked WC pan.'

CHAPTER SEVEN

GOING DOWN FIGHTING

Two years after his premiership began, Brown has arrived at an incredible point. Not only is he deemed widely to have failed so completely that he cannot recover; he is also deemed to be unassailable. It seems that hardly anyone outside his own circle believes he can win the election, now certainly put off to 2010, the last possible moment. Yet, in spite of that, the party cannot summon the will to replace him.

So is Gordon really to blame? Or is he the victim of timing – the right man for the wrong time? Few things are more agonizing than watching an apparent doom being played out, especially in such a public and sometimes excruciating glare.

At this moment the Guardian *sent its deputy editor, Kath Viner, to spend time with Brown to see if she could find the answer …*

20 JUNE 2009

'It's a strange life, really'

KATHARINE VINER

Gordon Brown meets me in the garden of No 10, and looks like a man without a care in the world. His skin is peachy and fresh. His 58-year-old face is surprisingly unlined, despite the sometimes windswept little pouch under his chin that makes him look so haggard in photographs. His stripy, liquorice-allsort hair is shiny. In a month in which the Labour party he leads has polled the lowest share of a national vote since the first world war (less than 16 per cent in the European elections), in which he has faced an attempted coup, mass resignations, a cabinet in turmoil, almost all the press turned against him, the prime minister is solicitous – 'Tea? Coffee? Sparkling water? You can drink too much tea ... Aren't you freezing?' – and jokes about the so-called Hotmail plot, brushing off suggestions that his political career is all but over. 'I wouldn't exaggerate how bad it's been,' he says.

I spend a morning and an afternoon with the prime minister, including two long one-to-one meetings, in the week in which he saw off dramatic attempts to unseat him. I expected to find a bloodied, beleaguered figure. Matthew Parris called him a 'living waxwork'; Suzanne Moore a 'zombie gurning ... less popular than pig flu'; and Richard Littlejohn wrote, 'If Gordon was a dog, he'd be put down.' A friend joked that it would be better to call up the late medium Doris Stokes than attend the interview. But Brown appears bouncy, even if his staff seem a little shell-shocked. Perhaps it's the relief of survival (for the moment), perhaps it's the adrenaline charge of adversity, perhaps it's the fact that the Tories had just made a rare gaffe on public spending, but the prime minister is apparently relaxed, and talks freely on a vast range of subjects, from the recession to his children, foreign policy to Simon Cowell, spin to how much sleep he's getting, even what he might do when he is no longer in charge.

Still, what a week. 'Interesting. Challenging. It feels like any other week,' he says. The shoulders of his jacket hunch up to his enormous ears.

Brown may sound sanguine about his current position, but what would it take for him to agree that, in the words of the resigned cabinet minister James Purnell, his 'continued leadership makes a Conservative victory more, not less likely'? He clearly doesn't consider himself a liability – he laughs uproariously when I tell him this – but if getting less than 16 per cent in an election isn't enough of a message, what would it take? Something that Peter Mandelson said? 'Something that the *Guardian* said?' He laughs again, referring to an editorial earlier this month that called on Labour to 'cut him loose'. This most serious of men simply won't take the question seriously. Come on, to whom would he listen? He levels his gaze, deploys his best growl. 'You', he jokes.

It becomes clear, as his answers to other questions reveal, that it's Brown to whom Brown listens most. His often-repeated mantra, 'I've got a job to do' sounds empty, but perhaps it isn't: what drives him appears to be this desire to complete a task. 'When things are difficult, you have to be sure of who you are and what you want to achieve,' he says. 'When people criticise you, you've got to listen to that criticism, and to learn from it, which I've tried to do. But you also have to be sure about what you are in this for.'

And this is in spite of doubts, which he talks about, quietly. 'To be honest, you could walk away from all of this tomorrow.' (He often says 'you' to distance himself from the intended 'I'.) 'I'm not interested in what accompanies being in power. It wouldn't worry me if I never returned to any of those places – Downing Street, Chequers. That would not worry me at all. And it would probably be good for my children.' He sounds almost wistful, as if imagining a life in which he was not compelled by the belief, perhaps instilled by his Presbyterian minister father, who worked seven days a week, that life is all about toil. (He once joked, 'I have seen the future, and it is work.')

Suddenly, Brown's younger son, Fraser, three next month, bursts down some steps and into the garden. 'Come here! Come on!' Brown shouts. Fraser, spotty with chickenpox, jumps up at his father and shouts something about Power Rangers. 'Ask him about his plants,' the prime minister suggests, and when I do, Fraser shows me the pots he's growing, including some ripe strawberries. He points to the pond: 'This is for fish, not for swimming.' Perhaps he could feed a strawberry to the fish? 'No, they don't like strawberries,' he shouts. 'They like poo! They like poo!' His father seems familiar with this kind of line: 'He's at the age where everything comes back to ... that.'

His children are cute and John, five, is already at the local state school. I wonder why he doesn't deploy them more to soften his dour public image. 'Sarah perhaps made a decision – and I certainly made a decision – to be in politics, and people are free to criticise Sarah and me. But my children, they didn't make that decision. I'd prefer them to grow up in a modest and ordinary background.' David Cameron, who is often photographed with his children, has taken a different path. 'Well, each to their own decisions. But I'm clear that although I talk about my children a lot, and clearly I want to do everything to support them, I don't feel they would benefit from being in the public arena.'

Nevertheless, the boundaries between Brown's home and work life seem curiously fluid. The maze of rooms, corridors and staircases in Downing Street, some parts official, some residential, is baffling. In the official areas, you are forever bumping into a racing child. In the flat, where the Browns live, there are staff wandering in and out, old-fashioned fax machines beside homemade Father's Day cards (early, or very late). Alongside the ordinary recycling bins is one that is locked and marked 'Confidential'. You step over toys, and Brown's wife, Sarah, brings tea – but in a Household Cavalry mug. And it's awkward: the flat is more relaxed than the formal areas, but not much; you have to reach it in an absurdly small lift. I was squashed into it with the PM and his special adviser; it was definitely necessary to breathe in.

With a job such as his, though, with its all-consuming demands, it must be lovely to work where his children are. 'That's one of the advantages,' Brown says. So it's a nice place to live? 'You wouldn't choose to live here.' The layout is confusing. 'Oh, it's ridiculous. I'd be happy enough living in the flat we had before, but I've discovered it's the only way you can do this job, by living here. There'd be huge security issues, the way things are. I wish it was more open.' Being behind such heavy security must cut him off from the electorate. 'Yes, but I've tried to get around the country more, it's much more interesting ... It's been very difficult to focus on [strategic planning] because you have to deal with immediate events like if a bank's going to go under. It's difficult to be running around the country if you're dealing with that.' In fact, Brown has a truly innovative idea for how the prime minister should live: 'If you could run No 10 from a train, getting round the country, that would be the best way.'

How does he cope with the stress of the job? Does he stop sleeping? 'I always sleep. But I have one child who hates going to bed, I've got another who gets up really early, and the gap between the two is getting narrower and narrower.' But he must have ways to find relief from it all? 'You're defining me as someone who feels under real pressure ... Obviously, when something happens that is surprising to you, you've got to respond to it.' Perhaps he goes for a run? 'That's one of the problems: I'd like to run in London in the morning, but I can't. When I'm in Scotland, I can run. We've got a hill and I can just run up it.' He was a talented sportsman before he lost the sight in his left eye in a rugby match, and still moves around with astonishing speed, despite an expanding paunch pushing at the buttons of his thick cotton shirt.

He has suggested that he doesn't feel under much pressure, but surely the past few weeks have been pretty bad. 'I've been through lots of things before.' As bad as this? 'Yeah.'

Brown looks severe, and from his expression I guess he might be thinking about personal setbacks, such as his 10-day-old daughter Jennifer's death in 2002, or the six months he was kept immobile in a darkened hospital as a teenager while doctors fought to save his sight. He has wept about Jennifer in interviews before, and I have no desire to get him to talk about the tragedy again: he told Suzie Mackenzie in 2004 that it was a year before he could listen to a piece of music. Has he ever been through anything this bad in his political life? 'Maybe not so much ... I've been through lots of different problems over the last 20-30 years, but this is one that's been more in the public eye. But you stop thinking about who you are and think about what you've got to do.' No indulgence of the ego allowed.

He is, of course, acutely aware of how his remarks might play in the media. For instance, when I ask him to concoct a 'fantasy cabinet' – to select his dream team from the past or present – he senses a trap: 'But then I'd be in a position of saying that the existing cabinet is not the one I wanted,' he says, hyper-alert to how the press could use such a story. 'I'll tell the home secretary he's going to be replaced by Gladstone!'

But he is frustrated with the way Westminster is seen. 'Politics is written up as the ins and outs, the infighting and the calculations, as if it's a game, right? Whereas I think of it as a purpose and a mission.' Surely it's both? 'I know it's both, but if we don't stand united, we just confirm the image the public has of us from the expenses crisis – that we're in it for ourselves, that it's about small ambitions, not big causes. It's the big causes that matter, that drive you on.'

Still, you need people with you to do that. 'You do, you do!' he agrees. And he himself is known as an expert at political machinations: he once said, when he became rector of Edinburgh University, that 'it was quite a revelation to me to see that politics was less about ideals and more about manoeuvres'. He protests: 'I'm not sure I'm that good at it ... I don't actually think I am very good at it at all.' Well, he certainly outmanoeuvred the so-called Hotmail plot of Blairite ministers and backbenchers. 'This was the email that nobody signed?' he jokes. But he claims his background means he finds the shenanigans of politics difficult. 'I never heard my father say a bad word about anyone.' (He has a coughing fit at this point. 'Water!' he shouts. 'I'm talking too much!') He recovers: 'It's incredible ... I wish I could be as good as he was. That's why it was shocking to me that politics could be so personality-driven.'

That may be true, I say, but he has employed other people to do his dirty work. This is a familiar accusation, most recently made by the environment minister Jane Kennedy, who resigned, alleging he 'rules by smear'. He responds: 'Look, find weaknesses in me, criticise me for my weaknesses – I'm not as great a presenter of information or communicator as I would like to be – but the one thing people should not say is that I'm surrounded by some group of conspirators.' What about Damian McBride, Brown's shamed spin doctor, sacked for sending an email suggesting planting scurrilous and untrue rumours about members of the opposition? 'Damian McBride doesn't work for me.' But he did. 'When Damian McBride made a mistake, he was out. He made a mistake and he had to go.' But he was notorious for sending abusive texts to journalists. 'I didn't know that. I didn't know that. It's not what I do. Anyway, I don't text. But when that behaviour was discovered: out! Gone! Away! No longer working for me. And I think if you look at the people who work in our office ... it's people who've come from charities, academic life, business ...' People around Brown say McBride and his predecessor, Charlie Whelan, acted on their own initiative to spin against the Tories; Blairites know they also spun against them. It's hard to believe Brown's insistence that he knew nothing about it; post-Campbell, post-*The Thick of It*, spin is hardly a hidden art.

What of Caroline Flint's excoriating resignation letter, in which the Europe minister accused Brown of having an inner cabal with few women in it and of using women as 'window dressing' – did that annoy him? 'It does, because I've tried not only to promote women, but also our egalitarian agenda is an agenda that helps women most of all: the minimum wage, working families tax credit, maternity rights, childcare, new chances in education for people who missed them. The majority of people who benefit are girls and women.' So why have only four women in the cabinet? 'Well, attending cabinet [there are] a lot more.' Only three more – of the 33 ministers who are either in cabinet, or able to attend cabinet in some capacity, only seven are women. 'Most of the people promoted to minister of state are women ... But we always need more women at every level.'

Even so, whatever way you look at it, it's not great. 'Obviously, we lost Jacqui [Smith], we lost Hazel [Blears], we lost Caroline [Flint].' (He makes it sound as if they were lost at sea.) Is he sad about that? 'Of course. They did a good job and I wanted them to stay.' So why didn't he, say, promote Flint? 'Caroline was minister for Europe and was offered the promotion to be present at all cabinet meetings. Every cabinet. But she wanted to run a particular department.' Which one? 'I don't know, we didn't get to that conversation. The point is, she'd been in that job for a few months, she was doing very well, Europe is a big job and she's going to be at cabinet. So it wasn't a demotion, it was a promotion.' Her letter? 'It was sad.' He uses a similar, it's-all-so-terribly-sad tone the next day, when discussing Blears. 'At some point I think Hazel should come back to government.'

Does he use women as window dressing? 'No. At Downing Street we've got women doing many of the important jobs. You ask all my staff.' I ask a few. One close female colleague says, 'He just doesn't differentiate between men and women in his conversation. He's just not someone who thinks about it.' Another says, 'For years he's worked closely with good feminist women like Harriet Harman and she has never complained of anything.' One talks of his kindness and discretion when she was ill. But a male colleague concedes, 'He is slightly a product of an older generation.'

Brown's intimate relationships with women were for many years kept fanatically secret; he didn't marry until he was 49 and rumours about his sexuality persisted, perhaps because some found it hard to understand that a straight man could have close gay friends (such as Peter Mandelson and Nick Brown). His exes were attractive, intelligent women such as Sheena McDonald, the television presenter, Marion Caldwell, a lawyer, and, most surprisingly, given his rather heavy reputation, Princess Margarita of Romania, Prince Philip's goddaughter, whom he met at university. She said of their relationship: 'It was a very solid and romantic story. I never stopped loving him, but one day it didn't seem right any more. It was politics, politics, politics, and I needed nurturing.' Brown married the former PR executive Sarah Macaulay in 2000, though he took a long time to commit; in 1995, when they had been seeing each other for 18 months, the journalist Lynn Barber asked him about Sarah and he said, 'No. That's wrong. It's just the way names get thrown up.' His marriage appears settled and happy, and even those who don't like him like her; she refuses all requests for interviews.

Sarah is widely regarded as an electoral asset, but nothing was able to offset an undeniably catastrophic Euro election result. 'Labour voters punished us by not coming out to vote,' he says, 'but I don't detect an enthusiasm for the Conservative party.' Brown refuses to accept that the next election is as good as lost. 'I don't believe the Conservatives can win in the way you're suggesting. The Tories have made, for them, a cardinal mistake in that they admitted the truth – that if you take 10 per cent off the health service or schools or policing, you've cut into the jobs, the services, the expectations. The Conservatives' mask has slipped. They cannot be a centre ground party any more, they can't talk about being mainstream. The choice has become a lot clearer.' But won't everyone have to cut public spending, as governments are forced to tighten their belts to pay off debt built up during the recession? 'No. It's a myth. Public spending will continue to rise. It's in our figures. We've costed it, and you're paying more in top rate tax to pay for it.'

He sees his trials in a global context (perhaps so they seem less to do with him). 'Every government in the world is having trouble. Lula from Brazil told me that when he was a trade unionist and something went wrong, he blamed the government. When he was an opposition leader, he blamed the government. And when he became the government, he blamed the Americans. And now that he can't blame the Americans, he blames the bankers.'

Yes, I say, let's blame the bankers! 'I'm not going to blame anyone else,' he says, suddenly sombre.

So what about Labour's poor showing? Is it all his fault? 'It's easy to find an individual to blame, and make that person the source of the trouble, but we've been hit by a world economic hurricane, by an expenses crisis unparalleled in the history of Westminster, and we've been in government for 12 years.' But he also gives another reason: 'Of course, unity in the party is an important element to this. People want to see parties united, not divided. All these elements are not present at the moment ... '

In nine months, Brown has gone from being popular – the man who saved Britain from financial meltdown – to a pariah. Has he found it upsetting? 'However much you feel responsible, and however much your integrity is ... is ... and you feel hurt by what people are saying, you've got to deal with it.' Friends say he can't understand why people have turned against him; that he's the same person he was when he was doing well in the polls. He thinks under his leadership Labour can win the next election, and perhaps because he's seen the tide turn so quickly, he thinks it can turn again. He is sure that, in time, his measures will turn the economy around. And he really believes that the age we're living in is a progressive one. He cites a bit of evidence for this: for the first time, he says, teaching is the most popular occupation for people leaving university. 'It's a great profession. I could move to teaching ... ' He beams, as if to say, You see! There's always something else I can do!

Brown is convinced that he is prime minister in a uniquely difficult period. He talks of the 'two earthquakes – one economic, unparalleled since the war, one political, the biggest parliamentary scandal for two centuries'. But it's more even than that: 'The changes throughout the world, whether you talk about the environment, or the nature of jobs, are dramatic. For centuries, individuals have been learning how to live with their neighbours. Now, uniquely, we're having to learn to live with people who we don't know. People have now got the ability to speak to each other across continents, to join with communities that are based not on territory, but on networks; and you've got the possibility of people building alliances right across the world. That flow of information means that foreign policy can never be the same again. You cannot have Rwanda again because information would come out far more quickly and public opinion would grow to the point where action would need to be taken. Foreign policy can no longer be the province of just a few elites.'

Returning to the idea that we live in a 'progressive age', he believes that the public's fury about MPs' expenses and bankers' pay is proof of this. But if so, and if Labour is the progressive party, why isn't everyone voting for them? 'People are in this difficult position – which I understand – where they know we've made these decisions to try to sort the economy out, but they don't yet see results. Same thing on MPs. People know there's a crisis in MPs' expenses, but they don't yet know we've sorted it out.' What's the timescale? 'It's going to take some time.' Will it all be done in time for, say, May (the last date at which Brown can call a general election)? 'In time for whenever,' he says. ('She's forcing me to be a politician,' he says, turning to an aide.)

Labour voters stayed at home because they're angry, mainly about MPs' expenses. 'I'm as angry as the public. I understand their moral outrage. I've said it offends my Presbyterian conscience, and it does.' But, he adds, 'One thing I didn't cause is the expenses crisis.' He sees a link between expenses and the economy: 'What people took out of the banking crisis is that bankers can act in a way that's irresponsible and unfair, and what people take out of the political crisis is the same thing.' So, private and public worlds have both shown themselves to be irresponsible. 'The public realm and the free market realm are subject to inherent weaknesses that have got to be underpinned by having shared values that lead to shared rules,' he says, in some version, many times. Values, values, values, rules, rules, rules.

I find this curious. Brown seems keen to show how both private and public sectors have revealed their profound flaws, so he can sort out both together, without making a distinction between the two. If anything, he seems to me almost relieved that it's not just the private sector that has been profligate – a bizarre idea when the expenses scandal has done him such damage. But perhaps it allows him to be all things to all people.

Hasn't the banking crisis led him to fall out of love with the unfettered capitalism that many Labour supporters saw him as having embraced, and found so hard to stomach? 'I don't think I was ever ... ' he starts, and doesn't finish. 'I've always argued that this global marketplace has got to be properly supervised. What I didn't want was Britain to be in a position where we were outside the mainstream.' He seems to be saying that the neoliberal model was simply the only option for Britain if it wanted to be part of the world economy. But did he really need to be such an outrider to the mainstream, pushing things further? 'To be honest, for the last 10 years when I was chancellor, my battles were always with those people who were telling me we should deregulate even more.' Does he wish he'd been tougher? Regulated more? 'Yeah ... but I was calling on the rest of the world all the time to create a global supervisory regime.'

Perhaps what we need is a return to old-fashioned banking? I give you £1 to look after, you lend out 90p of it to others. 'That kind of banking has been sound,' he agrees. 'But the international ambitions of these banks made them take risks that nobody could ever have contemplated.' Couldn't he, as chancellor, have stopped them? 'Well, we didn't know about a lot of it. People did not know that British, German, Italian, Austrian banks were buying subprime mortgages from the States.' But all that packaging up of assets, selling bits off so no one knows who owns what – that's no way to run a bank. 'But it will continue to happen.' So there's nothing that can be done? 'No, there's a lot that can be done. But it will still be in the interests of the economy to have many sources of money for investment in the future. But it must be in conditions where you have proper supervision and an understanding through transparency of what's happening.'

He has been criticised over inequality, which under many measures has risen under Labour: that he cares about reducing poverty, yes, but cares little about the vast sums the richest are paid. He concedes that that has been his focus: 'Poverty has fallen, and you'll see it continue to fall over the next year or so. And then there is the issue at the top. I've always said you can deal with some of it through taxation, our tax rates have gone up and the top 1 per cent of the population are paying more than before. Removing people from poverty must be our priority. Whatever you can or can't do at the top – because it's a global economy – you can as a government do a lot with the poor.' It's almost as if he wants to be a socialist for the poor and a free marketeer for the rich – also known as having your cake and eating it.

At first, during our conversations, I thought that Brown had moved away from his New Labour triangulated position – such as when he said, 'Free market solutions can't work. They can't work for the environment, they can't work for the economy.' But then he added, 'The old market v state debate is not sufficient to solve the problems that we have.' Despite the scale of the economic crisis, there's no doubt that Brown is still New Labour at heart.

Much has changed, though: perhaps most strikingly his relationship with Mandelson, who is widely believed to have saved the prime minister this month and now has more titles than we have space for here. Once close, Brown never forgave Mandelson for backing Tony Blair to be Labour leader when John Smith died in 1994; throughout a decade of New Labour infighting between Blairites and Brownites, they were at war with each other. And now? 'I get on with Peter very well.' After all those years? 'It's really interesting, isn't it? When there's a common purpose, people tend to work together ... Things go wrong ... ' And now? 'There is a common purpose. I think in a sense people are coming to appreciate his talents in a way the Labour party didn't before.' Even to love him? (Blair once said his mission would be complete only when the party learned to love Mandelson.) 'They're at least appreciating his talents.' But not loving him. 'I think there's a great affection for him now, to be honest.'

Another change is his new enthusiasm for reality TV and, just a little, for the celebrity culture he eschewed for so long. This month he ennobled Alan Sugar, businessman star of *The*

Apprentice; Amanda Holden, a judge on *Britain's Got Talent*, told of how she had been invited to No 10 for dinner ('Gordon was incredibly charming – it was a side of him you don't see on TV'); Piers Morgan, her fellow judge, claimed on *Desert Island Discs* earlier this month that he saw the PM every six weeks or so, and that he talks to Sarah once a week. Meanwhile, Sarah, a confident woman whose work on maternal mortality has had a real impact, has been photographed out with Naomi Campbell, Paris Hilton, Sharon Osbourne.

Why ennoble Sir Alan? Brown says he has known Sugar since 1997, and that his new role is to 'get the banks to act in a more open and forward-looking way to new business proposals'. But has Brown ever watched *The Apprentice*? The man is no sweet-talker. 'People respect the advice he gives them, even if it's harsh sometimes.' He's also the man who said of women who might have children, 'Just don't employ them.' 'I'm not here to defend every statement he's made,' Brown says.

And *Britain's Got Talent* – is it his new favourite TV show? 'I think *Britain's Got Talent* is really interesting. What annoyed me when I was at school was that there were lots of people with obvious ability who could've benefited from opportunities and were told, "It's not for people like you." And now they've got more open ways of coming forward. Surely the future for our country is more that Britain has got talent than it is that Britain is a broken society.'

What about the judges? Simon Cowell is so nasty. 'Do you not think the reason people like him is that he's honest about whether they've got a talent or not?' This sounds uncannily like why Sugar appeals to him, too. Others see their behaviour as bullying, and, of course, that's what Brown's critics say about him, too. Lord Turnbull called him a 'bully and a control freak', a sentiment echoed by those who have fallen foul of his relentless demands for loyalty. Close allies are more forgiving, such as the colleague who says, 'Look, it's not the easiest thing to be in a meeting with him. He doesn't mean to intellectually overwhelm you, but he'll always ask you the question you hadn't thought of ... which is very annoying. That doesn't make him empathetic. But so what? Can you imagine being taken through the banking crisis by Cameron or Alan Johnson? It's chilling. Fifty years ago he'd have been FDR. Did anyone ever notice that he had a wheelchair?'

Of course it would be noticed now. Brown would clearly prefer a political era of New Deals and Bretton Woods, rather than rolling news and YouTube. He talks with longing about the days when the BBC would announce, 'There is no news to report.' He doesn't relish 24-hour news, the constant media demands on politicians, what Sugar (of all people) calls 'the giant reality show this country is driven by'. Brown confesses here that he's 'not as great a presenter of information or communicator as [he] would like to be' – a dangerous shortcoming when presentation is such an essential skill of the 21st-century politician.

This must be particularly frustrating for Brown as he is able to communicate successfully, but more in private, where it is of limited use to him. I witnessed him prepare for a short TV interview and he seemed to rearrange his features into something stiffer and less appealing for the camera. He was asked about Cristiano Ronaldo's £80m transfer deal, a subject surely ripe for a joke, and he muttered something about English football emerging stronger as a result. During all our one-to-one conversations, I never once saw him perform that strange, lower-jaw breathing manoeuvre he so often executes in public. His image is fusty and secretive, but he's the first prime minister to sit in an open-plan office in Downing Street. To me he spoke fluently and with passion. He sounded like a normal person.

The prime minister is a man of such paradoxes. He is now convinced free market solutions can't work, but is still privatising parts of the Royal Mail and the health service. He passes strong legislation on women while appointing few to top positions. He sees himself as a good person, but employs others to do his dirty work. He wants to stay as prime minister, but longs to get out of No 10, govern from a train, become a teacher. As he says himself: 'It's a strange life, really.'

30 JUNE 2009

12 minutes, 12 bills – but one more battering for Gordon Brown

ALLEGRA STRATTON

It was billed as the moment Gordon Brown would define what his government would be about, a chance, after months of uncertainty and an attempted coup, to answer his party critics who say he is incapable of communicating a vision.

But last night, after delivering a 12-minute statement containing 10 main measures, Brown found his style and platform under attack from left and right as the Tories criticised the lack of detailed spending plans while unions and Labour backbenchers spoke out against plans to add more conditions to the benefits of unemployed young people.

New entitlements were the main theme of yesterday's draft Queen's speech, entitled Building Britain's Future.

The 'entitlement' agenda replaced the Blairite method of evaluating public services through Whitehall targets and an emphasis on consumer choice in public services. The Tories and the

Liberal Democrats said there was no sign of how new entitlements could be enforced and no method by which those public services that did not meet the entitlements of the public penalised.

David Cameron, the Tory leader, said: 'The prime minister is living in a dream world in which spending is going up, investment is going up, infrastructure is being boosted. When is someone going to tell him that he's run out of money?'

Nick Clegg, the Lib Dem leader, said Brown's statement was 'nothing more than a hotchpotch of unrelated Whitehall schemes, a ministerial cut and paste job'.

But criticism, ranging from gentle to more trenchant, also emerged from within Labour, a party keen for the prime minister to demonstrate that he cuts the intellectual mustard in order both to reaffirm his position and their own in deciding that it should him that should be lead them. The government could live with sniping about its Big New Idea if it gained good grace from its other big ticket items.

But given that the objective of Brown's day was to bring recalcitrant backbenchers into the fold for the next 12 months, the first big item on his draft legislative programme was a strange choice. He began with a plan to make those aged 18-24 and out of work for more than 12 months accept a job found for them or face a benefits cut.

Instead of pulling off a rapprochement, Brown ended up opening a new sore and he is, in all likelihood, on another collision course with his backbenchers, who have already recoiled from attempts to attach conditions to other welfare reforms. In April's Budget, the government announced a £1.2bn fund to create guaranteed employment for the young who find themselves out of work for more than a year. It hopes this will secure jobs for 100,000.

Though centrist members of the party are minded to support the prime minister in his effort to be tough on benefit claimants

– regarding it as kinder to demand things of the unemployed than to let them languish during a recession – the bulk of Brown's parliamentary party abhor the policy. As olive branches go it was a particularly twisted and gnarled stick the prime minister held out to his party yesterday.

22 JULY 2009

As he bows out at end of term, Gordon Brown leaves with some hope

PATRICK WINTOUR

Gordon Brown departed for his summer holiday today predicting that Britain may be able to avoid the large rises in unemployment that are likely to take place elsewhere in the world and has already prevented 500,000 people joining the dole queues.

Speaking at his closing press conference of the political season, the prime minister suggested that the government's interventions on fiscal policy had helped slow the pace of rising unemployment.

No 10 is understood to be looking internally at charts suggesting that the Job Seeker's Allowance count could hit a peak 500,000 lower than the Treasury had previously thought, saving as much as £2bn in benefit costs.

In the budget, the Treasury used an average of city forecasters to predict the unemployment claimant count would 'rise from … 1.39m to 2.09m at the end of 2009, and to 2.44m at the end of 2010'.

Although economic growth is thought to have been worse than the Treasury predicted in the spring, the latest figures from the

Office of National Statistics show the claimant count in June had risen to 1.56m, an increase of only 23,000 on the previous month, compared to monthly increases of 80,00 per month at the start of the year.

At his Downing Street press conference, Brown insisted he was not making predictions about unemployment, but noted that even last month 300,000 people had left the claimant register suggesting it was still possible to find work.

He added: 'I think as people look at the situation in the next few months they will find unemployment rising very fast in other countries. The question is whether we can prevent unemployment rising as fast. If we had not acted, and taken the fiscal policy decisions we have, unemployment would be higher.'

Brown was careful not to say that the recession was coming to an end, and repeatedly said he was not going to be complacent. But ministers are desperately hoping that the figures are revealing the economy as stronger than expected.

Normally, unemployment is a lagging indicator, suggesting the unemployment rate could be close to 3m at the time of the general election next spring. But there is uncertainty inside Downing Street. Brown insisted: 'If we had not intervened and acted decisively at least further 500,000 jobs would have been lost in this recession.'

He also argued the political debate should be turning on 'the here and now question' of whether the government had been right to take the fiscal action it had, rather than debating how much spending will have to be reined in after the election.

He insisted his was the first government to introduce a debt reduction programme, pointing to the budget's plan to raise taxes for high earners and to find £30bn in efficiency savings.

Without citing a source, he said: 'Because of the action we have already taken our debt in most of the years ahead will be less than the debt of America, France, Germany and indeed lower than many other countries.'

Brown remains reluctant to set out the measures his government is willing to take after 2010-11, the last year for which there are departmental spending totals. He also challenged polls showing that the electorate wanted to see big public spending cuts, saying if people were asked whether they wanted to protect frontline services, such as health, schools and police, they would say they did.

But Brown is under political and expert pressure to say more about how he will reduce debts. He is likely to set out some of his plans in the autumn, by which time he hopes the country will be clearly coming out of recession.

He said he understood people had not yet seen the results of the government's actions, and insisted by the time of the election the country will be making a choice, rather than as at present holding a referendum on Labour.

30 AUGUST 2009

Support for Gordon Brown falling as economic confidence grows

GABY HINSLIFF, THE *OBSERVER*

Gordon Brown's hopes of a late fightback based on recovery from recession have been dashed today by a new poll showing that economic confidence is surging back – but Labour is not reaping the benefit.

The Ipsos Mori research shows the proportion of people expecting the economy to improve in the next 12 months has staged the biggest recovery in nearly three decades of polling, with

43 per cent of Britons now believing the UK is emerging from recession compared with just 7 per cent in spring 2008.

The findings will be welcomed on the high street and in the property market, with consumers more likely to spend when they have faith in their future prosperity. Optimism was strongest among the middle classes and southerners.

However, poll analysis shows that Brown's ratings have actually fallen as confidence in economic 'green shoots' grows, with the Tories now on 43 per cent of the vote – representing a 17-point lead over Labour on 26, with the Liberal Democrats on 17. There is now an 'inverse correlation' between the fortunes of the economy and of Labour, suggesting the link between feelings of economic prosperity and support for the government has been broken.

Asked about the poll findings, Yvette Cooper, the secretary of state for work and pensions, admitted that Labour still had to convince voters its strategy of spending to beat the recession was reviving the economy faster than Tory proposals could. 'The challenge for us is to make clear that there is a political divide in economic policies and that actually makes a difference. I think [had we not intervened] the course of the recession would be much worse,' Cooper said.

The findings reflect growing government concern that the prime minister, burdened with some of the blame for the credit crunch thanks to his years as chancellor, may not get credit for any recovery. They also suggest that the Conservatives still lack the poll dominance that would mean they had completely sealed the deal with voters, with turnout at the next general election dictating whether David Cameron gets a commanding Commons majority and strong mandate for potentially painful, planned spending cuts.

15 SEPTEMBER 2009

New poll finds voters want 'anyone but Gordon Brown'

ANDREW SPARROW

Gordon Brown suffered a blow today following the publication of a poll suggesting nearly half of voters think 'literally anyone' would make a better leader of the Labour party.

The Populus poll, published in the *Times*, also says 61 per cent of voters see Brown as a liability to Labour, and only 34 per cent regard him as an asset.

And it appears to confirm the party is heading for defeat in next year's general election, with the Conservatives enjoying a 14-point lead.

Labour is on 27 per cent (up one point on the Populus figures for mid-July), the Conservatives are on 41 per cent (up 3 per cent) and the Lib Dems on 18 per cent (down 2 points).

The *Times* says no party that has been this far behind at this stage in a parliament has ever gone on to win the subsequent general election, although it also says that the Tories are not doing as well as Labour was in opposition in 1996 (when it was 50 per cent) or the Tories were in 1978 (when they were on 48 per cent).

Brown survived an attempt by his enemies to remove him as Labour leader in June and, although there has been talk in the party of another leadership challenger later this year, there is no evidence that any members of the cabinet are plotting against him.

But the Populus figures will embolden those who believe the party should have replaced Brown earlier this year.

29 SEPTEMBER 2009

Gordon Brown: the clunking fist thumps its last tub

MARTIN KETTLE

Gordon Brown definitely gave it his all. It was said this speech had been through 50 revisions and it very probably had – for good and ill. There was nothing in it that hadn't been thought about, argued over by his speechwriters, strengthened, honed and sharpened.

And with good reason. Never in his life has Brown made a speech on which more rested, for him and for his party, than the leader's speech he gave to the Labour conference in Brighton on Tuesday. But it's a sign of weakness that this was so. According to Labour polling, most voters think Labour stands for immigrants and single parents. He should not be in this position.

The speech had a theme – summed up in the repeated and inelegant phrase about 'the change we choose'. The phrase is meant to combine two things that are essential if Labour is ever to haul itself back into the political game – to be the party of change and to offer a distinct choice from the Conservatives. It's hard for any government that has been in power for 12 years, especially one led by a stolid figure like Brown, to be the party of change – and I don't think Brown managed that piece of alchemy. But there is no doubt that Brown made the case that the next election is a real contest of conflicting visions. A lot of people pretend there's nothing to choose between the main parties – but Brown reminded anyone with the stamina to listen to his speech that there is.

Someone once said that listening to Brown's speeches is like listening to the weather forecast on the radio. You intend to concentrate; you know there is important information there. But there's something about the event that means your mind is all too often elsewhere. Not even this speech, which was one of his better efforts, was free from that problem. Not for the first time, Brown tried to say something about almost everything and possibly ended up saying not enough – and not enough that was original or brave about some of the things that really matter. Climate change was an obvious example. So was Afghanistan. So was Europe.

Anyone hoping that Brown would somehow rouse himself to be something we never suspected he was capable of being will have been disappointed at this speech, too. So it was a better-than-average but standard Brown speech, with all the tics and characteristics that we have come to expect. The sentences without verbs. The repeated slogans. The growing tendency to legislate for purely tactical reasons – like the so-called fiscal responsibility legislation, which he trailed at the weekend. The addiction to announcements: some of them original and well worth making, others merely relaunches and repackagings.

If I could cure Brown of one particular bad habit – but it's way too late for that – I would tell him to stop saying 'And I can also announce today ...' It makes the speech sound like a report to the central committee, not a conversation with the people.

Brown remains a politician of the old school. He loves to pose as the moral exemplar, the man who can deal with everything, and solve all problems. His solutions have a touch of Oliver Cromwell about them, as well as a dose of Nye Bevan. In a sense, he tries too hard and thereby loses credibility over the things for which he really does deserve credit. I don't think he came up with a compelling new idea to guide Labour through the next election, let alone to steer Labour's course through another period of government, if it gets one. The emphasis in the extensive sections on social policy, care for the elderly, the NHS and neighbourhood policing was all about doing and spending more, not on reform and doing doings better or differently. This speech, it was clear, was aimed far more at the Labour core electorate than at the 'squeezed middle' (whatever that means).

All that said, Brown made some important announcements. They deserve to be taken seriously. As ever, there were some announcements for the *Daily Mail* – on antisocial behaviour and 24-hour drinking. Brown clearly sees no limit to the role of the state in taking over from parents; more practical people will be sceptical about that. Again, too, there was something for the *Guardian* reader – this time the promise of a referendum on electoral reform. But the referendum will only be on the minimum change and it won't happen until after Labour wins the election. In other words, it won't happen at all.

This was indeed the most important speech of Brown's life. But it was impossible to listen to it without reflecting that it is almost certainly his last speech to a Labour conference as leader. It came on the day when a poll showed Labour trailing third for the first time in a generation. That's a reminder that this may even be the last party conference speech by a Labour prime minister. Ever.

Brown is going down fighting. But he is going down. In the end, this speech was a rage against the dying of the light.

30 SEPTEMBER 2009

In defence of Gordon Brown

MADELEINE BUNTING

I can launch my own catalogue of complaints against Gordon Brown as well as the next columnist, but I've no appetite right now to join what increasingly sounds like a mob lynching. There is something about the assembled chorus of received wisdom which makes me go contrary; group think rarely produces good judgments. The Labour party is panicking and there is no better way to assuage their sense of failure than to heap the blame on Brown. Plus, the relish with which Brown's many critics are pitching in makes me suspicious.

So here are a few arguments in an unfashionable cause: Brown's defence. His speech to the Labour party conference was lambasted for its promise of change; the argument was that New Labour has had 12 years to deliver change and it shouldn't need more time. But this is absurd impatience. Who presumes that a government has the power to transform a country in little over a decade? Labour wanted a generation in power – the country needed it after a generation of chronic underinvestment in public services. So Brown is entirely right to talk of work unfinished, a job half done, and journalists are the least well-equipped to complain. Journalism is a profession built on impatience – most forms of social change are vastly harder and slower to achieve than filing an article.

Next up is the idea that the electorate doesn't like Brown. This is an odd thing to say about a politician. I don't expect to like prime ministers; they are hardly going to be my dinner guests. I want them to do a good job; what I feel about their personalities is irrelevant. Was Clement Attlee a bundle of laughs? Did Lloyd George treat women well? Surely after Tony Blair's energetic charm, which did so much to win 1997 and proved such a disillusionment, we might have opted for another way to measure a politican's worth.

Much of the criticism hurled at Brown seems odd. His speech tacked this way then that; he commits the crime of triangulation. But this is a peculiar accusation given that New Labour was all about triangulation. Blair did it all the time, facing both ways. The only difference is that Blair was more adept, Brown is clunky – but that is a difference of style not substance.

Another odd charge is that he lacks conviction. Yet his speech yesterday seemed evidence that he is one of those rare politicians who does have conviction. The commitment to 0.7 per cent for international aid is to be enshrined in law. And although the speech was spun as an appeal to the middle classes, he was proposing to take the childcare tax credit away from the middle classes to pay for free nursery care for the neediest two-year-olds. This is a man whose instinct for social justice is still evident after 12 years in power.

I'm not saying that Brown is faultless. Of course not. He lacks style; he lacks key political skills in building alliances and in conveying clarity. He probably has some major personality faults – too controlling – but there is a dangerous myopia afoot here. Think big picture and politics is always about the least worst option. In that frame, Brown is a no-brainer. In the midst of the financial crisis, the worst in decades, he didn't dither (as he is often accused of) and he didn't flinch from making decisions involving huge sums of money. Who can imagine that Cameron would have had the experience and confidence to have acted as decisively.

Be wary: scapegoating serves a deeply entrenched psychological need in human beings. The iniquities of Brown are being used and elaborated as a foil for a tumultuous year of failures. Far more deserving candidates for the collective frustration are lurking unnoticed at the back of the baying mob.

Index